# Physical Education in a Changing Society

# Physical Education in a Changing Society

*William H. Freeman*
*State University of New York*
*at Brockport*

**Houghton Mifflin Company**
Boston  Atlanta  Dallas  Geneva, Illinois
Hopewell, New Jersey  Palo Alto  London

Printed in the U.S.A.
Library of Congress Catalog Card Number: 76–10898
ISBN: 0–395–24408–0

Cover photo courtesy Nicholas Sapieha, Stock, Boston. Part-opening photos: Part I, courtesy Nicholas Sapieha, Stock, Boston; Part II, courtesy British Museum; Part III, courtesy Cary Wolinsky, Stock, Boston; Part IV, courtesy Constantine Manos, Magnum Photos, Inc.; Part V, courtesy Julie O'Neil, Stock, Boston; Part VI, courtesy Jeff Albertson, Stock, Boston.

# Acknowledgments

I want to express my sincere appreciation to the people who have influenced or contributed to the development of this book. Professor F. W. Clonts of Wake Forest University helped as an adviser and historian with his broad view of the scope of history, combined with his requirement of clear, precise prose. Professor Betty F. McCue of the University of Oregon has been an invaluable, supportive adviser and critic to a degree that is appreciated beyond words. Professor William J. Bowerman of Oregon assisted in many ways by providing an experience and association of lasting value. I would also like to thank the reviewers of early versions of the manuscript: Professor Scott Greer of Indiana University, Professor Richard Lauffer of East Carolina University, and Professor James Genasci of Springfield College.

My students at Gardner-Webb College graciously acted as guinea pigs for the earlier versions of these chapters, helping me to discover where I was failing to meet my intended goals.

The members of my family have been very helpful with their supportive assistance during my extended bouts of writing.

My wife, Janice, has been of great assistance during the work on this book, both in practical assistance and in moral support. The production of this book would have been extremely difficult without her.

I will welcome any suggestions for the improvement of this text.

# Contents

# Preface

This text was written as an introduction to physical education for under-graduate students. I have tried to present physical education as a very broad field of interests that are rapidly developing into specialized disciplines and subdisciplines. I have presented physical education as a field lying between the arts and the sciences, and thus able to use and benefit from both.

This text emphasizes the development of physical education and sport, separately and together, including the problems that have resulted. Philosophy is stressed more heavily than in many introductory texts, and the critical area of ethics and ethical problems relating to physical education and sport is treated in a separate chapter.

The scientific bases of physical education have not been treated in this text because in most programs of study the different scientific bases are studied in separate courses or course sequences, making such a study redundant. This text, however, is an attempt to cover ground that usually is not covered at length in other required courses.

Some of the definitions or explanations that are presented, such as the definitions of "play" and "sport," the discussions of the philosophies, and the critical area of ethical problems, may not agree with the ideas of some scholars. I have attempted to deal with these concepts and issues at an easy-to-understand level for the beginning student, rather than presenting a scholarly study for the upper-level student. I hope each student will pursue the subjects to the scholarly and philo-sophical levels, but my aim in these discussions is to introduce the topics in a clear and simplified manner, not to act as the last word of scholarship on the subjects.

The readings that are suggested as parallel references for the chapters are generally from materials that are available on most college campuses, including schools with newer libraries. Older references can usually be found in more recent anthologies that should be readily available.  The readings are not all-inclusive, rather they serve as a starting point for further investigation.

The readings cover the same area as the corresponding chapter, but they will either expand the discussion or approach the subject from a different viewpoint.  The student should develop the habit of seeking further information when a subject seems unclear.  The process of education works best when the student seeks to learn the views of a number of authorities, rather than accepting the version given by the first one encountered.

*William H. Freeman*

# I

## The Field of Physical Education

# 1 What Is Physical Education?

When we speak of physical education, to what are we referring? Many people are confused by the term and are not sure exactly what physical education is, or what its teachers do. In many cases this confusion is shared by the college students who have chosen physical education as their major field. The purpose of this chapter is to explain what physical education really is.

## A Broad Field of Interests

When we speak of physical education, we are referring to a broad field of interests. The basic concern is human movement, primarily in the sense of gross (larger) movements rather than the more minute or finer movements of the body. More specifically, physical education is concerned with the relationship between human movement and other areas of education—that is, with the relationship of the body's physical development to the mind and soul as they are being developed. This concern for the effect of physical development on other areas of human growth and development contributes to the uniquely broad scope of physical education, for no other single field is concerned with the *total* development of the human, except education, and then only within the broadest possible view of that field.

***Definitions of Physical Education.*** While many definitions have been given for physical education, one of the most lasting has been expressed by Jesse Feiring Williams: "Physical education is the sum of man's physical activities selected as to kind, and conducted as to outcomes." [1] He explains his definition by considering the question of

---

[1] Jesse Feiring Williams, *The Principles of Physical Education*, 8th ed., W. B. Saunders, Philadelphia, 1964, p. 13.

whether educating only the physical aspect of the body is sufficient to define the field:

> When mind and body were thought of as two separate entities, physical education was obviously an education *of* the physical . . . . with new understanding of the nature of the human organism in which wholeness of the individual is the outstanding fact, physical education becomes education *through* the physical.  With this view operative, physical education has concern for and with emotional responses, personal relationships, group behaviors, mental learnings, and other intellectual, social, emotional, and esthetic outcomes.[2]

Williams is stressing the point that even though physical education seeks to educate people through physical means by working with physical activities, it is concerned with educational results that are not entirely physical.  The goal of physical education is to influence all areas of educational development, including the mental and social growth of the student.  While the body is being improved physically, the mind should be learning and expanding, and there should be some social development, such as learning to work with others.

Other authors have sought to convey this broad definition of the goal of physical education.  John H. Jenny, for example, also discusses this "education *through* the physical":

> The unique contribution that physical education has to make to general education is that of general body development through physical activity.  When this physical activity is guided by competent teachers so that the other general outcomes of education accompany the physical activity, then, and only then, does the physical activity become more than physical culture or physical training.[3]

In this definition education that is simply "*of* the physical," or has a goal that focuses on only the physical aspects of education, is too limited in scope to really be considered physical education.

Harold M. Barrow puts physical education into the context of education's traditional goal of developing the liberally educated person:

> Physical education may be defined as education through big-muscle play activity, such as sports, exercise, and dance, where education's objectives may be achieved in part . . . . This product is a physically educated person.  This value should be one of

---

[2] Ibid., p. 8.

[3] John H. Jenny, *Physical Education, Health Education, and Recreation: Introduction to Professional Preparation for Leadership*, Macmillan, New York, 1961, p. 5.

many values of the liberally educated person, and it has meaning only when it is related to the totality of the individual's life.[4]

In placing physical education within the context of the total educational experience, Barrow stresses that the physical education experience should relate to the total educational process and to each person's whole life.  If the physical education experience makes no contribution to the other educational experiences, the proper function expected of a true physical education program is not being fulfilled.

John E. Nixon and Ann E. Jewett also stress the total educational experience in defining physical education as

> . . . that phase of the total process of education which is concerned with the development and utilization of the individual's movement potential and related responses, and with the stable behavior modifications in the individual which result from these responses.[5]

This definition is a bit more limited, as it does not include all the educational areas affected by a good program of physical education. The authors do, however, point out that the education is not purely physical, for "movement potential" is a broad area, particularly when the "related responses" are included in the educational process.

James A. Baley and David A. Field describe physical education with more emphasis upon its use of gross physical activities that are not generally of an easy nature:

> Physical education is a process through which favorable adaptations and learnings—organic, neuromuscular, intellectual, social, cultural, emotional, and esthetic—result from and proceed through selected and fairly vigorous physical activities.[6]

The activities noted here are selected, as in Williams's earlier definition, in relation to the desired outcomes they can produce in the student. That the education uses physical means is emphasized by the statement noting that the activities that are considered a part of physical education are "fairly vigorous physical activities."  While physical activities requiring little effort might be considered recreational or beneficial under this definition, they would not be considered genuine physical education.

---

[4] Harold M. Barrow, *Man and His Movement: Principles of His Physical Education,* Lea and Febiger, Philadelphia, 1971, p. 15.

[5] John E. Nixon and Ann E. Jewett, *An Introduction to Physical Education,* 8th ed., W. B. Saunders, Philadelphia, 1974, p. 73.

[6] James A. Baley and David A. Field, *Physical Education and the Physical Educator,* 2d ed., Allyn and Bacon, Boston, 1976, p. 4.

Jan Felshin has discussed the definition of physical education by suggesting that its body of knowledge is based on human movement, but not on all human movement; it has been focused upon gross muscular efforts and activities. The notion of physical prowess underlies physical education, as she defines it, and physical education has not been concerned with human use of movement in work, but primarily physical movement in play and sport, and the basic functioning of the human body.[7]

As we can see from these various definitions of physical education, the basic points that define the field are brought forth consistently by the different scholars. First, physical education is conducted through physical means—that is, there is some sort of physical activity involved. This physical activity is usually though not always moderately vigorous; it is concerned with gross motor movements; and the skills involved do not have to be very finely developed or highly skilled in quality for the benefits to be gained by the student. Finally, although the means of the educational methods—that is, the process by which the student gains these benefits—is physical, the benefits for the student include improvements or changes in such nonphysical areas within the spectrum of educational development as intellectual, social, and aesthetic growth.

In other words, physical education seeks to develop each person's whole being by the use of physical means, which is a characteristic that physical education shares with no other area of education. Since the educational results of the physical experience are not limited to the physical or body-improving benefits, our definition does not refer solely to the traditional meaning of physical activity. We must view the term *physical* on a broader, more abstract plane—as a condition of mind as well as body. Indeed, the physical education *should* realize improvements "in mind and body" that affect all aspects of the person's daily living, and the whole person should be the better for the experience.

**The Relationship to Play and Sport.** In defining physical education, we must also consider its relationship to play and sport. Numerous physical educators have begun to study play and its implications for human well-being. While many of these studies consider sport and physical education to be one and the same, we will consider play, sport, and physical education as three different but overlapping entities. *Play* is essentially activity used as amusement. We think of play as a noncompetitive type of physical amusement, though play does not have

---

[7] Jan Felshin, "Physical Education: An Introduction," in *Physical Education: An Interdisciplinary Approach,* ed. Robert N. Singer, Macmillan, New York, 1972, pp. 3–12.

Children get an early start in physical education in their play. Because play involves physical movement, elements of it are evident in both physical education and sport. (Boston Globe photo)

to be physical. Play is not necessarily sport or physical education, though elements of play may be found in both.

*Sport* is an organized, competitive form of play. Some persons view sport simply as an organized form of play, which might put it closer to physical education as we have defined it. However, close consideration will show that sport has traditionally involved competitive activities.

When we refer to sport as "organized" competitive activities, we mean that the activity has been refined and formalized to some degree —that is, some definite form or process is involved. Rules, whether they are written or not, are involved in this form of activity, and these rules or procedures cannot be changed during the competition, though new ones may evolve from one year to the next.

Sport is, above all, competitive activity. We cannot think of sport without thinking of competition, for without the competition, sport becomes simply play or recreation. Play can at times be sport, but strictly speaking, sport is never simple play; the competitive aspect is essential to the nature of sport.

*Physical education* has elements of both play and sport, but it is not exclusively either one nor a balanced combination of the two. By its very title physical education is physical activity with an educational goal. It is physical and it seeks to educate, but neither play nor sport —even though either can be used in the educational process—always includes the educational portion of the physical experience as a vital aim.

Play, sport, and physical education all involve forms of movement, and all can fit within the context of education if they are used for some educational purpose. Play can be for relaxation and entertainment without any educational aim, just as sport can exist for its own sake without any educational aim. For example, professional sports (some would use the term *athletics*) have no educational goals, yet we consider them no less sport, for an activity need not be amateur to be considered sport. Sport and play can exist purely for pleasure, purely for education, or for any combination of the two. Pleasure and education are not mutually exclusive; they can and should exist together.

## The Allied Areas: Health Education, Recreation, and Dance

In our attempt to explain physical education in its broadest sense, we should not overlook the areas allied to physical education. We have defined physical education as basically concerned with the development or education of the individual both *of* the physical and *through* the physical. To complete our description of this very broad concept, three areas allied to the field of physical education need to be introduced at this point.

*Health Education.* Health education is perhaps the largest of the areas allied to physical education. When we speak of health education, we most commonly use it in the sense of total fitness of the person, physical, mental, emotional, and social fitness, as Charles A. Bucher has described it.[8] Three subareas, which can be included in a description of the larger area of health education,[9] are also functions or goals of health education. The first of these areas is *health instruction,* which is concerned with teaching the basics of healthful living to students and the general public. This instruction is provided in various ways at every level from kindergarten through college and through various public information programs. Health instruction can include information on caring for the body and general disease prevention as well as sex instruction. It is also concerned with providing help for more specific problems, such as alcohol and drug abuse, or coping with death.

Providing *health services* is the second area included in health education. In educational institutions health services are necessary to develop and maintain a reasonable state of health among the students. The nurses and doctors who work in this area of health education pro-

[8] Charles A. Bucher, *Foundations of Physical Education,* 6th ed., C. V. Mosby, St. Louis, 1972, p. 6.

[9] Jenny, p. 25.

vide routine health care services, such as dental, hearing, and eye examinations, and outpatient services at the college level.

*Health environment* is the third area included within health education. Its goal is to present settings that provide better health and safety standards for the people involved. The services include, for example, provisions for examining the cleanliness of school or public facilities and seeing that people are not needlessly exposed to disease or injury.

Health educators are not necessarily teachers, but they are concerned with education and physical well-being, though the means by which they educate may not be physical.

**Recreation.** Recreation is the second of the three areas allied to physical education. We generally think of recreation as leisure-time activity. Recreation, however, has been defined as fulfilling the earlier educational goal of "the worthy use of leisure." [10] In this view activities are selected by the individual to serve a constructive nature, and they are not so much time-consuming as time-using. Jenny refers to them as activities that are physically, mentally, and socially healthful.[11] Jay B. Nash has referred to recreation as a complement to work and therefore a need of all individuals.[12] The emphasis of recreation in this sense is the re-creation of the person—that is, the revitalization of body and mind that is a result of getting away from the mundane things in life. Like physical education, recreation is a broad and rapidly growing field. For example, the growth of park programs across the country has led to an expansion of outdoor education and related activities. The educational base of recreation has also been broadened by increasing amounts of leisure time in people's lives, for they need to be educated in how to use their leisure time, just as other people need to learn how to provide leisure services.

**Dance.** Dance is the third area allied to physical education. Although dance is not necessarily large in terms of professionals within physical education, it is quite large in terms of the popularity of dance-oriented activities for people of all ages. Dance activities have been something of a stepchild for physical education, for dance hangs on the periphery of physical education. While dance activities can definitely be considered a part of physical education, dance itself is strongly a part of the arts. Possibly dance has come into the realm of physical education as a natural result of its body movement orientation, and perhaps this

[10] Jay B. Nash, "Education for Leisure: A Must," *JOHPER,* 31 (January 1960), 17–18, 62.
[11] Jenny, p. 43.
[12] Nash, pp. 17–18, 62.

Dancing, gymnastics, and other types of movement are allied to the general field of physical education. This ancient Greek vase shows such activities. (Courtesy Museum of Fine Arts, Boston)

bit of the arts can do much to temper the sometimes excessively athletic orientation of physical education with the aesthetics of art.

## Historical Terms for Physical Education

Physical education has been known by many other titles in the past, but most of these are now considered too narrow and exclusive to express the full scope of the field.

The earliest of these titles was *gymnastics.* During the nineteenth century gymnastics referred to exercises or activities that took place in a gymnasium, rather than the activities that today are a part of a particular sport. This term was very popular with European programs, but in the United States it came to be used for only one phase of the total physical education program. Because of the limited nature of its meaning, this term, where it is still used, carries an explanatory subtitle, such as Olympic gymnastics or corrective gymnastics.

Another popular term of the nineteenth century, *hygiene,* really referred to the science of preserving people's health. The definition of this term is similar to that of today's health education programs, which evolved as state legislatures at the turn of the century began passing laws requiring instruction in hygiene, or the teaching of basic health practices.

*Physical culture,* popular during the late nineteenth century, was often used in conjunction with the term *physical training.* Physical culture was a "fad" term often used in trying to sell programs of physical training designed to bring about certain physical, and often health, benefits. Physical training, which was also used as a sales promotional term, refers exclusively to physical conditioning exercises and programs. This term is still commonly used to describe programs in the armed services, but it is a far too narrow concept of physical education to be used by educators in the United States today.

## Physical Education: The Best Name for Our Field?

For years physical educators have been dissatisfied with the term *physical education,* because they feel that it does not make clear exactly what the concern of the field is. An allied problem is that many physical educators believe that the term recalls close ties between physical education and school athletics, or sports programs, which have all too often had little relationship to education in the schools. Many physical educators have wanted to divorce themselves of this tie to sports in the belief that only in this way can physical education show its true worth in the educational arena. For reasons such as these, physical educators have been seeking a new name for physical education—one that will clearly tell people what physical education is all about and one that will give a new image without any ties to the past.

Physical educators are currently attempting to resolve the name problem by seeking to establish the focus of the field. The American Academy of Physical Education devoted an issue of *The Academy Papers*[13] to the question of what constituted the theoretical base for physical education—that is, on what area of knowledge physical education is based. The discussions also considered whether the designation *physical education* should be replaced as the title for the field, and if so, what title should be used as its replacement.

***Defining the Theoretical Base.*** The discussions on the theoretical base of physical education presented in *The Academy Papers* centered on four different areas. Lois Ellfeldt stated the case for *movement* as the base of theory by stressing that we need to remember that movement is an open concept, more of a process than an absolute.[14] In this view there can be no physical education without movement.

---

[13] *The Academy Papers,* No. 7 (1973).
[14] Lois Ellfeldt, "Movement as a Theoretical Base for Physical Education," *The Academy Papers,* No. 7 (1973), 12–13.

The second area of theory was suggested by Paul Hunsicker, who proposed *fitness* as the theoretical base.[15] He discussed fitness as including mental and physical fitness and thus used a broadened definition of fitness. He suggested that one of the benefits of using fitness as the theoretical base is that the public generally understands and accepts the relationship between physical education and fitness.

Thomas J. Sheehan had earlier suggested *sport* as the focal point of physical education by discussing the difficulties involved in studying physical fitness, human movement, and social values derived from physical education activities. He suggested sport science as physical education's area of work and study.[16] Edward J. Shea continued the case for sport as physical education's theoretical base. He pointed out that his definition of sport does not exclude the less physically gifted person, thus it is broader than the traditional view.[17]

Other physical educators considered that the broad base of physical education is its greatest appeal. Warren Fraleigh took the viewpoint that physical education is *multitheoretical* and is not based on a single area of theory.[18] In essence, he stressed that several different kinds of theory are included in the broader context of physical education. Celeste Ulrich further elaborated on this point by noting that while each of the areas we have already cited stressed itself as the base that lies at the heart of physical education, each is basically part of a greater whole.[19] As she pointed out,

> . . . the concepts cannot be isolated. One moves to be active. Sport is based upon specific patterns of activity. Fitness results from activity carefully 'selected as to kind and conducted as to outcome' . . . . But there may be a way of putting it all together. If physical educators will stop seeking a uni-theoretical approach and agree that the uniqueness of physical education is in its multi-theoretical approach.[20]

According to this point of view, physical education draws from many areas of theory, which sets it apart from many other areas of educational

---

[15] Paul Hunsicker, "Fitness as a Theoretical Base for Physical Education," *The Academy Papers,* No. 7 (1973), 14–15.

[16] Thomas J. Sheehan, "Sport: the Focal Point of Physical Education," *Quest,* 10 (May 1968), 62–63, 66.

[17] Edward J. Shea, "Sport as a Theoretical Base for Physical Education," *The Academy Papers,* No. 7 (1973), 16–17.

[18] Warren Fraleigh, "Resolved that Physical Education is Multi-Theoretical Rather than Uni-Theoretical," *The Academy Papers,* No. 7 (1973), 10–11.

[19] Celeste Ulrich, "A Multi-Theoretical Crusade," *The Academy Papers,* No. 7 (1973), 18–20.

[20] Ibid., 19.

Suggested theoretical bases of physical
education.

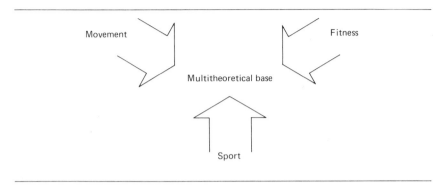

concern. In other words, we need not limit ourselves to any single area
of theory to say that we are working with the theoretical base of physical
education.

Daryl Siedentop considered these discussions on the focus of
study and theoretical base of physical education and pointed out the
risks of losing sight of the task of physical education. He believes
physical educators may get so carried away with the semantic battles,
fighting over the definitions and implications of the terms they use when
speaking of physical education, that they will forget what they are trying
to do with physical education. He suggested that physical educators
not spend so much time arguing over these questions that they fail
to concentrate on the battle to improve the teaching of physical education in the schools.[21]

**_Possible New Names for Physical Education._** The American Academy
of Physical Education also considered several possible new designations that would better define the field and by their very names enable
people to understand what physical education really is. There had
been some preliminary discussions of whether the older term needed
to be dropped for a new name, with Rosalind Cassidy leading the discussion,[22] and during the next year brief presentations in _The Academy
Papers_ were made in support of the various proposed designations.[23]

[21] Daryl Siedentop, "On Tilting at Windmills While Rome Burns," _Quest,_ 18 (June
1972), 94–97.

[22] Rosalind Cassidy, "Should We Drop the Designation _Physical Education_ in Favor of
a Different Name?" _The Academy Papers,_ No. 6 (1972), 1–4.

[23] _The Academy Papers,_ No. 7 (1973), 26–32.

*Movement arts and sciences* was suggested as one possible new name since movement is a vital concern of the field.  Physical education, however, goes beyond simple science; dance, for example, cannot be called a science so much as an art.  Nevertheless, while this designation is not broad enough in this area, it does give some indication of the breadth of physical education's concerns.

*Movement arts,* which was also suggested, is really a slightly less broad version of the movement arts and sciences title already mentioned.  Using this title can eliminate some of the overlap of study within the sciences that are concerned with certain aspects of human movement, but it causes the problem of disregard for the precision of science within physical education.  Much science is involved in physical education; it is not primarily an art, any more than it is purely a science.

*Movement education* refers to the broader meaning of physical education, but there has been some confusion over the use of the term, as Marion R. Broer pointed out.  Many educators have interpreted the term as referring primarily to dance activities, which is only a narrow part of physical education, while others have confused it with the movement education that has developed at the elementary school level and come to the United States from England.[24]  While movement education is not often used to refer to the broad field of physical education, nothing in its meaning contradicts what physical education seeks to do.

*Developmental motor performance,* another designation that was advanced, expresses physical education's concern with motor performance and its development.  The problems involved in using this designation lie in its breadth, as well as its clarity: Does it describe the whole work of physical education?  Would a typical educator in another field know what physical educators do according to this title?

*Kinesiology* is a term that many physical educators have been using as their designation for the field.  This term, which is primarily scholar oriented, refers to the study of human movement.  However, in the sense that the term refers to a particular study, it gives no indication of the breadth of what is taught.  A student in physical education does not necessarily study movement; movement is used to teach the student something, but he or she does not always study the movement itself.  Teaching the strategy involved in playing a team game, for example, is definitely a part of physical education, but it is not kinesiology or the study of movement per se.  Since we are not always involved in studying the movement itself, kinesiology is too narrow in scope to define the

---

[24] Marion R. Broer, "Movement Education: Wherein the Disagreement?" *Quest,* 2 (April 1964), 19–24.

The suggested components of a discipline based on the human movement phenomena. (From AAHPER, *Tones of Theory,* Washington, D.C., 1972, p. 13. Used by permission of the American Alliance for Health, Physical Education and Recreation, 1201 16th Street, N.W., Washington, D.C. 20036)

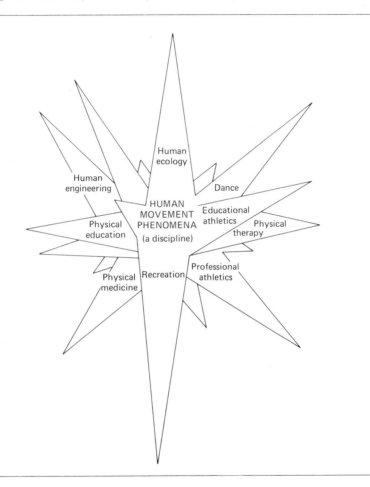

whole field, even though it does get at the heart of much of the physical education study.

*Human physical sciences,* as a suggested designation for physical education, points out a number of the characteristics of the field, for it is concerned with studying the areas of the physical sciences (such as physics and the laws of mechanics) as they relate to people. However, to understand its use as a descriptive title for physical education, people must know exactly what the physical sciences are as well as the difference between physical education and the overlapping areas within the sciences.

*Physical fitness,* or simply *fitness,* has been used at times to refer primarily to the bodily aspects of fitness, which makes it simply a more modern version of the older title of physical training. Physical fitness is basically a state of health or a condition of the body's ability to withstand the stresses of daily life, and since programs of physical fitness concentrate primarily on these physical goals, the term is too narrow to include the broader goals of physical education.

*Athletics* and/or *sport* have increasingly come into use as designations for physical education, as has *sport sciences,* but these titles are also too narrow by definition to represent the whole field of physical education. We have discussed sport and what it represents. Athletics is essentially the same thing, though some scholars will debate this statement at the philosophical level. Athletics refers to competitive activities, organized games and sports, either on a team or on an individual basis. Competitive activities are only one phase of education, and as we have mentioned, they need not be educational. Unless sport and athletics are properly channeled and oriented, they can easily result in education or learning directly contrary to what the physical educator is seeking to accomplish. Even though these titles have gained much favor in recent years, they must be rejected as being too narrow in concept to represent physical education in its broadest, best sense.

*Physical education and sport* is another suggested designation that is becoming more common. This title broadens the concerns of physical education by making it clear that sport is a concern of the field, but at the same time it shows that sport is not the only concern. This title has two inherent benefits: It retains the traditional designation, which is basically familiar to the public, yet it includes sport, which is vitally involved in physical education, and which is increasingly viewed by a large number of educators as the primary area of physical education's concern.

Lastly, some arguments were advanced for retaining the title *physical education.* Although many physical educators are not satisfied with this title, they realize that the public does at least have *some* idea of what physical education is and that it may be easier to develop a new image for the old term than to teach the public to recognize a new, unfamiliar title.

Although no agreement has been reached, this latter trend is the most likely direction for the next few years. However, when the arguments have all been studied and the dust has settled, perhaps the most likely replacement will be the title of *physical education and sport.* The largest movement away from the physical education designation at this time is toward the use of various designations that include the word *sport.*

No matter what the final designation, we should keep in mind that each of the proposals to define and represent physical education by a particular name depends heavily on individual interpretations of the focus within the field. Perhaps this diversity of opinion is a virtue in itself, for it represents our earlier definition of physical education as a very broad area of work and study that includes many people who seem to have little relationship to each other in their interests and tasks.

Physical education is indeed a house of many rooms, and though communications between those working and studying within each of the rooms may sometimes be difficult, it is still one house, and its inhabitants have but one goal—that of physical education as we have broadly defined it in this chapter.

## Suggested Readings

*The Academy Papers,* No. 7 (1973). Given largely to discussions of the focus and proper designation of the field of physical education.

*The Academy Papers,* No. 9 (1975). Discussions centered around the topic "Realms of Meaning."

Brackenbury, Robert L. "Physical Education, an Intellectual Emphasis?" *Quest,* 1 (December 1963), 3–6.

Caillois, Roger. *Man, Play, and Games.* Free Press, New York, 1961.

Cassidy, Rosalind. "The Cultural Definition of Physical Education." *Quest,* 4 (April 1965), 11–15.

Fallon, Dennis J. "Child's Play: Run for the Trophy." *Quest,* 24 (Summer 1975), 59–62.

Grebner, Florence, and Jack E. Razor. "Interdisciplinary Approaches to Physical Education." *Journal of Physical Education and Recreation (JOPER),* 46 (June 1975), 34.

Gulick, Luther. "Physical Education: A New Profession." Reprinted in *Chronicle of American Physical Education,* 1855–1930. Edited by Aileene S. Lockhart and Betty Spears. Wm. C. Brown, Dubuque, Ia., 1972, pp. 91–97.

Huizinga, Johan. *Homo Ludens: A Study of the Play-Element in Culture.* Beacon Press, Boston, 1950.

"The Language of Movement," *Quest,* 23 (January 1975), entire issue.

Metheny, Eleanor. "The Third Dimension in Physical Education." Reprinted in Arthur Weston, *The Making of American Physical Education.* Appleton-Century-Crofts, New York, 1962, pp. 237–241.

———. "This 'Thing' Called Sport." *Journal of Health, Physical Education, and Recreation (JOHPER),* 40 (March 1969), 59–60.

Mitchell, Robert Thomas. *A Conceptual Analysis of Art as Experience and Its Implications for Sport and Physical Education.* Microfiched Ed.D. dissertation, University of Northern Colorado, 1974.

————. "Sport as Experience." *Quest,* 24 (Summer 1975), 28–33.

Norbeck, Edward, et al. *The Anthropological Study of Human Play.* Rice University Studies, vol. 60, no. 3, 1974.

Pratt, Robert Lewis. *The Concept of Play in American Physical Education.* Microfiched Ph.D. dissertation, Ohio State University, 1973.

Pullias, Earl V. "The Education of the Whole Man." *Quest,* 1 (December 1963), 37–42.

Schrader, Carl L. "The Deeper Meaning of Physical Education." Reprinted in Arthur Weston, *The Making of American Physical Education.* Appleton-Century-Crofts, New York, 1962, pp. 245–248.

Siedentop, Daryl. *Physical Education: Introductory Analysis,* 2d ed. Wm. C. Brown, Dubuque, Ia., 1976, Chapters 5–8, 10.

Ulrich, Celeste. *To Seek and Find.* AAHPER, Washington, D.C., 1976.

Whited, Clark V. "Sport Science." *JOHPER,* 42 (May 1971), 21–25.

Williams, Jesse Feiring. "Cultural Aspects of Physical Education." Reprinted in Arthur Weston, *The Making of American Physical Education.* Appleton-Century-Crofts, New York, 1962, pp. 227–230.

————. "Education Through the Physical." Reprinted in *Chronicle of American Physical Education, 1855–1930.* Edited by Aileene S. Lockhart and Betty Spears. Wm. C. Brown, Dubuque, Ia., 1972, pp. 1–5.

————. *The Principles of Physical Education,* 8th ed. W. B. Saunders, Philadelphia, 1964, Chapter 1.

Zeigler, Earle F. "Five Stances That Have Got to Go." *JOHPER,* 44 (September 1973), 48–49.

# II The Historical Development of Physical Education

# 2 Physical Education in the Ancient World

Scientists have difficulty determining where humans originated—that is, if life began in one single area of the world. Scholars have theorized that human beings gradually evolved from simpler forms of life, but they have been unable to find concrete examples of all stages of the evolutionary process. Traces of early humans have been found in Africa, Asia, and Europe, though current theory suggests that people most similar to modern people first appeared in eastern Africa, in the vicinity of the Great Rift Valley.

During prehistoric times the world went through long periods of great changes in climate. In time, these changes, which varied from periods of tropical conditions to great ice ages and back to tropical conditions, forced prehistoric human beings to gradually disperse across the face of the earth in search of havens from nature's harshness. Primitive people gradually reached the major continents and appeared on many of the earth's islands. Because of the differences in the level of the seas, many areas that are now below water level were at one time dry land; these dry areas provided many "land bridges" to areas that are now separate islands or continents. A prominent example of the land bridge theory is the Bering Strait, which might have been a dry land connection by which Asian people moved into North America and then eventually on into Central and South America.

## Primitive Times

Primitive human beings lived in a harsh environment, and in order to survive constant battles with nature, they gradually developed crude tools, such as axes, knives, and bows and arrows, which elevated them above other forms of animal life. The primitive human's cranial capacity —which was larger than that of other creatures in relation to body size—permitted the full development of the human intellect and capacity

The emphasis of education in primitive
times was survival; prehistoric cave paint-
ings often depict hunting and warfare.
(Courtesy American Museum of Natural
History)

to reason and thus improved the chances of human survival over that
of the animals.

More advanced patterns of speech developed as people became
able to differentiate among shades of meaning. This greater precision
and refinement in communication skills was a necessary step toward
civilization, for it allowed people to begin working together to improve
their group situation. While only the toughest and fittest individuals
could survive the harsh life in primitive times, the formation of increasingly larger groups eased the difficulties of survival for the individual
members, who were then able to develop their defenses.

Primitive human beings gathered first in family groups; then
several family groups would band together into a tribe under a stronger
leader or chief. The groups overcame the difficulties of providing food
by learning to plant and harvest crops, and thus led more settled
lives than the migratory prehistoric people who constantly searched
for food.

As farming developed and people were able to live and feed in
one area for much longer periods of time, villages grew and society
became more stable. People were no longer forced to move when
game animals became scarce, for the sources of food had expanded.
Living in settled villages sped up the process of civilization by leading

to improvements in the crude standards of living and a gradual eleva-
tion of the type of education provided for the young.

The basic aim of the education within primitive society was
survival—both individual survival and group survival. The education
provided young males was primarily physical education, for it was
oriented strongly toward physical strength and cunning. Good hunting
and fighting skills were necessary if early man was to feed himself
and his family and provide protection from other forces.

Deobold Van Dalen and Bruce Bennett suggest that primitive
education was concerned with learning in two areas: the survival skills
and conformity conduct.[1] The survival skills included the ability to
defend oneself and others; the ability to provide food, clothing, and
shelter; and the skills necessary to live as an individual in the world.
The conformity skills were designed to insure the survival of the group
by putting the skills of the individual into the service of the group.
People had to be able to work with others to fill the needs of the group
or the group would not survive. If the group did not survive, then human
life would eventually pass from existence.

Dance activities and other ceremonial forms had meaning in
primitive societies as forms of prayer or means of communicating to
the forces that could not be explained. Primitive people both feared
and revered the forces of nature, and in trying to influence what they
could neither understand nor explain, they gradually developed religious beliefs and customs. Through dance the primitive people
sought religious communication and experience.

Among the physical activities of primitive people were the hunting skills of archery, spear and rock throwing, and stalking animals.
Survival skills included such activities as running, jumping, and swimming, while hand-to-hand combat—primarily wrestling—represented
the fighting skills.

As societies grew more advanced and life became easier, recreational activities developed. These activities often grew from earlier
survival skills—such as archery and running contests—but they became aimed more at children or for use by adults as entertainment.
As games and sports developed, ball games became a popular activity
in early societies. Despite differences caused by climate, local customs,
and available natural materials, the games that developed around the
world were basically similar, for they often served as training methods
in skills the children would need as adults.

---

[1] Deobold B. Van Dalen and Bruce L. Bennett, *A World History of Physical Education,*
2d ed., Prentice-Hall, Englewood Cliffs, N.J., 1971, p. 1.

The character of this type of education changed with the development of far more complex cultural patterns than existed in village societies. As civilizations grew, the world moved closer to the state concept, and large groups of people sharing many similar characteristics—such as racial group, language, customs, and mode of living—developed loose governmental forms and leaders. Rather than aiming education, which had been primarily physical education in primitive cultures, toward the survival of the individual and small groups, the new states oriented the educational process toward their own strength and survival, and often toward their expansion.

## Ancient China

The Chinese civilization was not the earliest civilization, and while it had almost no effect upon the development of Western civilization and patterns of education, it was the major civilization of the Far East. Chinese history extends more than two thousand years before the Christian era, and its civilization remained stable well into modern times, which thus makes it one of the longest lasting of history's civilizations.

Early China was a society of agrarian people governed by tradition. All persons fulfilled assigned tasks just as those tasks had been carried out before their birth and would be performed long after their death. The very strong societal organization was based on a strong family unit, which was controlled by its eldest member. Every individual had strong family ties and followed the tradition of ancestor worship, for individual obedience and subservience to the family or group, rather than individuality, was stressed.

The nation's feudal system was based on a group of major lords who had many vassals who owed them their allegiance. The dominant interest of the government was the maintenance of the status quo, or keeping things as they had been in the past.

The educational process, which was primarily for the upper classes, gradually became book oriented and formal. The emphasis on memorizing ancient writings required oral tests in which entire passages would be recited from memory; the result was a widespread system of rigorous examinations that left no time for physical activities. Many of the ancient writings, or teachings, were based on the works of Confucius and Buddha, and an attempt was made to develop the student's intellectual, moral, and aesthetic senses. During the earlier period of China's history the educational process had included physical training, but as the process became more ritualistic, there was less time available for such activities.

Although vigorous physical activities were generally of little interest in ancient China, the Chinese did participate in early versions of modern sports. The ball game here is similar to modern-day soccer. (From H. A. Giles, Adversaria Sinica, I, 92. Courtesy Widener Library, Harvard University)

In many societies the military needs of the nation were often a reason for developing a program of physical training, but this reason was not generally true in ancient China, for the Chinese developed a policy of isolationism that was maintained almost intact until the nineteenth century. The country was also blessed with many natural barriers that made invasion by outside forces extremely difficult. The towering Himalaya Mountains, which were all but impossible to pass, blocked much of the southern approaches to the land, and further complications were presented by the Gobi Desert. In answer to the few unprotected borders, the Great Wall (completed about 200 B.C.) was later built to protect much of the northwest border of China.

Many social problems resulted from the static nature of Chinese society, for it could accept no innovations unless they were justified by ancient authorities. The system of respect for the past and honor of elders of the family was upheld and implemented, however, by the teachings of Confucianism, which stressed the self-restraint and moderation necessary to survival in such an unchanging society. As religions developed, they were the sort of teachings that emphasized a life of contemplation as the ideal. Accordingly, the combined nature of the various aspects of Chinese life made vigorous physical exercise an idea of little interest to the society.

However, such recreational games and sports as early versions of soccer, polo, chess, and competitions in archery and wrestling were practiced by the people. A program of mild physical exercises, similar to gymnastics-oriented calisthenics, was developed and called *Cong Fu*. These activities were designed to prevent disease, which the Chinese believed could result from a lack of physical activity. Dancing was also popular. The dance was used primarily for ceremonial purposes, though there were both religious and popular forms. The popular forms were informal dances that the people used for recreational purposes.

## Ancient India

India was not a major influence in the development of Western civilization, but it represents an important civilization that is almost as ancient as China's.

India was invaded and largely taken over by an Aryan people around 1500 to 1200 B.C. The primary religion was Hinduism, which was also a social system and thus a factor of importance in the development of Indian civilization. The caste, or class, system within this religion eventually became very rigid and severely limited the flexibility of Indian society. The people were divided by the system into castes, or social classes, which were a part of their lives. Because they could not move either upward or downward in caste, their positions in life were unchanging.

The primary aim of a person under Hinduism was to be virtuous. Asceticism, which was also stressed by the religion, could take almost any form from a simple moderation of the wants of the individual to self-torture (only occasionally) depending on the strength and direction of the person's religious views.

Education was based upon a person's caste, for the castes dictated the type of occupation the members could follow, though the occupation might not have any relationship to the person's talents or abilities. There was no stress upon individuality; emphasis was placed on the future life. The Hindus believed in reincarnation—that is, in the soul of the person returning to earth after the body's death to inhabit another body, which might be human or animal, depending upon how well that person's previous life was lived.

There was little interest in physical education, though there were some recreational sports and games, and dances were used for ceremonies and religious observances. Some physical training was necessarily provided for the members of the military, who entertained themselves with hunting activities when there was no war. Physical exercises were sometimes used to promote health, but the dominant view under Hinduism was not toward the care or exercise of the body.


## Ancient Egypt

The predecessors of Western civilization were found in the Middle East, an area around the eastern end of the Mediterranean Sea that spreads inland into the area of the ancient Fertile Crescent along the valleys of the Tigris and Euphrates Rivers. Egypt furnished a natural place for an ancient civilization to flourish. The annual floods of the Nile River provided a rich soil for farming, while the water was always available for irrigation.

Although the civilization of ancient Egypt goes back for thousands of years, it reached its peak around 1500 B.C., when it controlled large areas of the Middle East. The Egyptian people were a very advanced civilization for the times. They developed writing and paper, produced great feats of engineering, developed a twelve-month calendar, and did much work in the sciences, farming, and the arts. Egyptian society was very religious, for the people believed in many gods and a life after death. It was also one of the earliest to give women a role and status roughly equal to that of the men; the women had many more rights and powers than were available to them in other societies.[2]

Much of the educational process in early Egypt was aimed at professional training, particularly for the position of scribe, which required the important skills of reading and writing. The education was primarily oriented toward the practical aspects of learning a trade, and students often served apprenticeships.

There was little interest in physical education. As the Egyptians were usually not military oriented, there was little impetus for physical training from that direction. However, some sporting contests existed as religious observances, and dance had a religious orientation.

Many games and sports were popular with the Egyptians, and women frequently participated in physical activities. Swimming was popular—for the civilization's life was based on the river—as were gymnastic activities, hunting, games using the skills of fighting and war, and many types of ball games. The Egyptians also had a great love for activities involving dance. Although physical education was not a major part of Egyptian life, physical activities were very important to the Egyptians.

---

[2] C. W. Hackensmith, *History of Physical Education,* Harper & Row, New York, 1966, pp. 16–18.

## The Ancient Middle East

The Middle Eastern civilizations included the Sumerians, Babylonians, Assyrians, Persians, and Macedonians. Their area of the world spread eastward from the Mediterranean Sea across the Tigris and Euphrates valleys and ranged northward to present-day Turkey, southward to the Arabian peninsula, and eastward to an area near modern India.

The Assyrian civilization began before 2000 B.C. and reached its peak of power about 1200 B.C. Thereafter one civilization followed another until about 100 B.C. when the Macedonians faded from the scene.

Much of the emphasis within these successive civilizations was on military conquest. Because of this military orientation, physical education in the Middle Eastern civilizations consisted primarily of warring activities, such as handling weapons and developing the ability to engage in hand-to-hand combat. Much of the fighting of the Persians was done on horseback, so much work in their civilization was devoted to developing the skills needed for good horsemanship. A strong emphasis was also placed upon swimming.

The physical training process for the men, which began in early youth and lasted well into the adult years, was very rigorous. Since little emphasis was placed on intellectual training, the educational process was more training than true education. Dance, which was largely a part of ceremonial exhibitions, was discouraged as a recreation activity for the people.

## Ancient Greece

The first Greek-speaking people were the Achaeans. They were invaders who settled in the northern areas of the Greek peninsula about 1900 B.C. and replaced the society and culture of the Minoan civilization of Crete. By about 1500 B.C. the Achaeans controlled most of the peninsula and had established Mycenae as their capital. Their economy was based on trade, and they established a number of commercial alliances with such other prominent cities and states of the eastern Mediterranean area as Troy, Cyprus, Palestine, and Egypt.

After several hundred years, however, prolonged warfare and a declining Mycenaean economy permitted another invasion of the Greek peninsula from the north. These invaders, the Dorians, referred to themselves as Hellenes and the area they had invaded (the peninsula of modern Greece) as Hellas.[3]

---

[3] Arthur Weston, *The Making of American Physical Education,* Appleton-Century-Crofts, New York, 1962, pp. 1–2.

The period of the Achaean or Mycenaean culture, from about 1500 to 800 B.C., was the Age of Homer. Many descriptions of Greek life and customs in this time appear in the two epic writings—the *Iliad* and the *Odyssey*—attributed to him.

Rule was by an oligarchy—that is, by a small group of aristocrats. Women were not considered equal to men in this society, but were considered the property of the men, with a certain value in livestock.[4] The education of the men at this time was essentially military, for there was no formal education, as we think of it today. The emphasis was on developing military skills, by such activities as running, boxing, and wrestling.

The people had developed rituals for the burial and entombment of the dead, which were similar to the customs of the Egyptians. Games had some religious aspects, for the people had also developed funeral games that were meant to honor the dead. Prizes were given to the winners of contests in footracing, boxing, wrestling, and chariot games. Most other contests and sports at this time were informal, rather than regularly occurring, organized events.

As the Mycenaean influence declined, the Greek peninsula gradually split up into a number of small city-states, or independent units. Within each city-state a town controlled the territory in its immediate vicinity but had no ties or obligations to any other city-state. As the city-states grew in strength, the classical Greek civilization with which most people are familiar gradually began to appear. During the Hellenic time period the major city-states were Sparta and Athens. These two city-states, though similar in many respects, were in marked contrast in their methods of government and their philosophies of education.

**Spartan Education.** The Spartans, located in the southern Peloponnesus, were a totalitarian society. The state was oriented entirely toward the military life. Education, which was controlled by the state, was a harsh process of training for the males, and weak children were abandoned to die in the wilderness so that the strength of the state would not be threatened by weak citizens.

The educational process was almost entirely physical. The emphasis on preparing the male child for the military life included diligent programs of running and throwing activities (javelin and discus), swimming, wrestling, boxing, and gymnastic activities. Dance was popular in Sparta because it not only was used to imitate military movements, but was part of the ceremonial and recreational occasions as well. Music was also important, for much of the exercise was performed to

---

[4] Emmett A. Rice, John L. Hutchinson, and Mabel Lee, *A Brief History of Physical Education,* 5th ed., Ronald Press, New York, 1969, pp. 11–14.

music.[5] Many songs were composed to honor dead heroes, and the laws of the state were set to music.

The male children went through three stages of military training. They left their homes to live in barracks at the age of seven years and trained in packs under an older young man until they were about fourteen. They then underwent more intensive military training until they were about twenty years old, at which time they became regular members of the military. Even as military men, they had to live in the barracks until they were thirty years old. At that age they could marry and leave the barracks, though they were still required to eat with the other soldiers, rather than in their own homes.

Because of their emphasis on military training, the Spartans developed the best war machine in Greece, but they did not develop the ability to rule well politically. The boundaries of the areas that they ruled successfully were never very large, even though they did defeat the Athenians in the Peloponnesian Wars.

The education of the girls was not neglected, for it was also controlled by the state from the time a girl was seven years old until she was about eighteen. The training, which emphasized weight control and conditioning to prepare the girls for motherhood, used many of the same activities used by the boys. The girls participated regularly in athletics, just as the boys did, and many markers honoring their athletic feats were put up in ancient times by proud fathers and brothers. Unlike the men, however, when a woman married, her physical activities were ended, and she was expected to stay in the home.

While the Spartans were important participants in the games and sports at the many festivals of the times, they discouraged boxing and the *pankration* (a sort of free style, no-holds-barred fighting) because the fighter had to admit defeat to prevent death or severe injury. Spartans were taught never to admit defeat. They considered victory very important, and their records of their victories provide many of the earliest clues to the nature of sport in Greece.

The Spartans placed no real emphasis upon intellectual forms of education. The Spartans were trained for war, but they were not equipped to survive a successful peace. Their inability to rule well in times of peace eventually led to the conquest of the Greek people, first by the Macedonians and then by the Romans. The Spartan failure points out the severe shortcomings of the unbalanced approach of the Spartans toward education.

**Athenian Education.** Athens of classical times has long been the favorite model for the theoretical balance necessary in education, par-

---

[5] Hackensmith, pp. 26–31.

ticularly so to physical educators because of its emphasis upon physical education.

Athens contrasted strongly to Sparta in many ways. While the state had begun as an oligarchy, the Athenians became a democratic society oriented toward the individual rather than toward the state. Their concept of democracy, however, was basically for the men rather than the women.

Athenian education was the first system of education that we think of as modern. It was the first system to be concerned with the all-around development of the individual, both mentally and physically.[6] The old motto that stresses the goal of education as "a sound mind in a sound body" expresses the essential balance that was the best quality of Athenian education. The process stressed physical training, public worship (which included music), and learning the traditions and customs of the state. Later, "book learning" was added to this list, as reading and writing came to be considered more necessary skills.

Weimer speaks of Athenian education as stressing *paideia,* which meant the "beautiful and the good." [7] This represented the ideal characteristics of the Athenian citizen: aesthetic sensibilities, knowledge, physical skills, and a strong sense of ethics.

The educational system in Athens, like democracy, was primarily for the men; the women were educated in the home and had few rights. Plato had suggested that the educational process for boys should begin with physical education at about the age of six years, with grammar added at the age of ten and music added at the age of thirteen. In reality, however, all three portions of the process were begun at about the same time and continued until the boy reached the age of about eighteen and entered the military.

The program of physical education for older males was concentrated at the *gymnasium.* The name for this type of training school came from the Greek word meaning "naked," for the Greeks exercised and performed in the nude. The gymnasium was relatively elaborate, and because considerable room was needed for running and throwing activities, it was built outside the city. A smaller version of the gymnasium, the *palestra,* or wrestling school, was located within the city and was used primarily for the training of the schoolboys. Despite these differences, the designations *gymnasium* and *palestra* are frequently used interchangeably.

A teacher of physical exercise at the *palestra* was called a *paido-tribe* and was similar to today's physical education instructor. The men

[6] Hermann Weimer, *Concise History of Education,* Philosophical Library, New York, 1962, pp. 3–11.

[7] Ibid., p. 8.

who coached or trained the athletes for competition were called *gymnastes* (the terms *paidotribe* and *gymnaste* are also often used interchangeably).[8] These instructors were often retired champion athletes, and their duties were similar to today's coaches.

The basic aim of the educational process at the gymnasium was not the development of the physical for its own sake; it was designed to develop the qualities of the individual *through* the use of physical means.[9] The activities used by the Athenians at the palestra and the gymnasium were essentially the same as those used by the Spartans, but with the addition of exercises designed to improve the movement skills, such as posture and the mechanics of graceful movement. The Spartans stressed the development of the man of action, while the Athenians sought a harmonious development of the individual across physical and intellectual lines. Because of this balance, physical education was a more important part of the education and was better integrated into the educational process than in any other civilization before or since Athens.

**Athletic Games and Contests.**  Many of the religious games and festivals held by the Athenians and other Greeks during this period (1000 to 300 B.C.) were generally celebrated by athletic contests, dances, and music. Some of the festivals were celebrated within a single city-state and by only one sex, as in the case of honoring local gods, for example; other festivals, however, were broader in appeal and sometimes were celebrated by all the Greek people.

The greatest of these festivals was the Olympic games, which were celebrated in honor of Zeus, chief god of the Greeks.[10] The festival lasted for five days in late August and was held on every fourth year (which resulted in the term *Olympiad,* meaning a four-year period).

The first recorded Olympic games took place in 776 B.C., though there were undoubtedly contests prior to that date. The games took place near the village of Elis in western Greece.

Each year a month-long peace was declared (the *pax Olympica*) around the time of the games. It required each city-state to cease any fighting with any other city-state and to allow all athletes passage through its territory. No women were allowed to view or compete in the games, and as was the custom of the day, the athletes competed in the nude.

---

[8] E. Norman Gardiner, *Greek Athletic Sports and Festivals,* Macmillan, London, 1910 (Wm. C. Brown Reprints, Dubuque, Ia., 1970), pp. 468, 503.
[9] Van Dalen and Bennett, pp. 46–67.
[10] Ibid., pp. 51–56.

Generally the games might be considered the greatest cultural exchange among the various Greeks of that period. The multitudes of people who came to watch the games mingled during the week of competition and all the athletes were required to spend the last month of training prior to the games in a common training camp with all the other Olympic competitors.

The games were originally held on a field beside a statue of Zeus, and the footraces started at its base. Later, over a period of years, a stadium was constructed. The primary footrace of the games was the *stade,* which was a race for the length of the long, narrow stadium, or about 180 meters. Another race was twice that long, while other races of up to three miles in length were held in some festivals. The shortest race was the most important race, however. Starting places were carved into stone for the sprinters, and javelins—and later, stone pillars—were used to mark the turning points and finishing lines.

Other events in the Olympic games included the discus throw, the javelin throw (thrown with the aid of a leather strap), the long jump (with hand weights to assist the takeoff), wrestling in several different styles, boxing, the very rough *pankration,* chariot and horse racing, and the pentathlon. The pentathlon consisted of five events: a short run, the long jump, discus and javelin throws, and wrestling. The manner of determining the winner has not been settled by scholars,[11] though H. A. Harris suggests that it required victory in three of the five events.[12]

The prize for an Olympic victory was simply a wreath or crown of olive leaves. However, the victorious athletes were usually feted by their city-states when they returned home. Triumphal parades were held, and many privileges were given to them, including gifts of money. Often statues of the Olympic champions were erected.

There were many other Greek festivals that included athletic competitions. The most prominent ones were the Pythian games at Delphi, the Isthmian festival (on the Isthmus of Corinth), and the Nemean festival. Evidence is clear that there were also separate athletic competitions for women.

Scarce records indicate that a festival of Hera was held every four years at the Olympic stadium at a time separate from the Olympic games.[13] In this competition the racing distance for the women was shortened by one-sixth. Apparently the women's competitions were

---

[11] Gardiner, pp. 359–371.

[12] H. A. Harris, *Sport in Greece and Rome,* Cornell University Press, Ithaca, N.Y., 1972, pp. 34–35.

[13] H. A. Harris, "The Greek Athletic Programme," *Proceedings of the First International Seminar on the History of Physical Education and Sport,* Wingate Institute for Physical Education and Sport, Nitanya, Israel, April 1968, p. 7-2.

expanding by the first century A.D., for their events are recorded at the other competitions we have mentioned.[14] Although many of the competitions were at times of religious holidays, Harris suggests that this has little actual religious significance in terms of the origin of the games. He theorizes that the festivals simply allowed convenient leisure time for the competitions, just as the American football bowl games were not founded as religious celebrations of Christmas and New Year's Day.[15]

Over a period of hundreds of years the interest in the Greek athletic competitions declined. The Olympic games in particular gradually fell into disrepute as professional athletes began to compete. The athletes with more money were able to devote more time to training for the games, which gave them an advantage over the athletes who did not have similar training. This professionalism became more prevalent after the Romans conquered the Greeks. The games were finally abolished by the emperor of the Byzantines (the Eastern Roman Empire), Theodosius I, in A.D. 394, partly because as a Christian he considered the games, which were held to honor the Greek gods, to be pagan events, though their corruption by professionalism had also changed the character of the games considerably by then.[16]

The Greek civilization, particularly as represented by the Athenians, was a high point in the history of education. This period marked the first time in Western civilization that the educational process had developed beyond predominantly military or trade designs and needs. For the first time education had a balanced goal: the development of a "whole" man, a person who was well and equally developed in mind and body, a man who was acceptable to the military needs of his day, but who, unlike the Spartans, could also fulfill the civic or governmental needs of his time.

Philosophy had entered education (see Part III) in this period, for people such as Socrates, Plato, and Aristotle had sought to develop or discover an "ideal" educational process to develop the well-rounded product of education that they believed should be the goal of education. Such a balanced educational process as the Athenians had was not to be seen again until the Renaissance, and when it did appear, it was a deliberate attempt to copy the newly rediscovered Greeks. As Greek civilization declined and Roman civilization grew to replace it, much of the glory of its culture was lost to Western civilization. As the power of the Greek people declined (largely because of prolonged wars between the city-states), they were conquered by the Macedonian empire of Alexander the Great. When Alexander died

---

[14] Harris, *Sport,* pp. 40–41.
[15] Ibid., p. 17.
[16] Hackensmith, pp. 54–55.

around 320 B.C., his empire broke into smaller nations. The Greek civilization went through a process of blending with the civilization of the Middle East over the next two centuries. The resulting diluted Greek culture was encountered by the Romans as they became powerful in the eastern Mediterranean between 200 and 100 B.C.

## Ancient Rome

Roman civilization grew at a hilly point on the Tiber River in the central part of the Italian peninsula. Founded by shepherds and traders, Rome began as a republican society with the government of the state shared by the citizens. This state gradually expanded its control of the surrounding territory until it had conquered the entire peninsula of Italy. It then looked to other parts of the Mediterranean, always with the excuse that Rome was only protecting itself against potential invaders.

The essential characteristic of the Roman civilization was practicality: What would work in a given situation? While the Greeks had been thinkers and philosophers, the Romans were doers. The Greeks built philosophies, and the Romans built roads.

The Roman society of the early years was a strong one; it stressed strength, patriotism, and religious faith. Character, or morals, was also stressed strongly. Women were more important and equal in the Roman society than they had been in Greece.

During this time the education was received at home. The object of early Roman education was to produce children who would be true to the Roman ideals and religion.

Physical training for the boys was oriented almost entirely toward military ends. Unlike the Greeks, the Romans had no real interest in beauty, harmony, or the balanced development of the individual, though a strong sense of morals was considered important. Much of the contact with literature came from the memorization of the Twelve Tables, Rome's codification of the laws.

As the power and influence of the Romans grew and they gained control of more provinces in the eastern Mediterranean, they saw more need for the education that would enable them to administer their territories. There was also a trend away from the military orientation of physical training as the old part-time army of citizens became more of a full-time army of "mercenaries," or noncitizens who were paid to serve in the army.

While education in the home had made early Rome strong, schools were developed outside the home as the empire grew. Much of the instruction was by Greek slaves, who had a broader education than the Romans.[17] They provided the grammar part of the traditional Greek education, but since the Romans saw no practical use for the gymnastics or music, these studies were not included in the program. The educational program was unbalanced, for the Romans were interested primarily in education that had practical uses. Their practical contributions to civilization were notably in law and engineering.

The great wealth that came into the Roman Empire from the conquered nations and the many slaves who did much of the work previously done by the poorer Romans led to a breakdown of the societal morals of the Roman people. A Roman did not need to work to live, for the state provided free food. Political corruption grew with the luxury, and the old Roman ideals of patriotism and self-sacrifice died.

The Romans saw little reason for physical training. Rome became a nation of spectators. The people would go to the circus or the amphitheater and watch chariot races or gladiatorial fights to the death. As they demanded more variety in the death-struggles, they used fights between animals and men, larger groups of men, and eventually even waged small sea battles by flooding the arena.

This emphasis on spectatorship and the growing professionalism in athletics destroyed much of the strength of Roman society, just as it had eventually destroyed the Olympic games of the Greeks, as professionals took over the games. The moral and educational values of the games had disappeared. The Romans were more interested in the violent sports—and only as spectators—and they were little interested in personal competition or in personal excellence.

The Romans were also very interested in baths. The ruins of old Roman baths, many of which were built and operated by the government, can be found in many areas of the Western world today. Some facilities were provided for exercise at the baths, but not on the scale of the Greek facilities. Exercise was only a minor part of the experience at the Roman baths, for the emphasis was upon the sedentary pleasures of hot and cold baths and massage.

The wealth and sedentary decadence of the Romans eventually brought down the empire. When the barbarians began to try to take it over, the Romans no longer had the internal strength to oppose a strong outside force. Although the Romans had gained control over most of western Europe, the Mediterranean, and the Middle East, the conquests began to reverse as the barbarians nibbled at the edges of the empire. By A.D. 400 the Romans were in full flight; they withdrew their outlying garrisons and came home to defend Rome, but to no avail. Riches and

---

[17] Weimer, pp. 11–16.

moral laxity had made Roman culture too weak for a successful defense. Although the last true Roman emperor passed from the scene in A.D. 476, the empire continued, controlled by the newcomers and split into two parts: the western empire, centered about Rome; and the eastern empire, centered at Constantinople. Henceforth there was little influence from the Roman Empire. Most of its former territories had fallen to various barbarian groups who had hoped to get a piece of the rich Roman life for themselves.

## Suggested Readings

Bazarnic, Steve George. *The Ancient Greek Pentathlon and Aspects of the Greek Ideal.* Microfiched M.S. thesis, Pennsylvania State University, 1970.

Cichy, Edward C., Marie Matsen, and Carolyn R. Surface. "Views from the Acropolis: the Development of Attitudes Towards Physical Education in Ancient Greece." *Canadian Journal of History of Sport and Physical Education* (hereafter *Canadian Journal*), 2 (May 1971), 31–43.

Fairs, John R. "The Influence of Plato and Platonism on the Development of Physical Education in Western Culture." *Quest,* 11 (December 1968), 14–23.

Forbes, Clarence A. "Athenian Physical Education in the Fifth Century, B.C." In *Proceedings of the Big Ten Symposium on the History of Physical Education and Sport.* Edited by Bruce L. Bennett. Athletic Institute, Chicago, 1972, pp. 151–159.

Gardiner, E. Norman. *Greek Athletic Sports and Festivals.* Macmillan, London, 1910 (Wm. C. Brown Reprints, Dubuque, Ia., 1970).

Gregory, C. Jane, and Darwin M. Semotiuk. "Hypothetical Relationships Between Zeus and Athletics in Ancient Greece." *Canadian Journal,* 5 (May 1974), 14–22.

Harris, H. A. *Greek Athletes and Athletics.* Indiana University Press, Bloomington, 1966.

————. *Sport in Greece and Rome.* Cornell University Press, Ithaca, N.Y., 1972.

Kleinman, Seymour. "Will the Real Plato Please Stand Up?" *Quest,* 14 (June 1970), 73–75.

Piper, David L. *Historical Study of the Concepts Underlying Health Education: Ancient Times to 1800.* Microcarded Ph.D. dissertation, Yale University, 1948.

Robinson, Rachel Sargent. *Sources for the History of Greek Athletics.* Privately published, Cincinnati, Ohio, 1955.

Siedentop, Daryl. "Differences Between Greek and Hebrew Views of Man." *Canadian Journal,* 2 (December 1971), 30–49.

Stull, G. Alan, and Guy Lewis. "The Funeral Games of the Homeric Greeks." *Quest,* 11 (December 1968), 1–13.

Zeigler, Earle F., ed. *A History of Sport and Physical Education to 1900: Selected Topics.* Stipes Publishing Company, Champaign, Ill., 1973. Includes a number of pertinent articles on research in several periods of physical education history, ranging from ancient times to about 1900.

# 3 Physical Education in Medieval and Early Modern Europe

The Roman Empire fell because most of the Romans made little effort to prevent its fall. While the incoming barbarians wished to share in the advantages of the empire and had considerable respect for Roman traditions, they did not really understand the Roman culture and were thus unable to preserve it. The rapidly growing Christian Church was the only stable institution in Europe after the fall of the Roman Empire. Its strength lay in its uncompromising dogmatism and its rigid organizational structure. Consequently it was the strongest political force in Europe during the medieval period.

## The Middle Ages

The Middle Ages is a period that many people misunderstand. Some have called it the Dark Ages in the belief that little was supposedly known about the period, or in the belief that the people of the times were uncivilized, or unenlightened; these beliefs, however, are really incorrect. Essentially the Middle Ages was a transition period between a time when a large, unified nation or civilization (the Roman Empire) had disappeared and a later period (the Renaissance) when nations regained strength and stability. The people of this period nevertheless seemed to be retreating from civilization.

The feudal system was the dominant form of social and political organization. Some scholars have suggested that the system had Germanic origins and had developed from a form of tribal organization that tied the fighting men to a single chieftain. In the pyramidic structure of feudalism the greater partners (lords) furnished financial support or political support to the monarch and protection or some manner of making a living to their many vassals, while the lesser partners (vassals) provided military and political support for the lords and the monarch.

The vassal owed a set period of military service for each land holding with which he was provided. The monarch owned *all* the land and had the right to evict any person who broke an oath of fealty or loyalty. The land holdings were not hereditary, so the monarch could disown the heirs of a vassal (lords were considered vassals to the monarch). Within this system the land was divided into large manors or farms, and the lords held the domain and all its products, plus a share of the products of the tributary lands that were worked by their vassals (in this case, similar to tenant farmers).

The towns were decaying for economic reasons from the fifth to the eighth centuries, the early Middle Ages. Trade in the Mediterranean Sea area was hampered by the rising Moslem tide, for its converts at their peak of power had gained control of the sea from Turkey around the south shore across Africa and into Spain. Travel was risky because of pirates at sea and barbarians and highwaymen on land. No strong, protective governments existed to assist free trade.

As the Moslem strength declined, however, trade became more open on the Mediterranean. Towns gradually began to grow in areas where they could find protection, such as beside castles and monasteries, and trade fairs sprang up across Europe as the barbarians began to settle down. Thus during the ninth to eleventh centuries the signs of a stable civilization began to reappear, and the growing trade across the face of Europe led to the peak of medieval development around the twelfth to thirteenth centuries.

During this time the need for money to wage wars led many monarchs to sell charters for towns, along with the rights of a lord. These towns, surrounded by walls for safety, became growing commercial and industrial areas. Traders and skilled artisans developed guilds, or trade unions, designed to insure the quality of their products, train apprentices in the skills of the trade, and limit the competition in the field to maintain price levels.

Between 1096 and 1270, a series of eight crusades, or military expeditions, were called for by the popes of the Church. These campaigns were in response to several recurring problems: the Holy Land, around Jerusalem, was captured by the Moslems, who hated the Christians; the Western world was threatened by the Turks; and the papal strength and control was challenged by the Holy Roman Emperor, whose territories were concentrated in the area of today's Germany.

People responded to the call for the crusades for many different reasons. Some were simply religious, while others were greedy. A fortune might be made in the booty of victory, fame could be gained, adventure was available. Some went for wealth or fame, while others went simply to gain salvation. As more crusades were called, their religious appeal diminished until they finally amounted to little more than self-seeking expeditions of greedy knights. A major effect of the crusades on late medieval Europe was the reestablishment of contact with areas beyond Europe.

Perhaps the best-known tradition of the Middle Ages is chivalry, or the tradition of courtly love, based on heroic fancy and romantic notions. The fiction that chivalry ruled the world resulted primarily from a thirst for honor and glory and the nobility's desire for praise and lasting fame. It implied the qualities of compassion, piety, austerity, fidelity, heroism, and love.

The Church frowned upon chivalry because of its erotic elements, for the romantic ideal was actually adulterous in that the knight was expected to pine away for a married woman. The Church did approve of some of the other ideals of chivalry, such as the ascetic tendencies implied in suffering for one's faith.

Education during the Middle Ages usually was education of the nobility, for what little education there was for the common people was oriented toward learning a trade and surviving. However, the male nobility was educated for knighthood.

The noble youth was trained in the house of another noble, rather than being trained by his own family. At about the age of seven he became a page. Until the age of fourteen he would be trained by the women and household workers. Women did not usually rate very highly in the Middle Ages, although among the nobility they were expected to organize and administer large households and estates, particularly during the frequent absences of the men.

Following this phase of training in which emphasis was on learning to serve people, the boy became a squire, usually by serving a knight or group of knights until he was twenty-one years old. During this period he concentrated on learning the arts of war, developing his body, and performing acts of obligation to his lord.

Around the age of twenty-one, perhaps earlier in cases of unusual bravery, the young man became a knight. Knighthood was usually bestowed in a serious religious ceremony. A ceremonial bath followed by an all-night religious vigil in the company of his lord and a bishop preceded the investitures that were usually held at major religious holidays and were accompanied by tournaments or other festivities. Physical education lay at the core of the training for knighthood at all stages, with goals of acquiring military prowess and developing the social graces and sports skills.

Much confusion surrounds the question of the views on physical education held by the Church in the late Middle Ages. No clear definition of its position has emerged from what is known about the trends within the Church and the civilization at that time, but the traditional view is that the Church was opposed to physical education for three

Many of today's popular games have ancient origins, such as this medieval rendi-
tion of bowling shows. (Courtesy Biblio-
theque Municipale, Troyes, France)

particular reasons. First, the Church was disturbed by what it considered the debased character of the Roman sports and games.
Second, it closely associated the Roman games with pagan religions,
and the Church was far from tolerant of other faiths. Third, a growing
concept of the evil character of the body was developing in the Church.
The body and soul were increasingly viewed as two very separate entities, in which case the soul should be preserved and strengthened,
while the body should not be catered to in any way, including enter-
taining or beneficial physical exercises. The Church attempted to
suppress many games and sports at this time, for they were considered
frivolous and perhaps tinged with sin. Dance was also strongly discouraged because of its sensual appeal.

A number of advocates of physical education were within the
Church prior to the Middle Ages. Usually these men had been exposed
to a classical education and thus viewed the body as a unity of parts,
rather than as separated and perhaps antagonistic parts. In the first
several centuries of the Church's existence, and again after the Middle
Ages, physical education was not opposed.

During the Middle Ages, however, the view of the Church, and of
much of society, was very "other worldly." The primary concern of this
life was for preparing for the afterlife; a future life of justice and peace
was promised. Asceticism, or denial of the pleasures or needs of the
body, was thus a popular concept among the more religious people.

At this time the Church was the savior of education, for education
as an intellectual process was generally connected to the Church.
Usually the educational process had no physical side. The common
system consisted of the seven liberal arts, composed of the *trivium*

(grammar, rhetoric, and logic) and the *quadrivium* (arithmetic, geometry, astronomy, and music). The monasteries preserved much of the learning that survived the Middle Ages and played a major role in education at that time.

In the fourteenth and fifteenth centuries medieval civilization began to fade in the light of the new forces it had created. Europe was waking up and progressing rapidly. Its culture was flourishing; the towns were becoming strong; education and the arts were developing new directions. Kings and queens began to consolidate their power and form nations similar to those we know today. This period of rebirth for civilization led to the term by which we know the era—the Renaissance.

## The Renaissance and Reformation

The Renaissance was a period of rebirth and transition in Europe. It began in Italy around the thirteenth century and spread gradually to the north and west across Europe for the next two centuries. It was a time of vast growth in learning and culture. Through contacts with the Arab world, the Western world was rediscovering many long-lost classical writings of the Greeks and Romans. The Arabs had preserved many of the ancient writings, and the European scholars retranslated them from the Arabic and shared them across Europe. The classical writings became very popular, and many of their teachings were imitated by the Europeans.

The universities, which were first established during the late Middle Ages were growing into a potent intellectual force, with major centers of learning in Paris, Bologna, Salerno, Oxford, and Cambridge. New universities were developing in other areas of Europe, especially in Germany, as the orientation toward church-controlled education lessened and secular education grew. Along with the growth of the universities came the growth of humanism, which emphasized the development of man's human-ness or humanity. The humanist scholars studied the classics closely because the ancient writings expressed humanistic ideas about education. This study of ancient writings, which the Church considered clearly pagan, created many scholarly problems in reconciling the humanities, or humanistic studies, to religion, which was still a dominant force in European life.

Europe was also making the transition to "modern times." The political institutions were making a gradual transition from feudalism to the more powerful monarchies, and a belief in the monarch's divine right to rule was growing. Europe was changing from a system of many small personal alliances to one in which the nation was the dominant unit. The governments were gradually being centralized, and the people were beginning to think of themselves as English or French or

German, rather than as Londoners or Parisians or Hessians. The birth of nationalism wholly changed the complexion of European affairs. Towns were becoming the new center of life as the economy began to edge away from its old feudalistic, agrarian orientation.

The invention of gunpowder changed the face of feudalistic military tactics. It helped to blow Europe into modern times, for with it a small force of men was vastly superior to a much larger force of bowmen.

The discovery of knowledge was enhanced by Johannes Gutenberg's invention of the printing press. The availability of books enabled knowledge and information to spread rapidly across Europe and provided a great impetus to education, for the need to be literate had increased immensely.

The Renaissance was a period of discovery of the outside world as well, for people began to question the old teachings about the nature of the world and what lay beyond Europe and northern Africa. They undertook voyages west across the Atlantic Ocean and south and east around Africa to India and beyond. The circumnavigation of the world showed how limited human knowledge had been.

The education of the period began to develop along the lines of the Greek ideal; it stressed a classical education combined with physical education. A major early leader was *Vittorino da Feltre* (1378–1446), who founded a school for the children of nobility that imitated the Athenian model of classical studies taught according to the model set by Quintilian.[1] The subjects included Greek and Latin literature, swimming, fencing, riding, and dancing. Education was primarily for the men, though women were treated as relative equals in Italy.

The Renaissance ideal was the "universal man," who had many talents and interests in the arts and literature, politics, games and sports, and the social graces. He was supposed to be interested and moderately skilled in almost every aspect of contemporary life. The goal of Renaissance educators was to develop an "all-around" person with a balanced education.

Education was beginning to be considered valuable for its own sake, regardless of how immediately practical it was. The barriers between separate areas of learning were beginning to break down, for the Renaissance ideal stressed training across any narrow divisions between areas of learning. The ideal was similar to the current concept of interdisciplinary studies in which the student tries to avoid the hazards of overspecialization that might result in an educational imbalance.

---

[1] Hermann Weimer, *Concise History of Education*, Philosophical Library, New York, 1962, pp. 38–42.

After the Renaissance this trend reversed and moved back toward specialization.

The humanistic impulse was strongly tied to the Reformation, the Protestant struggle against the Catholic Church, in the sixteenth century. The humanists' retranslations of the Scriptures indicated many areas of disagreement between the new translations and the Church's teachings. Many of the humanists were very antagonistic toward the Church, and some, who were convinced that the Church had strayed from the early Christian teachings, began to break away and form new churches. Because they "protested" the actions of the Catholic Church, these humanists were called *Protestants.* Martin Luther, founder of today's Lutheran church, was a major leader in this movement in Germany.

The Protestants were often more supportive of physical activities than the Catholic Church had been. The Protestants believed the activities would help prevent corruption of the body in word and deed and were therefore of moral value. The Protestant belief that everyone had the right to read and interpret the scriptures for himself or herself, which required some degree of literacy, enhanced education for the general public. Most education under the Church in the past had been the education of church leaders and scholars. The idea that each person should have any say in his or her beliefs and actions was a new concept for the time; the Church had previously told people what to believe and what to do. The Protestants were interested in education for both sexes, but women were not considered equal. Their status had been raised some in the Catholic Church by the emphasis on the Virgin Mary, but the emphasis was on the woman in the home setting, rather than as an equal and a partner to man.

As the struggles over religion spread across Europe, they were used by some rulers as one more way to consolidate their powers. An example was Henry VIII, who made himself head of the Anglican Church, the English national church that replaced the Catholic Church. As the nations gradually became "modern states," similar to the nations today, the stage was being set across Europe for the gradual move into the "modern era."

## Seventeenth-Century Europe

The seventeenth and eighteenth centuries saw more progress toward our current educational practices than any previous age, except perhaps ancient Greece. To see this progress we must look not at the different nations at that time, for there were still no national programs of education, but at the people who were the most prominent educational theorists of their time.

The seventeenth century, from about 1600 until the early 1700s, saw the rise of the "realists," whose goal was to tie education to reality, or life as it really was. They had questioned the humanists' total reliance upon ancient languages and teachings for the contemporary educational process. They believed that education should teach more useful things to prepare the students for life. They also began to stress teaching in the student's native language, rather than in only the classical languages, such as Latin. They wanted to get away from imitating the past.

Three slightly different groups of realists can be defined according to the degree to which they wanted to break away from the theories of the humanists.[2] The first group, the *humanist realists,* wanted to retain classical education as the foundation for all education. Although most similar to the humanists, this group wanted to modify the process of the classical studies by emphasizing the content but no longer copying the style of the ancient writers. The humanist realists' ideas were heavily classical.

The second group, the *social realists,* wanted some modification of the classical tradition. This group believed the goal of education should be preparation for a career, rather than the humanist aim of simply training scholars. The social realists wanted education to develop closer ties to contemporary needs and problems.

The third group, the *sense realists,* believed that knowledge was best obtained through the senses—that is, by observation and experience. This group wanted the schools not only to teach in the vernacular, the language the students spoke every day, rather than in the classical languages, but to teach useful arts and sciences as well. The sense realists tried to base their educational methods upon scientifically proven principles.

These groups consisted of many different people, and their ideas are examples of the progress in educational thought and practice that evolved during this time. Education was still primarily limited to the upper classes and to males, but the theorists were beginning to suggest that such a concept of education was far too limited. While physical education was still at best a minor part of the educational process, as educational theory developed, so did the idea that physical education could be a valuable part of the curriculum. More theorists were beginning to call for the use of physical activities in education, though their primary reason was for improved health.

---

[2] C. W. Hackensmith, *History of Physical Education,* Harper & Row, New York, 1966, pp. 98–107.

One of the earliest of the humanist realists was the Frenchman *François Rabelais* (1495–1553).[3] He wrote of the education of the boy named Gargantua, who studied the classics for their content but was not concerned with their style. His education included practical training and physical education activities as well. The emphasis of the physical activities was to prepare him for war, for he was being trained to be a scholar and a knight. In earlier times he would have been trained for one or the other, but never for both. The physical activities were to strengthen his body and to serve as recreation, and objects in nature were used in the educational process.

Another prominent humanist realist, also a forerunner of the Enlightenment period of the eighteenth century, was *John Milton* (1608–1674), the English writer.[4] He believed that a classical education was useful, but he thought the eight years of study could be condensed to a single year. He wanted to include physical exercises in the studies and divide each day's activities into three parts: study, exercise, and meals. His exercises were basically war oriented. The humanist realists thought that play and games were good training for skill and alertness, but they had only limited interest in their potential for developing social or recreational values. Their education was still planned as an education of the aristocrats, with little concern for the middle or lower classes.

One of the great theorists of the social realists was the Frenchman *Michel de Montaigne* (1533–1592). His theories concerned the education of aristocratic boys. He believed that experience and reason were the roads to knowledge. He expressed strong opposition to rote memorization by saying that "To know by heart is not to know." [5] His use of physical activities to further the pupil's experiences was very similar in manner to John Dewey's later theories of "learn by doing." He stressed the education of the mind and the body at the same time, but he was not interested in providing learning experience through games. Much of modern educational theory can be traced to Montaigne's ideas.

An English social realist, *John Locke* (1632–1704), used the now-popular phrase of physical educators, "a sound mind in a sound body," [6] which was originated by Juvenal, a Roman writer. He believed that mind and body were separate entities and that all ideas come from personal experiences, which might be better described as the experiences of the

---

[3] Ellen W. Gerber, *Innovators and Institutions in Physical Education,* Lea and Febiger, Philadelphia, 1971, pp. 54–56.
[4] Hackensmith, pp. 99–100.
[5] Quoted in Gerber, p. 57.
[6] Ibid., p. 70.

senses combined with mental reflection or thought based on the experiences. He stressed physical exercise as a way to health and also believed that dancing helped to develop grace. He thought of recreation as a useful and beneficial break in the normal pattern of activity, which is similar to Nash's twentieth-century statement of recreation as the "re-creation" of the person through a change in the pattern of his activities. Locke's ideas not only were a major factor in the development of contemporary educational theory but were also widely used in the development of other educational theories during his time.

Despite such forward-looking ideas, however, education under the social realists remained oriented toward the aristocracy and not toward the common people. For this reason many of the ideas of physical activity were an attempt to overcome the tendency of the aristocrats to pamper their children, who usually became overweight, unhealthy students.

A leading sense realist was *Richard Mulcaster* (1531–1611) of England. He believed that students should be taught at a school with other students rather than individually by a tutor at home. He was also convinced that teachers should be trained professionally. He suggested that both men and women should receive some education rather than just the males,[7] and he was one of the first to suggest coeducational activities among children. He was interested in physical and moral training through exercise, and thought that mass education, unlike the more common tutorial system, could lead to the development of social values through the use of physical activities. Mulcaster, who was one of the strongest early proponents of physical education, urged its use far more than any other person of his time. Although he did not have much influence in his time, his works were rediscovered during the late 1800s.

*Wolfgang Ratke* (1571–1635) of Germany was another great theoretician of educational reform, though like many of the other theorists he was unable to successfully translate his theories into action.[8] The major points in his attempt to develop education as a science included such ideas as following nature in its teaching methods (teach the students what they need to learn, and teach it at an age when they are ready to learn it); going only one step at a time with new information, utilizing much repetition; not forcing learning or stressing memorization; learning through experience; and educating *all* children, without exception. Although Ratke was unable to translate his formulas into

[7] Ibid., pp. 61–64.
[8] Weimer, pp. 73–77.

personal success, he is considered the father of modern educational theory.

*John Comenius* (1592–1670), a Czechoslovakian, became a Moravian minister in Bohemia.[9] For religious reasons he was forced to move frequently; he lived at times in Poland, England, Sweden, Hungary, and finally Holland, where he died. He wrote books on education that included illustrations to improve teaching methods. He wanted to have children exercise to develop and preserve their health, but he also believed they could learn much through recreational activities, which was not a widespread idea at the time. Comenius believed in the importance of play in educating young children, and he believed that *all* children should be educated.

## Eighteenth-Century Europe

The realism of the seventeenth-century was followed by the Enlightenment of the eighteenth century, a movement to spread rationalism and knowledge to all people. The concurrent trend toward the belief in the essential equality of all men, however, still did not necessarily apply to women. The educational theorists were beginning to move away from the idea that only the aristocracy should be educated. These theorists of the Enlightenment helped to reinforce the work begun in the seventeenth century; they used many of the realists' theories as the starting points for many of their own theories. Hermann Weimer writes of John Locke as the founder of the English Enlightenment, for Locke's stress on educating people through rational, natural means led to the later theories of Rousseau.[10]

*Jean-Jacques Rousseau* (1712–1788) of France was one of the most important theorists of the Enlightenment.[11] In 1762 he published two extremely influential books, *Emile* and *Social Contract. Social Contract* expanded upon his view that all humans were free and equal by nature, that inequality developed only after they had got away from nature and developed governments. He considered people good by nature but corrupted by so-called civilization.

In *Emile* Rousseau wrote that the task of education was to develop all of a child's capabilities freely, as nature intended, and to avoid anything that would hamper this "natural" development. The book was considered a revolt against the education and society of the day and

---

[9] Gerber, pp. 65–69.
[10] Weimer, pp. 98–103.
[11] Ibid., pp. 104–110.

was at first banned by the Catholic Church and then condemned by governments.

Rousseau's plan of education for the imaginary Emile required a tutor, for the child was educated alone; nature was the primary teacher and the tutor was the guiding force. He believed that the child could not be taught by logic, as Locke had suggested, because as a youth the child would not yet have developed common sense. He wanted to let children progress naturally—learning what they wanted to learn, when they were interested in learning it. They were given tasks that were considered appropriate to their ages and that were geared toward learning from nature and experience. When young adults, they would be introduced to languages and the classical authors, who were considered closer to nature than the contemporary writers.

Rousseau also discussed the education of Sophie, Emile's future wife, but it was much closer to a traditional education for girls; it took place in her parents' home, unlike Emile's education in the country. She was educated primarily to be a wife, so she could make her husband's life pleasant. While Rousseau had many liberal tendencies in his theories, he was not liberal where women were concerned. He said that all men were born equal before nature, and he did mean men.

Rousseau considered play to be both healthful and educational, but he did not think it should be forced. He was opposed to compulsion in any area of education; he believed it was in opposition to the ways of nature. Although he stressed equality of men in his educational theories, his idea of a tutorial educational process required a one-to-one pupil-teacher ratio and thus was beyond the reach of all but the wealthy.

Rousseau's theories that made the education of the mind and the body almost the same thing moved very close to contemporary educational thought, but the influence of his works cannot be estimated. The most visible immediate influence was upon the Germans, who followed rapidly in developing his theories of "naturalism" into actual educational practice.

*Johann Basedow* (1724–1790), a German educator, had experimented with an educational system that was based on the theories of Locke and others and that involved physical activity.[12] His discovery of Rousseau's work *Emile,* however, was the basis for the development of his own version of an educational system, and with the help of a number of financial supporters, in 1774 he was able to start a coeducational school called the *Philanthropinum,* later known as the Dessau Educational Institute. He tried to educate the children free from the influence of any particular church and he preferred to treat the children

---

[12] Gerber, pp. 83–86.

as children, rather than as small adults.  Basedow published several illustrated books explaining his educational theories and given examples of the methods and content to be used when teaching children.

He stressed physical activities heavily, for the ten-hour day in his school included five hours of classes, three hours of recreation (including fencing, riding, dancing, and music), and two hours of manual labor aimed at learning a craft.  He also planned a camping experience that was similar in nature to the later ideas of outdoor education.

The school hired *Johann Simon* as the teacher of physical education, and he might be considered the first modern physical education teacher.  He taught fencing, dancing, and games, and some crude "gymnastics" activities that he developed, and he held a contest similar to the ancient Greek Olympics.  In 1778 he was succeeded by Johann Du Toit, who expanded upon the gymnastic activities.  The exercises were performed outdoors with apparatus made from natural materials.

Basedow, who was unable to make the school work under his direction, left in 1778, but the school, which reached its peak in the early 1780s, continued until 1793.  Although the school did not last, its experimental program, which recognized the importance of physical activities to the child, was very influential throughout Europe, particularly so to *Christian Salzmann* (1744–1811), who founded the *Schnepfenthal Educational Institute* in 1785 near Gotha, in present-day East Germany.

Salzmann's institute was a good copy of the Philanthropinum, and his copy worked.  One year after the founding of the school Salzmann hired a new, young teacher, *Johann Guts Muths* (1759–1839), who taught there for fifty years and became one of the most influential of German physical educators.[13]  Strongly influenced by the writings of Basedow, Guts Muths developed an outdoor gymnastics program that included many activities, with exercises in tumbling, climbing, jumping, vaulting, the horizontal bar, balance beam, and rope ladders.  He organized his activities by age level and difficulty and kept careful records of each student's progress.  His book, *Gymnastics for the Young,* published in 1793, was reprinted in many countries, including the United States in 1802 with Salzmann listed as the author.  His work set the pattern for the German gymnastics, which was introduced into the United States around 1825, and which was a less formal German system than the one that developed later in Germany.

Guts Muths' influence was widespread across two continents both because of his writing skill and because of the interest of many prominent theorists and practitioners of the day. Friedrich Jahn, Adolf

---

[13] Ibid., pp. 115–121.

*The Leap in height with & without a pole*

An example of outdoor gymnastics activities popularized by Guts Muths in Germany. (Reproduced from the English translation of Johann Guts Muths' *Gymnastics for Youth, or a Practical Guide to Healthful and Amusing Exercises,* Philadelphia, 1803. Courtesy Francis A. Countway Library of Medicine)

Spiess, and Immanuel Kant were among those who visited Schnepfenthal to study the work he carried out at the school until he retired in 1835. Many of his practices are similar to those suggested and followed in today's schools.

*Johann Pestalozzi* (1746–1827) was a Swiss whose school at Yverdon in Germany was also extremely influential among the educational reformers of the early 1800s.[14] He taught at the school at Yverdon from 1804 to 1825 and wrote a number of books on his theories. His most important book, *How Gertrude Teaches Her Children,* was an expansion of the educational ideas he had introduced in an earlier novel, *Leonard and Gertrude.*

Pestalozzi stressed the early education in the family by writing of humans as social creatures. He tried to connect education with life and make it useful. He believed the learner had to be stimulated to *want* to learn and the teacher should act as a guide, rather than force the child to learn. He wanted learning to follow the natural process from easy to hard activities according to the child's level of development.

---

[14] Ibid., pp. 87–92.

He saw education as having three aspects: intellectual, practical, and, most importantly, moral. Physical education was also important to Pestalozzi in bringing the mind and body into full harmony.

His school provided many physical activities, including one hour of gymnastics five days a week. While the gymnastics program, which gradually became formalized as the influence of the formal German system became more widespread, was not advanced it provided a great impetus for the development of physical education activities on the part of people from many nations who visited the famous school.

*Philipp von Fellenberg* (1771–1844), who based many of his ideas on Pestalozzi's writings, began one of the first European schools for vocational education, which were sometimes referred to as schools of manual labor.[15] There was one essential difference between Fellenberg and most of the educational theorists: His ideas worked. Fellenberg's activities were a practical success throughout his life; his school, started in 1804 at Hofwyl, was an immediate success.

Fellenberg believed in the value of physical activity, though he felt that his vocational students received enough activity without having a planned program. He considered their manual work sufficient exercise, and it kept them outdoors, which he considered important. He encouraged outdoor activity and allowed his students a free choice of activities in their free time.

*Friedrich Froebel* (1782–1852) built a theory of play based on his experiences of studying and teaching at Pestalozzi's school at Yverdon from 1808 to 1810. He stressed that play was essential to the education and development of children and developed a philosophy of play that went far beyond previous ideas.[16] He expressed some of his ideas in a book entitled *Education of Man.*

In 1837 his interest in the education of children and play activities led to his founding a school, which he called a *Kindergarten,* for young children in Germany. His ideas on education, which along with those on the kindergarten were carried out by his disciples, became a major influence upon the early education of children.

During the last part of the Enlightenment period, the ideas of the European theorists were beginning to influence the development of education in the United States. From about 1800 onward, educational theories in Europe moved rapidly to the United States as immigrants brought many of the new ideas with them to the huge and growing land. While many educational developments were concurrent on both continents by 1850, the developing American educational practices were

---

15 Hackensmith, pp. 124–126.
16 Gerber, pp. 93–99.

strongly based on the work of the nineteenth-century European theorists.

## Nineteenth-Century Europe

We cannot really draw a line separating the eighteenth century from the nineteenth century when we study the development of physical education, for the philosophies and experimental schools of the late 1700s in Europe produced the progress of the 1800s. We have already mentioned several of the educators who were more a part of the nineteenth century; others who were equally influential during the nineteenth century had their foundations in the events of the eighteenth.

During the late eighteenth century revolution was in the wind. The young United States had rebelled against Great Britain and Rousseau's ideas still had much of Europe in shock. The educational theories that leaned toward Rousseau's views on the equality of men were given a popular boost by the French Revolution. As the year 1800 came and went, Napoleon had gained power in France and was trying to gain control of all Europe. As nations allied to block him, the feelings of national consciousness rose to an all-time high.

After Napoleon was put to rest and the Congress of Vienna had tried to reestablish the old Europe, many changes became manifest. The people were less content, and many rebellions took place between 1815 and 1850. The people were also bginning to clamor for national systems of education, but in large numbers they were also fleeing the Old World, frequently to take a chance on a better life in the United States. Those who remained sought systems of education that would strengthen their nations and have some effect on national pride.

*Friedrich Ludwig Jahn* (1778–1852), a German educator, is often considered the "Father of Gymnastics." [17] Jahn was an ardent Prussian patriot opposed to the provincialism that kept Germany separated into a multitude of small kingdoms. He began teaching in a Pestalozzian school, where he tried to use Guts Muths' ideas in an outdoor gymnasium setting.

In 1810 he began using an open area that he termed the *Turnplatz*, or exercise group, which was basically a playground with apparatus for exercises, and the formal organization of his program gradually became the Turner movement. Although some persons have considered his system too formal, Jahn opposed artificial activities in the early years of its development and sought to use natural activities instead. A book by a follower described his work in 1816, the same year Jahn wrote *German Gymnastics* to explain his system.

---

[17] Hackensmith, pp. 133–134; Gerber, pp. 126–133.

The popularity of Friedrich Jahn's turnplatz reached the United States in the
early nineteenth century; this Turner gymnasium in the United States shows activities typical in about 1890. (Courtesy the
Bettmann Archive)

Jahn's emphasis upon German nationalism eventually put him in
prison.  The rulers of the separate states considered his views on a
unified Germany a threat, and Jahn was out of favor until the 1840s
when the political climate changed.  The success of the Turner movement depended upon other men during that interval.

*Adolf Spiess* (1810–1858) was the man who had the greatest impact upon educational gymnastics in Germany.[18]  Having met both Guts
Muths and Jahn, he experimented with gymnastics as a teacher by
applying the movement to the formal classroom situation.  He also
worked with Froebel in Switzerland, where he was strongly influenced
by Froebel's views on the part of play in education, and his later
writings, especially his *Gymnastics Manual for Schools,* which had the
exercises classified by difficulty and by appropriate age and sex, were
a strong influence in the schools.

He devised a system of "free exercises" that required almost no
apparatus.  He also used musical accompaniments for these activities

---

[18] Gerber, pp. 139–144.

and stressed the idea of professionally trained specialists to teach the gymnastics classes. He wanted indoor exercise areas in addition to the traditional outdoor areas so the winter weather would not limit the program. He also stressed gymnastics for girls, and his free exercises were a great benefit for them, for less strength was required than for the apparatus activities. Although he considered the existing formal systems of gymnastics inappropriate for the schools, his own system also included much marching and stressed discipline and obedience. Traces of his system, which served as a lasting model for the later German system of school gymnastics, can still be seen.

*Per Henrik Ling* (1776–1839) was the founder of Swedish gymnastics,[19] though he was also well known for his literary works. While living in Denmark he was influenced by Nachtegall, and he later decided to try to train teachers of fencing and gymnastics to strengthen Sweden's army. A fierce Swedish nationalist, he became the director of the new Royal Gymnastics Central Institute in 1814, where he later developed his program of gymnastics, sometimes called the Swedish system but also called Ling gymnastics. His emphasis upon simple, fundamental movements and exercises was a change from Jahn's complicated exercises.

Although the Ling exercises were developed for both educational and military purposes, they worked better as military training. While Per Henrik Ling's medical and military gymnastics were successful, his son, Hjalmar Ling, really did the major work in developing the educational aspect of the Swedish system.

*Franz Nachtegall* (1777–1847) was considered the father of physical education in Denmark.[20] Inspired by the writings of Guts Muths, he gradually became known as a leader in Danish gymnastics and physical training. In 1804 he was made director of the newly established Military Gymnastic Institute, which had the task of preparing teachers of gymnastics first for the military and then later for the schools, and which is the oldest institution training gymnastics instructors in Europe. Although Nachtegall did not design his own system, he was most instrumental in the development of school gymnastics and physical programs in Denmark and was also an influential factor in the development of Ling's Swedish system of gymnastics.

*Archibald MacLaren* (c. 1820–1884) was a major early influence on physical education in England.[21] Asked to design a physical training

[19] Hackensmith, pp. 142–144.
[20] Gerber, pp. 177–180.
[21] Ibid., pp. 215–219.

These examples of the Swedish system, or Ling gymnastics, show the simple, fundamental movements involved. (Reprinted from *The Gymnastic Free Exercises of P. H. Ling,* arranged by H. Roth-stein and translated by M. Roth, M.D., Groombridge & Sons, London, 1853. Courtesy Francis A. Countway Library of Medicine)

program for the military, he stressed a gymnastic program, similar to Jahn's, which made heavy use of apparatus activities. Above all, MacLaren stressed a balance between recreational activities (physical play) and educational physical activities, which he wanted in a regular class as a part of the educational process, in addition to the noneducational play time. Although his ideas on gymnastics never really took hold in England, his writings were a major influence in the development of physical education in England in the late 1800s. His military system of physical education also spread across England as the instructors he had trained for the military left the military service but continued to teach across the nation.

During the first half of the nineteenth century the European theorists and systems were a powerful influence on the development of physical education in the United States. After the U.S. Civil War the European influence declined rapidly, for American physical educators were beginning to pass the point of needing the European ideas as impetus for developing their own programs and systems. By the end of the century U.S. leaders were calling on their fellow teachers to work together to develop an "American System," rather than rely on the European systems, which were after all designed for Europeans. The turn of the century saw the beginnings of that distinctly American system, though it was not stressed in writing for several more decades.

## Suggested Readings

Bennett, Bruce L. "The Curious Relationship of Religion and Physical Education." *JOHPER,* 41 (September 1970), 69–71.

Broekhoff, Jan. "Chivalric Education in the Middle Ages." *Quest,* 11 (December 1968), 24–31.

———. "Physical Education, Sport, and the Ideals of Chivalry." In *Proceedings of the Big Ten Symposium on the History of Physical Education and Sport.* Edited by Bruce L. Bennett. Athletic Institute, Chicago, 1972, pp. 9–31.

Edmondson, Cornelia. *A Continuum of Thought on the Value of Health, Physical Education, and Recreation from the Time of John Locke Through the Early Twentieth Century.* Microcarded Ph.D. dissertation, University of Washington, 1966.

Gerber, Ellen W. *Innovators and Institutions in Physical Education.* Lea and Febiger, Philadelphia, 1971.

Hardy, Stephen T. "The Medieval Tournament: A Functional Sport of the Upper Class." *Journal of Sport History,* 1 (Fall 1974), 91–105.

Medlin, William K. *The History of Educational Ideas in the West.* The Center for Applied Research in Education, New York, 1964.

Moolenijzer, Nicholaas J. "Our Legacy from the Middle Ages." *Quest,* 11 (December 1968), 32–43.

Park, Roberta J. "Concern for the Physical Education of the Female Sex from 1675 to 1800 in France, England, and Spain." *Research Quarterly,* 45 (May 1974), 104–119.

———. "Education as a Concern of the State: Physical Education National Plans for Education in France, 1763–1795." *Research Quarterly,* 44 (October 1973), 331–342.

Piper, David L. *Historical Study of the Concepts Underlying Health Education: Ancient Times to 1800.* Microcarded Ph.D. dissertation, Yale University, 1948.

Zeigler, Earle F. *A History of Sport and Physical Education to 1900.* Stipes Publishing Company, Champaign, Ill., 1973.

# 4 The Development of American Physical Education

We have discussed the evolution of physical education in the ancient world and in Europe to 1900, for we must understand the origins of our current forms of physical education. To understand the development of physical education in the United States, we must also look at the developmental period of the country itself and the ways it was influenced by the European ideas of the nineteenth century. After the mid-1800s, however, Europe began to lose its influence in the United States, and we need to see how this period of declining influence affected the later directions that American physical education took.

## Colonial America (1607–1783)

In Colonial America there was no physical education as we think of it. The colonies made attempts to start schools, but their primary concern was to provide the rudiments of a practical education—that is, learning to read, write, and handle mathematics. Physical education activities, such as were being developed in Europe, would have been considered a "frill" at that time. The colonies of the New World were expanding into wilderness areas, and the pioneers, who frequently faced the threat of attack by the Indians whom they were displacing, usually got more outdoor exercise than a European would receive in the most educationally advanced school of the day. During this period the nonworking physical activities of the people were primarily recreational activities.

The developing colonies were a diverse culture—a mixture of many nationalities and religious groups. The Puritans in New England were opposed to most activities that could be considered pleasurable; they considered them either sinful or questionable activities that might eventually lead to sin. While the Puritans were the most negative group of the colonial settlers regarding the pursuit of physical pleasures, the Quakers, who later settled in Pennsylvania, were also strict. The

Virginia colony, predominantly Anglican, was opposed to many recreational activities in its early days, but other groups in the New World, such as the Dutch in today's New York City and Hudson River valley areas, were more inclined to appreciate such activities.

The colonies, which were widely separated in their early days, might be likened to ancient Greek city-states: all of the same "nation," but more competitive than cooperative. After the Revolutionary War the nation was still very spread out, so there was little spirit of nationalism. People were from Massachusetts, or Virginia, or Pennsylvania, rather than from the United States. The spirit of cooperation among the states was noticeably thin even during the Revolutionary War.

The hard nature of the life of the settlers led to the gradual development of a society far more tolerant of differences among people than in their native European countries. Ancestors had little to do with the settler's ultimate survival or value to colonial society. As the political development of the colonies proceeded, however, strong regional antagonism developed between the three groups of people that were established in many states.

In colonial society the new elite were the residents of the coastal areas that had been settled first. These people were well-to-do traders. They were better educated than the other groups, and they had regular contact with what was going on in Europe. The second social group included the people of the piedmont and foothill areas who were primarily farmers. They lived in less-settled areas than the coastal dwellers and had little in common with them, either in wealth or in politics. The third group—the settlers of the still-unopened areas—was gradually moving into the mountains and beyond. These people were far out of touch with the coast, much less Europe. They had some ties with the piedmont farmers, for they were often farmers themselves, but they had nothing in common with the people on the coast. The result was a long period of political struggles in the legislatures of almost every state between the people in the east, who had the power, and those in the west.

The schools in the colonies were copies of the European schools of the time. The first schools were Latin grammar schools, which proved to be of little value in the colonies and were gradually replaced by academies that were concerned primarily with basic instruction, as mentioned previously. Advanced education, also modeled after European schools, was primarily for those who were going into the ministry, as at Harvard University, formed in Massachusetts in 1636.

Physical activities served almost no official function in colonial education, but many unorganized recreational games and sports were carried on for entertainment. The daily life activities of the pioneers involved the survival skills used in hunting, fishing, and swimming and required such physical activities as running, jumping, lifting heavy objects, and fighting. Dance also gradually became more acceptable as the Puritans became more affluent.

Although no real education of the physical existed in colonial times, the idea was supported by some prominent men. Thomas Jefferson wrote in support of physical education, and Benjamin Franklin was a swimming enthusiast, though swimming was then considered a quaint but questionable custom. One of the few schoolmen who supported physical activities in the schools was *Samuel Moody,* headmaster of one of the first private boarding schools in America.[1] He promoted physical activities as vital to the health of the students, but most activities were strictly traditional ones inherited from European backgrounds.

There was little real spirit of nationalism in the United States until after the War of 1812. The people shared a basic reluctance to submit to any centralized form of government (an independent spirit that is still a noticeable characteristic of the American people). Thus nationalism was not the strong impetus toward physical education that it was in the European nations in the late 1700s and early 1800s. The second impetus in Europe, pursuing physical training to help serve the military needs of the country, was also weakened in the United States. The Americans were usually concerned with the strength and fitness of the military only in times of war, and thus physical training was not an overriding concern in this period of rapid expansion across the Appalachian Mountains and on toward the great American Midwest. While some military schools were being formed during the early 1800s, the idea of military instruction did not become popular until the time of the Civil War in the 1860s.

## The Early National Period (1783–1820)

Colonial America and the early national period were not times when educational theory was of great concern. The major concerns before 1800 were survival and politics, in that order. As the nation became more settled and the larger population centers became more stable in their lifestyles, the interest in education beyond the rudest beginnings grew. The first real attempts to put physical education into the educational curriculum were just developing in the 1820s and 1830s, as experimental schools and academies began to open under the direction of men and women who had been influenced by the growing interest in physical education within new European schools.

Much of the impetus for the improvement of programs involving

---

[1] Emmett A. Rice, John L. Hutchinson, and Mabel Lee, *A Brief History of Physical Education,* 5th ed., Ronald Press Company, New York, 1969, p. 146.

physical activity before the Civil War came from Europe.[2] Three movements within the United States, however, enhanced the effects of these pre–Civil War European influences. First was the women's education movement, seen particularly in the female seminaries. Second was the move of religious groups into education and later physical education. Third was the growth of sport in the United States during the years before 1860.

The major European influences in the United States at this time were the ideas of Johann Pestalozzi, Joseph Lancaster, Philipp von Fellenberg, and the German gymnastics system. Pestalozzi's ideas have already been discussed. His internationally famous school was visited by people from many nations. One of his visitors from the United States was *William McClure,* who also visited Fellenberg's school. McClure, who wanted to open a Philadelphia school that would follow Pestalozzi's methods, hired *Joseph Neef* (1770–1854), an instructor at Pestalozzi's school. The Philadelphia school, which opened in 1809 and offered many physical activities and much military exercise, was among other U.S. schools that were beginning to follow Pestalozzi's example in the 1820s.

*Joseph Lancaster,* an Englishman, developed a system of instruction that used student assistants to do much of the teaching, much as contemporary theory has suggested that teacher's aides or paraprofessionals be used. Lancaster's assistants were called *monitors,* and after they had learned a lesson, they would teach the same lesson to a group of students. His ideas, published in 1803, included a recommendation for the use of playgrounds and play activities as a part of the educational process. Most of the U.S. schools of this type that later developed in New England followed his teaching handbook, which was reprinted in Philadelphia in 1820. As free public education gradually developed, the Lancastrian schools gradually dwindled in number.

Fellenberg, whose methods and views on physical activity have already been discussed, also influenced the development of U.S. schools. His model was considered a good combination of the academic and the useful in education that included physical activity as an important part of the process. Schools with Fellenberg's ideas became popular in the 1830s, though many teachers thought the manual labor requirements removed the need for any other physical activities. These manual labor schools gradually lost popularity about the time of the Civil War, though after the war their basic plan reappeared in the manual arts schools.

The German gymnastics system, which was based upon the work of a number of men (notably Friedrich Jahn), was brought to the United

---

[2] C. W. Hackensmith, *History of Physical Education,* Harper & Row, New York, 1966, pp. 332–345.

States during the early years of the nineteenth century by the numerous German immigrants. Three prominent leaders appeared in the United States to do much of the work toward making German gymnastics popular in this country. Two of them were *Charles Beck* (1798–1866), who taught at Round Hill School in Massachusetts,[3] and *Charles Follen* (1796–1840), who taught at Harvard University; both arrived in the United States in 1824. *Francis Lieber* (1800–1872), who also taught at Harvard, came from Germany in 1827. All three generally followed Jahn's teachings in their programs and helped spread his system, which became a major facet in the development of U.S. physical education programs prior to 1900.

During the late 1700s and early 1800s women's education was growing in popularity, though the growth was not rapid. First supported strongly by Dr. *Benjamin Rush* (1745–1813), "female seminaries" or academies were founded in many communities during this period. Tuition was required at these private institutions, for providing free public education to women was not yet considered worth the expense. Attempts to open public high schools for women in Boston and New York City in the 1820s were failures because too many women wanted to attend and the citizens thought the cost was too high.

During the first half of the nineteenth century interest in sports was also beginning to grow rapidly. Most of the Puritan-based objections to games and sports were gradually disappearing as the nation grew larger and more settled. Various nationality groups had been bringing their own favorite games to the United States, and the "melting pot" of peoples became a melting pot of sports. The time when sport would begin to organize had not yet come, however.

## Antebellum Physical Education in the United States (1820–1860)

The period from 1820 to 1860 saw many new developments in both education and physical education. The *Round Hill School* was opened in Northampton, Massachusetts, in 1823 by *Joseph Cogswell* and *George Bancroft*.[4] This college preparatory school was the only school in the nation that was concerned with the idea of individualized instruction. It also recognized the importance of physical activity as a part of the educational program. The founders had observed the programs of the German gymnasiums and of Fellenberg and had decided to try an experimental school based on those ideas.

The Round Hill School provided a classical education, but also included dancing, riding, and gymnastics. The classes were small,

---

[3] Ellen W. Gerber, *Innovators and Institutions in Physical Education,* Lea and Febiger, Philadelphia, 1971, pp. 245–251.

[4] Gerber, pp. 245–251.

Roper's gymnasium, an example of an
early American gymnasium in Philadelphia in about 1830. (Courtesy New York
Public Library)

usually about six persons, and the instruction was individualized at the
level of each student. Cogswell, who ran the school, tried to be like a
father to the students. He abolished most systems of punishment and
rewards, and led much of the exercise himself, for he especially liked
long hikes and running. Gymnastics was taught regularly, and the
physical activities were emphasized at the school.

Charles Beck taught Latin and gymnastics at the Round Hill
School from 1825 to 1830. Following Jahn's system (he had translated
a gymnastics book of Jahn's into English), he started the first outdoor
school gymnasium as well as the first school gymnastics program in the
United States when he began teaching at Round Hill. His program
served as the introduction of German gymnastics into the United States,
for as Albertson has noted:

> During the late 1820s many academies and colleges provided
> German gymnastic apparatus for students to use during recess or
> idle time. A small number of academies followed the example of
> Round Hill and included gymnastics in their regular curriculum.[5]

---

[5] Roxanne Albertson, *Physical Education in New England Schools and Academies
From 1789 to 1860: Concepts and Practices,* Microfiched Ph.D. dissertation, University
of Oregon, 1974, pp. 90–91.

The Round Hill School closed in 1834. Although the school had some financial problems, the primary reason was that the school was so different compared to other U.S. schools. Its educational work had been of superior quality, and its graduates were ready for the last year or so of work at most colleges. However, students were required to pay for the full four years of college work even though they entered college as advanced students. This practice made the Round Hill School a financial hardship for many of its graduates.

During this period before the Civil War there was a gradual increase in school gymnastic programs and the construction of gymnasiums. The first college gymnasium, which was furnished with the sort of equipment generally used in German gymnasiums, opened at Harvard in 1820. By the 1850s, many colleges began providing gymnasiums for their students, and the gymnasium construction boom really began.

This period also saw increased interest in swimming and a boom in the building of swimming pools. Benjamin Franklin, who had long been a disciple of swimming, was quoted liberally in William Turner's *The Art of Swimming* in 1821. In 1827 Francis Lieber opened the first public swimming pool under the control of the Boston gymnasium. The first college to construct swimming pools was Girard College, which opened in 1848. The college's four indoor pools in the dormitory basements as well as its outdoor pool were all planned by Lieber.

Public education was also beginning to develop during this time. Although many public schools for elementary education were being opened, much of the secondary education remained in the private academies, or schools that charged tuition. The academies, which were frequently coeducational, stressed terminal education—that is, they were not college preparatory, and they were more practical than classical. Because of the large numbers of private academies, the first public schools were often mocked as schools for the poor.

By the 1830s, the aristocratic tendencies of the rapidly growing nation and the educational system were beginning to disappear. With the help of President Andrew Jackson, more democratic feelings began to emerge. The people wanted more useful education than they had received at the classically oriented private schools, and by the middle 1800s most people were beginning to feel that education should be free and that it should be provided for both sexes.

In 1818 the first public high school for boys had opened in Boston, and by 1852 Massachusetts became the first state to pass legislation requiring all children to attend school. The problems of public education for girls have already been mentioned, but the similar disinterest in forming colleges for women was overcome in 1853 when the first full four-year college for women, Elmira (New York) College, was established.

In 1832 *John Warren,* a Harvard professor of anatomy, published a book supporting physical education in education. This work, *The Importance of Physical Education,* can be considered the first theoretical book on physical education, for it was philosophical in nature. However, most colleges were not very interested in physical education. Although they had begun to provide gymnasiums and other facilities for physical activities, the improvements were primarily the result of student agitation for the facilities, rather than the result of any administrative or scholarly interest in the value of exercise for students. The outdoor gymnasiums that developed in many schools in New England followed the leadership of the German gymnastics model set up by Charles Follen at Harvard in 1826. These gymnasiums were not recognized as a part of the official school programs, however.

A prominent leader in physical education for women in the antebellum period was *Catharine Beecher* (1800–1878).[6] She was conservative in most areas concerning women, for she basically believed that woman's place was in the home, which was a popular idea with the men. Unlike other women of her time, however, she felt that women should be educated for the position. She viewed the mother as the core of the family, needing to be educated if she was to do a good job of her difficult task. Beecher objected to the clothing styles of the time as too restrictive and heavy to permit good health and she emphasized the idea of exercising to improve the health. For her students, both women and children, she prescribed exercises similar to Ling's Swedish gymnastics, which were not widely used in the United States until the 1860s.

Although Beecher was in favor of sports and games as good exercises and considered them useful in promoting family unity, she was very puritanical in her opposition to other activities. She considered hunting for recreational purposes to be sinful and was suspicious of the directions in which dance might lead people. She was more interested in women's role in the home than in their intellectual role. Because women were beginning to struggle for their rights at this time, her ideas were never extremely popular; however, they were refined and spread by Dio Lewis after the Civil War.

Colleges were beginning to grow rapidly in number before the Civil War. The earlier colleges had been formed by religious groups, except for Benjamin Franklin's school, which later became the University of Pennsylvania. The government had provided land in each state to be used in providing education for the people and this impetus had led to the founding of many state colleges.

Religious groups were also beginning to get involved in physical education and recreational activities at this time. The recreational life

---

[6] Gerber, pp. 252–258.

of many people centered about the church, which was a common gathering point in rural areas. The Young Men's Christian Association (YMCA), founded in London in 1844 by George Williams to help young men to lead a more moral life, was first brought to U.S. cities in 1851. These YMCA programs in the United States moved into the area of physical education, when interest grew in gymnastics and other health-oriented activities after the Civil War. A women's version, the Young Women's Christian Association (YWCA), was organized in Boston in 1866, while the Young Men's Hebrew Association (YMHA), which had been founded in 1854 as a literary society, also began moving into the area of physical education activities.

During the 1830s and 1840s a developing trend in the heavily-populated cities concerned public health.[7] Doctors began to notice the multitude of unhealthy citizens, particularly the children, and assessed the problem as one primarily caused by a lack of exercise. There was nowhere in most cities for people to get any "country-type" exercise away from the city's crowded, dirty environs.

Boston was fortunate in having its large common, but it was an exception among the cities. Gradually other cities in the United States began to look into the matter of providing public parks for the citizens' exercise. European parks were studied by a number of people who began to develop the architecture of public parks. This civic concern for low-level recreation of its citizens was the start of a long period of gradual growth toward the important field of recreation.

The United States was gradually becoming a land of large cities that were complete with slums, and it was beginning to face for the first time some of the problems that the European cities had been facing for centuries. Fortunately, most American cities were young enough or small enough to be able to set aside land for parks in the middle of the towns, which was impossible in the European cities. This period of interest in public health and public parks continued until the Civil War, and it progressed with increased vigor after the war was over.

Perhaps the most influential factor in the development of physical education in the United States in the last decade or so before the Civil War was the example of the turnvereins, or German gymnastic societies. The turnverein movement grew within the United States as the unsettled political situation in the multitude of states that later became Germany caused increasing numbers of Germans to come to the United States. As we have mentioned, these immigrants brought many of their customs

---

[7] John Rickards Betts, "Public Recreation, Public Parks, and Public Health Before the Civil War," in *Proceedings of the Big Ten Symposium on the History of Physical Education and Sport,* ed. Bruce L. Bennett, The Athletic Institute, Chicago, 1972, pp. 33–52.

with them, and by 1848 the Turners had established their first group in the United States in Cincinnati, Ohio, as well as a second group in New York City. (The first national turnfest, a large, organized, outdoor gymnastics meeting, was held in Philadelphia in 1851.)

The popular Turner groups might almost be called family physical and social clubs, for they were as much social organizations, which included entire families, as they were physical activity–oriented groups. The goals of the Turners in this country were to promote physical education, improve the individual's intellect, and provide opportunities for socializing with other members.

The demarcation point in the nineteenth century development of physical education might be set at 1861. In that year Dr. *Edward Hitchcock,* recently graduated as an M.D. from Harvard, was hired by Amherst College as a professor of hygiene and physical education, the first such recognized position in the United States. He was asked to develop a program to contribute to the health of the students at Amherst. His program began as heavy gymnastics, using large, fixed apparatus in the German manner, though he later modified it to light gymnastics, using light hand apparatus and exercising to music, which he felt was more beneficial to the students. He also began to take extensive measurements of the students' bodies and gradually developed a large pool of anthropometric measurements for later physical educators. He also started one of the nation's first intramural school sports programs.

Dr. Hitchcock was head of the Amherst physical education program for fifty years, until his death in 1911. His hiring was a turning point in U.S. physical education, for it was the first sign of recognition by a college of the value of physical education in the educational program of the students, and the Amherst program served as a major example to other U.S. schools for many decades.

Another major factor in the development of physical education in the year 1861 was the start of the Civil War, which marked the beginning of a period of drastic change in the United States. The country began to move from a heavily agricultural nation toward a highly industrialized one. Over the next half-century radical changes in the complexion of the nation led to a greatly increased demand for physical education activities and gymnastics.

## Physical Education after the Civil War (1865–1900)

By the close of the Civil War many changes were taking place in the country. The teaching of physical education was beginning to expand more rapidly. *Dio Lewis* (1823–1886) was a major influence on the development of American physical education at this time.[8] Although his only degrees were honorary, he practiced medicine. He had some academic studies and practical experience in the medical field and he was an enthusiastic, attractive supporter of health-related activities, particularly physical education and temperance activities (against alcohol).

Lewis developed his own system of gymnastics that he referred to as the "New Gymnastics."[9] He was particularly concerned with the development of the upper body, and he tried to develop a system of exercises that would be applicable to men, women, and children. He used no large or fixed equipment, preferring free exercises and activities using wands, Indian clubs, rings, and even bean bags. In his program the students performed the activities to music.

He started the *Normal Institute for Physical Education* in Boston in 1861 to prepare teachers of this system of gymnastics. The course was a ten-week training session with instruction in anatomy, physiology, hygiene, and gymnastics. This first teacher-training institution in the United States for physical education remained open until 1868 and graduated between 250 and 400 teachers during its existence.

Lewis was something of a charlatan-salesman, for although he practiced medicine without a degree, gave many lectures based upon little experience, and made many unscientific claims that could not be supported, he was an excellent salesman of physical education. He did more to popularize gymnastics than anyone in his time. His system became a major influence in the use of gymnastics in the schools for it required a minimum of equipment and minimal expenses for the schools, and his book of instructions for his system, first published in 1862, went through ten editions in six years. Lewis also devoted much of his life to the work of the Women's Christian Temperance Union (WCTU), which he founded and which became an avid supporter of physical education in the schools.

**The Turner School.** The German Turners also formed a school to train teachers of their system, though their school had many early difficulties.[10] The school, which opened in New York City in 1866, was called the *Normal School of the North American Gymnastic Union.* (The Turners had been split by politics before the Civil War, but they dropped all political concerns afterwards and changed their name to the North

---

[8] Fred E. Leonard, *Pioneers of Modern Physical Training*, 2d ed., rev., Associated Press, New York, 1922, pp. 83–88.
[9] Gerber, pp. 259–266.
[10] Ibid., pp. 267–275.

American Gymnastic Union.) Their primary objective of physical training was evident in the new school. The one-year course included the history and aims of physical education, anatomy, first aid, dancing, and gymnastics instruction combined with work in teaching methods. The classes met during the evenings, so the students could have jobs during the day. The first class began with nineteen students, five of whom graduated.

In the years that followed, the teacher's course varied in length from four to ten months, and the site of the school shifted from New York to Chicago and back, then to Milwaukee (for thirteen years), to Indianapolis, and back to Milwaukee, where the course was a two-year program from 1895–1899. The curriculum gradually became diversified and more like a junior or senior college program as the Turners discovered that they needed to broaden their program if they wanted their influence to reach beyond the German community. By 1907 the school was in Indianapolis to stay; it offered a four-year degree program, which resulted in a B.S.G. degree (Bachelor of Science in Gymnastics), and later became affiliated with the University of Indiana.

***Development of Other Schools and Systems.*** *Dudley Sargent* (1849–1924) was made director of the Hemenway Gymnasium at Harvard University in 1879.[11] He had received an M.D. degree at Yale and had taught there and at Bowdoin College. He developed a gymnastics program based on the German and Swedish systems, constructed many types of apparatus to be used in his program, and also did much experimentation in anthropometric measurements. He referred to his system as the "Sargent System," an eclectic system that drew from all other systems. He used a thorough medical examination as the basic preliminary to any program of physical activity.

The school he formed in 1881 to prepare teachers of physical education, which he called the Sanatory Gymnasium, later became the *Sargent School for Physical Education,* which eventually merged with Boston University. In 1887 he introduced a summer session, which met at Harvard, to prepare physical education teachers. Sargent became a key figure in the development of modern American physical education, along with Dr. Edward Hitchcock of Amherst and Dr. Edward Hartwell of Johns Hopkins University, who also formed major American schools of gymnastics and physical education.

Other plans and systems of physical education were being introduced into the United States in the 1880s. The Swedish system of

---

[11] Arthur Weston, *The Making of American Physical Education,* Appleton-Century-Crofts, New York, 1962, p. 34.

gymnastics based on Ling's work was first taught by *Hartwig Nissen* (1855–1924)—who taught in Washington, D.C., then at Johns Hopkins, and later in Boston—and then taught by *Nils Posse* (1862–1895) who also taught in Boston.  A graduate of Sweden's Royal Central Institute of Gymnastics, Posse came to Boston in 1885.[12] He was hired by *Mary Hemenway* to teach the Swedish system to twenty-five women teachers. Later he was made director of the *Boston Normal School of Gymnastics* when it was founded in 1889.

The Swedish system, which began to replace the German system in popularity, used no apparatus and was more free and less rigid than the German system.  This flexibility was the strongest point of the Swedish system, for it allowed the program to adapt to more conditions than the German system could meet.  Posse added exercises with Indian clubs and other objects because they were popular in America. His primary concern was achieving the desired health benefits rather than maintaining the "purity" of the Swedish gymnastics.

Baron Posse wrote three popular books on his version of the Swedish system and published a journal that rapidly spread the word throughout the United States before his death at the age of thirty-three. He had formed his own school of teacher training in 1890, and he was succeeded as its director by Nissen.  Posse's influence was great in developing the popularity of Swedish gymnastics.

The so-called system of *Francois Delsarte* (1811–1871) of France enjoyed some popularity in the late 1800s also. Delsarte had worked with the use of body movements to express feelings.  His exercises were aimed at training actors, singers, and public speakers, but since he left no writings about his ideas, his followers interpreted his work into a program of physical exercise that they called the "Delsartean system of physical culture."  His system of expressive exercises were used as a counter to the German and Swedish systems, though the influence was much smaller.  The system was later absorbed by dance, to which it was more applicable.

**The Physical Education Requirement.** After the Civil War the first moves were made toward requiring physical education activities and instruction in the public schools.  Under the leadership of *John Swett,* Superintendent of Public Instruction, the state legislature of California passed the first law requiring physical education in the public schools in 1866.[13] This first law did not signal a dramatic surge in the number of such laws, however.  The second law requiring physical education was

---

[12] Gerber, pp. 314–318.
[13] Ibid., pp. 100–105.

not passed until 1892, when Ohio required such instruction, but only in the larger schools in the state. Much of the work leading to the passage of such state laws around the turn of the century was done by the turnvereins and the WCTU. The WCTU, in seeking to gain more public recognition of the place of physical education in the educational process, was also instrumental in having a physical education division organized within the National Education Association in 1895.

***The Move toward Professional Organization.*** A focal point in the history of U.S. physical education was the 1885 formation of the Association for the Advancement of Physical Education (AAPE). Most teachers of physical education were then called gymnasium teachers or directors of gymnasiums. At this time there were few leaders in physical education, and few of the better-known teachers had received formal training in the work they were doing. Most teachers had learned more through trial-and-error, plus reading, than they had learned through teacher-training programs.

*William Anderson,* M.D., teacher of physical training at Adelphi College in Brooklyn, wanted to learn what other teachers were doing, so he called for a meeting in Brooklyn of people interested in gymnastics who wanted to discuss what they were doing. The group met on November 27, 1885, with sixty persons present. Dr. Edward Hitchcock was appointed chairman and later elected the first president as forty-nine people joined the new AAPE. Most of the leaders in the new organization held M.D. degrees and were most often interested in physical education for the health benefits they believed it could provide.

The group met in the same place during the following year but changed its name to the American Association for the Advancement of Physical Education (AAAPE). The members stated that their objective was "to disseminate knowledge concerning physical education, to improve the methods, and by meetings of the members to bring those interested in the subject into closer relation to each other." A New member was *Edward Hartwell,* M.D. and Ph.D., who had helped to define the field of physical education and show the extent of its practice with the publication of his 1885 report to the government called *Physical Training in American Colleges and Universities.*

The Boston Conference of 1889 might be considered an outgrowth of the AAAPE. Whether or not it is true, the AAAPE canceled its convention that year so the members could go to the Boston meeting, and most of them did show up in Boston.[14] The meeting was called by Mary

---

[14] Weston, pp. 37–39.

Hemenway, assisted by *Amy Morris Homans*. The two women were advocates of the Swedish system, but the conference was called to discuss all the systems. While many prominent leaders of physical education spoke on the German, Swedish, and Sargent systems, it is interesting to note that no spokesman was called upon for games and sports, probably because those activities were not really in the curriculum used by the schools and colleges at this time. The 1889 conference is significant, for it was the first meeting to bring together the leaders in the field of American physical education specifically to discuss the various systems and what might provide the best help to the American people.

By this time the Battle of the Systems between the German and Swedish systems of gymnastics was growing to fever pitch. During the 1892 convention of the AAAPE many arguments were presented on both sides, with Nils Posse, champion of the Swedish system, suggesting that the greatest need was to develop an "American system" based on the needs of the American people, rather than totally adopting either the German or Swedish system as their own.

Another speaker at the 1892 convention was *George Fitz* (1860–1934), who pushed hard for physiological research into the benefits of physical activity to provide proof of the benefits and at the same time to help determine which activities are actually beneficial to the body.[15] An M.D. who taught physical education in Harvard's short-lived (1891–1899) bachelor's degree program in physical education, Fitz was the impetus behind the formation of the *American Physical Education Review,* as well as its first editor. He also founded the first physical education research laboratory in the United States, at Harvard in 1892.

**American Physical Education at the Turn of the Century.** By 1900 there were 1076 members in the AAAPE, though there were no members west of Nebraska.[16] The association was playing an increasingly important role in providing channels of communication among physical educators as physical education continued to spread and evolve. By the turn of the century the Battle of the Systems was being decided in favor of the Swedish system, but this issue was becoming less important. As the new century dawned, the influence of sports, including games and play activities, moved irresistibly into programs of physical education, to the point of almost replacing the traditional activities.

Thus at the close of the nineteenth century physical education was becoming recognized for its value in the educational process. States

---

[15] Gerber, pp. 302–307.
[16] *JOHPER,* 31 (April 1960), 33.

Walter Camp's Home Defense Guards, a turn-of-the-century exercise class formed to get usually sedentary businessmen into shape in case of war. President William Howard Taft (right foreground), the heaviest U.S. president, joined in to popularize the program. (Courtesy Brown Brothers)

were beginning to require its inclusion in the public school programs (though most states did not do so until after 1900), and in turn the increasing use of physical education in the schools was beginning to require more physical education teachers.

Although regular four-year degree programs designed to prepare teachers of physical education had not yet emerged, several institutions had begun training physical education teachers. The list of these schools starts with Dio Lewis's school and includes the school of the Turners, Sargent's regular school and his Harvard summer session, the Boston Normal School of Gymnastics, the Posse–Nissen School, and the newly expanding International YMCA School (later Springfield College) at Springfield, Massachusetts. The first graduates of such programs were appearing at the close of the century, and the most recent research indicates that the first baccalaureate degree in physical education was awarded to James F. Jones by Harvard in June of 1893.[17]

[17] Walter Kroll and Guy Lewis, "The First Academic Degree in Physical Education," *JOHPER,* 40 (June 1969), 73–74.

Other early four-year degrees were offered at Stanford University (which graduated Walter Davis in 1897 and the first woman graduate in the United States, Stella Rose, in September of 1899)[18] and at the University of Nebraska. This first state university degree was also awarded to a woman, Alberta Spurk, in June of 1900. The big boom in four-year physical education degree programs was to come in the next thirty years, from 1900 to 1930.

## Twentieth-Century Changes in American Physical Education

Before 1900 physical education was more narrowly defined than today. To most teachers it meant gymnastics, or physical training, or physical culture. Its primary orientation was toward developing good health for the student, rather than looking at the total educational program. A philosophy of dualism was present—educating the mind and training the body—but educators viewed the process as two separate processes, related but not very similar. Thus most of the ideas for unified programs of instruction had come from foreign sources.

***The Move toward a Unified American System.***    At the 1892 convention of the AAAPE, Posse had stated the need for American leaders to quit trying to use foreign systems of training and develop an American system based upon the characteristics and needs of the American people. Such efforts actually began to occur around the turn of the century as new leaders moved into prominence in education and physical education.

A major leader in what came to be called the "progressive movement" in education was *John Dewey* (1859–1952), who was teaching at the University of Chicago when his ideas on education first became known.[19] Later a professor of philosophy at Columbia University, he sought social changes through an experimental form of education that was centered on the child. He was best known for a work on education called *Democracy and Education*, published in 1916.

Dewey, who had a strong belief in the unity of mind and body, suggested that a major reason why the system of Greek education had been so good was because the Greeks never tried to separate the mind from the body in the educational process. His teachings included the concept of the "whole child" and combined the mental and the physical as areas that could not be separated in education. This concept led to

---

[18] Mabel Lee, "Further Discussion of the First Academic Degree in Physical Education," *JOHPER,* 44 (April 1973), 89.
[19] Gerber, pp. 106–111.

a gradual shift in the aim of physical education in the United States—from a health-centered concern with the student's body to a concern for *all* educational values—that is, to a unified view of the child and of education.

Because Dewey considered the school a social institution, he believed that education had social goals and outcomes. He included physical education in this role and followed a philosophy sometimes referred to as the "learn by doing" method of education. He considered play quite important in education, because children were interested in play activities. If children were interested in the activity, they would become more involved, which would result in greater accomplishments, he believed. His was a pragmatic approach, for the teacher could take useful things from many activities to form a better activity or group of activities.

**The New Physical Education.** Dewey's work in physical education was carried on by *Thomas Wood, Clark Hetherington,* and *Luther Gulick.* Wood developed the "New Physical Education" during the first several decades of the twentieth century and referred to it as "a program of naturalized activities for education toward citizenship." [20] He included games and sports, as well as other new, nongymnastic activities, in his program, which was aimed at meeting the needs and interests of his students. Hetherington emphasized in turn that the physical education program must be a product of American society, if it was to contribute to the total education of the American child. Gulick's work in the area of recreational activities included camping and outdoor education and stressed the social values of education.

Although the trend away from the older, more rigid systems of physical education was beginning, the move toward the New Physical Education was delayed during the gradual transition by a lack of trained teachers of physical education who could teach the newer program. After World War I, however, the newer system began to catch on in the schools. Wood's textbook led the work of spreading the New Physical Education between World War I and World War II, as did the efforts of *Jesse Feiring Williams,* known for his work in the philosophy and principles of physical education, and *Jay B. Nash,* whose major work was in the field of recreation.

During the period from about 1900 to 1930 sports were gradually included in the school curriculum, partly in response to the problems

---

[20] Thomas Denison Wood and Rosalind Frances Cassidy, *The New Physical Education,* Macmillan, New York, 1927.

out-of-school sports created for the schools and partly because of the very strong student interest in sports. This student interest showed itself not only in the changes in the physical education curriculum but also in the rapidly growing development of intramural sports as many colleges began responding to the student interest in sports participation.

***A Growth in Programs.*** At the same time sports was moving into the school program as a result of its popularity with the students, another activity was moving into the program with equal vigor: dancing. Dance, particularly folk dancing, had been presented in depth at the 1905 convention of the renamed American Physical Education Association (APEA, formerly the AAAPE). This convention might in fact be called the "Dancing Convention," for the bulk of the program was devoted to explanations and demonstrations of various dancing programs and their education benefits. Some educators feared that the rapid growth in popularity of dancing programs would push gymnastics from the school curriculum.

Many new programs of professional preparation were also being developed—first at the undergraduate level, then at the graduate level—during the early years of the twentieth century. The need for trained teachers of physical education was great at this time, for more schools began to require that their teachers hold bachelor's degrees and few such programs were available in physical education. Many state normal schools (colleges to train teachers) were built at this time, while existing state schools expanded their programs and many universities and private schools added physical education majors to their programs. Teachers College of Columbia University in New York City awarded the first master's degree in physical education in 1910, and along with New York University, offered the first Ph.D. program in physical education in 1924.[21]

The recreation movement, led by people like Luther Gulick, was also beginning to grow at the turn of the century. The larger cities in the United States were beginning to expand their recreational facilities, and programs of recreation and play were coming more into the attention of the federal government. After World War I great interest in recreation was evident, and during the Depression the government provided jobs for out-of-work citizens in constructing recreational facilities.

The National Park Service, formed by the government in 1911, led to more national interest in public parks and recreational opportunities,

[21] Deobold B. Van Dalen and Bruce L. Bennett, *A World History of Physical Education,* 2d ed., Prentice-Hall, Englewood Cliffs, N.J., 1971, pp. 441–443.

and camping and outdoor education was becoming a large movement. Many schools began camp programs, the most prominent being the program in New York City, while many other interested groups, especially the new youth groups such as the Boy Scouts, Girl Scouts, and Camp Fire Girls, moved into the area of camping.

The physical educators also began to form new professional groups according to their more specialized interests. The Academy of Physical Education was formed in 1904 (no relation to the later group), and other groups were formed for people interested in men's college physical education, women's college physical education, camping activities and recreation, and school health activities. The old AAAPE, which had become the APEA in 1903, changed its name twice in the next thirty-odd years, first to the American Association for Health and Physical Education (AAHPE) in 1937, then to the American Association for Health, Physical Education, and Recreation (AAHPER) in 1938. Although the initials representing the organization are the same today, the name was changed in 1974 to the American Alliance for Health, Physical Education, and Recreation.

On an organizational level across the country, new groups of physical educators united to form smaller versions of AAHPER on state and district levels and eventually established six districts (each containing several states), as well as many state associations. On the national level, the older divisions of interests themselves became associations, such as the Division of Physical Education and the Division of Men's Athletics, which combined into the National Association for Sport and Physical Education (NASPE).

**Effects of the Depression and World War II.** The onset of the Depression in the United States, which became a powerful factor in the nation's life during the early 1930s, created great social changes in the country. The United States gradually shifted from its old idea of "rugged individualism" to a newer concern for equality of opportunity and a concern for the group (society). It was a difficult time for physical education in the schools; the money shortage led to the belief that many physical education programs were expensive "frills" and that they represented money better spent elsewhere. The move to drop physical education as a requirement in many states forced physical educators to have to defend their program for the first time.

The trend toward social and recreational goals in physical education programs continued through the Depression, but began to slow down in the years just prior to World War II. The new programs in many European nations, which showed their aims to be fitness for war and the development of a stronger sense of nationalism, resulted in a gradual shift of the U.S. programs back to emphasis on physical fitness.

During World War II the physical education programs in the United States basically became programs of physical fitness oriented toward the military needs of the nation. Sports were strongly pushed as a phase of fitness, and many prominent physical educators became involved not only in developing programs of physical training for the armed forces, but also in developing intramural sports programs for the military as well. The tendency for the school programs to adopt the physical training programs of the military and thus change from programs of physical *education* to physical *training* was the greatest problem created for physical education by World War II.

**Changes after World War II.** The period from World War II to the present day exhibits several notable features. The first was the work done toward improving the standards of teacher preparation in the United States on both the undergraduate and graduate levels. Major conferences concerned with developing the undergraduate professional preparation curriculum were held at Jackson's Mill (1948), Washington, D.C. (1962), and New Orleans (1973); written reports on curriculum suggestions were published after each conference. Other conferences on graduate study in physical education were held at Pere Marquette, near Chicago (1950), and in Washington, D.C. (1967).

Physical education was also beginning to split into a number of separate areas of concentrated interest in the decades following World War II. Major interest groups whose concerns were health education, safety education, recreation (including park activities), and dance developed during this time. Fitness also became a major concern several times after World War II, first at the time of the Korean War and then soon afterward when the results of the much-publicized Kraus–Weber Tests suggested that U.S. youngsters were much less fit than their counterparts in other nations.

In 1955 President Eisenhower formed a Council on Youth Fitness, and although it was allowed to fade from the public eye, during the late 1950s and early 1960s AAHPER worked to develop a program of physical fitness tests with norms for American school children. The Eisenhower Council on Youth Fitness was revived under President Kennedy as the President's Council on Physical Fitness. This action was an example of the increasing governmental concern for the state of fitness not just of the children, but of all the citizens.

In 1957 physical educators also discovered that the required program of physical education must be defended again. When Russia orbited the first Sputnik satellite, the United States went into educational shock and for the first time became convinced that its schools were "behind." The result was a concentrated push toward the sciences and bread-and-butter education. Many educators began going for the old dualistic concept of the mind and body as separate entities. The problem of dualism reappeared in the late 1960s as an opposition to specific requirements in the educational process. The net result was to show physical educators that they had sadly neglected public relations in their dealings with the public as well as with their fellow educators.

**Characteristics of U.S. Physical Education.** In reviewing the history of physical education in the United States, Daryl Siedentop has suggested that there were seven important characteristics visible during its development:[22]

1    Physical education as an "umbrella" concept, with a multitude of activities, such as sports, games, dance, recreation, and health education (which is the "broad field of interests" interpretation of physical education this text has suggested).

2    The downward movement of innovation from the college level to the high school level and, finally, to the elementary level (which he suggests is the normal direction for most new programs to take since they are learned by the future teachers at the college level)

3    The development of sports and games through sources outside the schools (which is discussed more fully in Chapter 9 of this book).

4    The selection of physical education activities dictated by the trends in adult leisure (which was a major direction of many required programs during the late 1960s in response to the concept of "lifetime sports"—activities that could be practiced throughout the individual's life—as opposed to strenuous fitness activities, which could not be utilized as well by older persons).

5    The unclear relationship between physical education and athletics (which has been a continuing problem in American physical education since the late nineteenth century—when students began organizing their own sports programs—and which is discussed in Chapter 10).

6    Periodic returns to a major emphasis on fitness (which was the direction of the physical program in times of war, but also at other

[22] Daryl Siedentop, *Physical Education: Introductory Analysis,* 2d ed., Wm. C. Brown, Dubuque, Ia., 1976, pp. 38–44.

irregular intervals, such as when the results of the Kraus–Weber Tests were made known).

**7**    Increased specialization in professional training (which can be seen today even at the undergraduate level, as some students are asked to specialize in either elementary or secondary physical education, while larger schools have undergraduate majors in other areas, such as health education or recreation). This trend will cause increasing problems for physical educators, for while such programs last longer and longer, the public is calling for programs that are shorter and less expensive.

American physical education has seen many changes during the one hundred and fifty years since the start of the earliest programs that we think of as physical education. It has moved from an emphasis that was purely on the health of the student to a concept of concern for the education and state of the "whole" person—mind and body unified. It has come from a system pushed by self-taught "amateurs" to one supported by science and the medical profession, from one with teachers with ten weeks or less of professional training to one with trained teachers who hold degrees up through the doctorate. It has come from a field interested in a small area of physical concern to a diverse body of people who might at first glance seem to have little connection with each other; they are, however, united in physical education as a broad field, though individually they may be health educators, park administrators, recreational program directors, or teachers of dance. Physical education has become a broad and complex field, but it has become no less a satisfying field for the practitioner.

## Suggested Readings

Albertson, Roxanne M. *Physical Education in New England Schools and Academies From 1789 to 1860: Concepts and Practices.* Microfiched Ph.D. dissertation, University of Oregon, 1974.

Barton, Helen M. "History of the Development of Physiology and Hygiene Texts." *Research Quarterly,* 14 (March 1943), 37–45.

Bennett, Bruce L. "Biography of Dudley A. Sargent." *Research Quarterly,* 19 (May 1948), 77–92.

———. "The Making of Round Hill School." *Quest,* 4 (April 1965), 53–63.

Betts, John Rickards. "Public Recreation, Public Parks, and Public Health Before the Civil War." In *Proceedings of the Big Ten Symposium on the History of Physical Education and Sport.* Edited by Bruce L. Bennett. Athletic Institute, Chicago, 1972, pp. 33–52.

Billett, R. E. "Evidence of Play and Exercise in Early Pestalozzian and Lancastrian Elementary Schools in the United States." *Research Quarterly,* 23 (May 1952), 127–135.

Blaikie, William. *How to Get Strong and How to Stay So.* Harper and Brothers, New York, 1899. (Reprinted by Wm. C. Brown, Dubuque, Ia., n.d.)

Butler, George D. *Pioneers in Public Recreation.* Burgess Publishing Company, Minneapolis, 1965.

Chapman, Sara A. *Development of Movement Education in the United States: Historical and Theoretical Bases, 1900–1960.* Unpublished Ed.D. dissertation, Temple University, 1974.

Cieplik, Raymond. *Physical Work and Amusement as Concerns of the Young Men's Christian Association, 1851–1884.* Microcarded M.S. thesis, University of Massachusetts, 1969.

Davis, Thomas R. "Puritanism and Physical Education: the Shroud of Gloom Lifted." *Canadian Journal,* 3 (May 1972), 1–7.

Drew, A. Gwendolyn. *A Historical Study of the Concern of the Federal Government for the Physical Fitness of Non-Age Youth with Reference to the Schools.* Microfiched Ph.D. dissertation, University of Pittsburgh, 1944.

Gerber, Ellen W. "The Ideas and Influence of McCloy, Nash, and Williams." In *Proceedings of the Big Ten Symposium on the History of Physical Education and Sport.* Edited by Bruce L. Bennett. Athletic Institute, Chicago, 1972, pp. 85–100.

————. *Innovators and Institutions in Physical Education.* Lea and Febiger, Philadelphia, 1971.

Gulick, Luther Halsey. *Physical Education by Muscular Exercise.* P. Blakiston's Son, Philadelphia, 1904. (Reprinted by Wm. C. Brown, Dubuque, Ia., n.d.)

Hackensmith, C. W. "Contributors to the Scouting Movement in North America." *Canadian Journal,* 4 (May 1973), 48–57.

Hartsoe, Charles Edwin. *The Contributions of Charles K. Brightbill to the Recreation Movement.* Microfiched Ph.D. dissertation, University of Illinois, 1970.

Hoepner, Barbara J. "John Swett's Experience with Physical Exercise at the Rincon School: Foundation for the First State Physical Education Law in the U.S." *Research Quarterly,* 41 (October 1970), 365–370.

Hunter, Adelaide. "Contributions of R. Tait McKenzie to Modern Concepts of Physical Education." *Research Quarterly,* 30 (May 1959), 160–166.

Hyde, William J. *The Round Hill School, 1823 to 1834: an Early Experiment in American Physical Education.* Microfiched M.S. thesis, University of Massachusetts, 1970.

Jable, J. T. "Pennsylvania's Early Blue Laws: A Quaker Experiment in the Suppression of Sport and Amusements, 1682–1740." *Journal of Sport History,* 1 (Fall 1974), 107–121.

*JOHPER,* 31 (April 1960), 10–126. Special historical issue written for the 75th anniversary of the AAHPER by Mabel Lee and Bruce Bennett, with contributions by many other people. Includes a history of AAHPER, plus brief biographical sketches of eleven of the early leaders.

Kennard, June A. "Maryland Colonials at Play: Their Sports and Games." *Research Quarterly,* 41 (October 1970), 389–395.

Ladd, Wayne M. *The Athletic Institute: A Study of an Organization and Its Effect on and Reflection of the Development of Sport, Recreation, and Physical Education in the United States.* Unpublished Ph.D. dissertation, Ohio State University, 1974.

Leaf, Carol Ann. *History of the American Academy of Physical Education, 1950–1970.* Unpublished Ph.D. dissertation, University of Utah, 1974.

Lee, Mabel. "The State of the Profession from World War I to Women's Lib." In *Proceedings of the Big Ten Symposium on the History of Physical Education and Sport.* Edited by Bruce L. Bennett. Athletic Institute, Chicago, 1972, pp. 101–120.

Leonard, Fred E. *Pioneers of Modern Physical Training,* 2d ed., rev. Associated Press, New York, 1922.

Lockhart, Aileene S., and Betty Spears, eds. *Chronicle of American Physical Education, 1855–1930.* Wm. C. Brown, Dubuque, Ia., 1972. Contains many valuable articles by early leaders.

Osbourne, Barbara J. *An Historical Study of Physical Education in Germany and Its Influence in the United States.* Microfiched M.Ed. thesis, Woman's College, University of North Carolina, 1961.

Peavy, Robert Darwin. *History of the American Academy of Physical Education, 1926–1950.* Microfiched Ph.D. dissertation, University of Utah, 1973.

"Pioneer Women in Physical Education." *Research Quarterly,* 12 (October 1941 Supplement).

Posse, Nils. *The Special Kinesiology of Educational Gymnastics.* Lothrop, Lee and Shepard Company, Boston, 1894.

Shults, Frederick D. "Oberlin College: Molder of Four Great Men." *Quest,* 11 (December 1968), 71–75.

Struna, Nancy, and Mary L. Remley. "Physical Education for Women at the University of Wisconsin, 1863–1913: A Half Century of Progress." *Canadian Journal,* 4 (May 1973), 8–26.

Swanson, Richard A. "The Acceptance and Influence of Play in American Protestantism." *Quest,* 11 (December 1968), 58–70.

Van Wyck, C. B. "Harvard Summer School of Physical Education." *Research Quarterly,* 13 (December 1942), 403–431.

Wacher, Hazel M., Mark A. Pankau, John R. Schleppi, and Mary Womack. "Bicentennial Celebrations: Presenting 200 Years of Activity." *JOPER,* 47 (January 1976), 32–36.

Wood, Thomas Denison, and Rosalind Frances Cassidy. *The New Physical Education.* Macmillan, New York, 1927.

Zeigler, Earle F. "Clearing Up Some Confusion about the First Teacher Training Program in Physical Education in the United States." *Canadian Journal,* 5 (May 1974), 38–46.

––––––. "An Historical Analysis of the Professional Master's Degree in Physical Education in the United States." *Canadian Journal,* 3 (May 1972), 44–68.

––––––. "Historical Perspective on Contrasting Philosophies of Professional Preparation for Physical Education in the United States." *Canadian Journal,* 6 (May 1975), 23–42.

Zingale, Donald P. *A History of the Involvement of the American Presidency in School and College Physical Education and Sports During the Twentieth Century.* Microfiched Ph.D. dissertation, Ohio State University, 1973.

# 5 International Physical Education Today

The advances in technology during the twentieth century have resulted in a shrinking world. We find ourselves increasingly caught up in events around the world because communications have become almost instantaneous, with travel not for behind. Nations are forced into contact with each other, often with awkward results because neither nation really understands the other. The study of comparative physical education is an attempt by physical educators around the world to learn about each other and share an understanding of their national programs.

## Why Study Comparative Physical Education?

This chapter is concerned with what physical educators are doing in other nations around the world today. Such a study is sometimes called a cross-cultural study of education, or comparative education.[1] Lynn Vendien and John Nixon give five reasons for making comparative studies of the physical education programs in other nations. First, the studies help educators to learn about the different programs around the world. Second, the studies can assist in developing talent in constructive leadership by studying other systems in a way that will enable educators to make comparisons. This requires educators to decide whether one system might be better than another one, or whether their own systems are necessarily best for their respective societies. This process is necessary to the continual improvement of any educational system. Third, the educator is able to learn about the goals, ideas, and experiences of other cultures or societies. This knowledge is helpful in

---

[1] C. Lynn Vendien and John E. Nixon, *The World Today in Health, Physical Education, and Recreation,* Prentice-Hall, Englewood Cliffs, N.J., 1968, pp. 5–6.

determining whether the system that has evolved is fulfilling the needs of the society, or if it is not doing so, the knowledge can assist in determining how the program has moved away from the needs of a society. Fourth, comparative studies can help educators assess and improve their own educational systems by allowing them to see how other nations with similar and dissimilar systems have tried to meet their educational needs. Fifth, such studies can help to promote international professional collaboration, particularly within the areas of educational research. Comparative studies of international education can thus be one more facet of international understanding that leads to better and more peaceful relations between the many nations on the earth.

Our comparative study has been based on several assumptions. First, we assume that any educational system is patterned at least partially by the traditional values and practices of its culture. Any nation's educational system is expected to be largely a reflection of that nation's interpretations of its history, traditions, and the cultural practices it has followed throughout its history. The educational system will be an attempt to maintain the traditions of a nation and pass them on to the nation's youth.

Second, if the country was at one time the colony of another nation, we assume that its educational system was strongly, and perhaps permanently, influenced by the former colonial power, and therefore it will be less strongly developed according to its own cultural traditions. A colony usually inherits an educational system very similar to the native educational system of the ruling country, for the ruling power believes its own system is the best one. However, because the system was developed by the ruling power, and has little or no regard for the culture or tradition of the colony, it is often almost useless for mass education of the "natives," as it takes little account of their cultural needs and patterns. This pattern is most easily seen in the former colonies of the British Empire where very "English" schools were started. Usually these schools preserved British social class distinctions that did not even exist in the colony where the schools were located; the schools were based on the cultural traditions and social patterns of the English, though they could serve almost no genuine cultural function in the colony.

The third assumption in our comparative study is that if the country is what we refer to as a newly emerging nation, it often faces two dangers, either of which is risky to the nation's educational future. The first danger is that the new country will perpetuate the inherited educational system developed by the colonial ruler and thus continue a system that has little true relationship to the culture of the new nation. The problems are essentially those noted above. The other side of the coin constitutes the second problem: The new nation will drop the old colonial system of education that it has inherited, but will at the same time simply adopt a copy of some other Western nation's educational pattern, with little regard for whether that new educational system will fully meet its needs. However, each nation's educational system should meet the cultural patterns and traditions of that nation if it is to be a truly effective system of education.

Fourth, the newly emerging nations face the risk of assuming that the quality of their new programs is acceptable and thus leaving their new educational system in its original state. Any educational system should be in a constant state of change, even though that change is very gradual, for societies and cultures themselves are constantly in a state of change. The educational system must be gradually evolving to meet society's changing needs and prevent education's gradual obsolescence. The new nations need to be continually assessing their programs and revising them in an attempt to bring them closer to the needs of their own culture, just as the older nations must do if they are to continue to improve. No educational system can remain static, unless the nation wishes to stop progressing, for cultural life depends upon change and growth. By failing to grow, an educational system begins to die.

Most educational programs that are now developing in the non-Western nations are under the influence of Western ideas and educational patterns. Unfortunately, these educational patterns are based on Western culture, which may not be consistent with the cultural patterns and needs of a non-Western nation.[2] When the barbarians invaded the Roman Empire, they often wanted to adopt the Roman system, which they considered very good. The end result was the destruction of the Roman system, for it was not culturally suited to the barbarian nations. The strength of the Romans' system came from their adopting a bit of the native culture of each conquest, while leaving the basic traditional cultural patterns of the conquered people largely unchanged. The Romans were able to strike a happy medium between preserving their own culture and preserving the native culture, which permitted the conquered people to be ruled with a much greater stability than might otherwise have been the case. Neither the Romans nor those they conquered were expected to adopt a system radically different from the one they had traditionally followed.

Several problems may be created by wholesale adoption of Western educational patterns by non-Western nations. One problem may stem from whether the native country has a people who are either

---

[2] Ibid., pp. 8–9.

basically competitive or noncompetitive. Many nations are not competitively oriented, and if this is the case, adopting Western educational patterns may cause many inconsistencies. The Western patterns are usually strongly oriented toward competition, both inside and outside the classroom.

Another problem concerns the program for women in the schools. In some cases the program might simply be copied from the men's program, while in other cases it might be a separately developed program. The difference can be quite important, for much depends upon the place of women in a particular country. In some nations women do not hold the same rank or relative equality with the men, as they do (increasingly so) in the Western societies. The schools should reflect the cultural patterns of the native country, for otherwise the result may be rather unpleasant to a nation that discovers its national educational system produces a massive change in its cultural patterns.

A third problem concerns the differences in the *need* for physical activity in different nations. Most of the Western nations whose educational patterns might be copied are composed of relatively affluent people who greatly need programs involving considerable physical activity. Most newly emerging nations and many non-Western nations are less affluent, however, and their people, who are more involved in physical labor in their daily lives, need less physical activity in their physical education programs. The educational pattern thus needs to reflect the needs of the local people, rather than the needs of an unseen nation far away.

A fourth area that can cause problems is dance. It is used far more in non-Western societies than in the West, and any program of physical education should reflect this cultural difference. Since dance is an important part of the culture of many nations, it should play a much greater part in the educational process of those nations than in others where it is not. Again, the educational patterns of any country should reflect that country's own culture and needs.

A study of the practices of other nations around the world can be a major contribution to international understanding. The idea of improving international relations has been a concern for centuries. Baron Pierre de Coubertin of France was concerned with this lack of understanding between nations when he began working to revive the Olympic games. When the games were revived in 1896, a major concern was to develop fellowship and understanding among the athletes of many different nations. During the time of the ancient Greeks the Olympic games had been a time of peace and harmony, when people from all nations could meet and mingle in peace. Coubertin stressed this aspect of free movement by the athletes, their getting to know their opponents from around the world. As a result of his emphasis of the

National boundaries momentarily forgotten, Rafer Johnson of the U.S.A. and C. K. Yang of Taiwan collapse against each other after finishing first and second in the Olympic decathlon in Rome in 1960. It was this kind of international fellowship that Coubertin wanted to promote when he worked for the revival of the Olympic games in the late nineteenth century. (*Sports Illustrated* photo by John G. Zimmerman © Time Inc.)

cultural aspects of the Olympic games, the modern games were also tied into displays of art and other cultural activities.

This contribution to international understanding was an important part in the formation of the United Nations in 1945. Previous attempts to provide a place for the world's nations to meet and exchange their views, such as in the League of Nations, all eventually failed. The United Nations was formed after World War II as an attempt to provide a forum where the nations could discuss their common problems and explain their views to the other nations.

Many of the conflicts in the modern world have been a result of misunderstandings or failures of nations to communicate clearly with each other. As the world advances technologically, such misunderstandings become increasingly risky, for acts that might be interpreted as aggressive moves by a nation can be spotted almost immediately, and retaliation can be instantaneous. The risks of accidental war in a world filled with guided nuclear missiles set to go into action almost automatically are great indeed. The nations of the world need a forum where they can learn what their counterparts around the world have, want, and are doing. There *must* be some channels of communication between nations, if only as an attempt to prevent accidental wars.

Each of the many international groups in the world today has some particular area of special interest. Our primary concern is with the international organizations that function in the areas of education, physical education, and sport. As there are multitudes of organizations in these areas, we will concern ourselves primarily with the larger and more important of the international organizations.

We can advance no claim that international understanding and good will are the only goals of international relations, especially in the area of sport. Sport is an international language, and as such it can serve many other national interests. The commonly expressed reason for international sports competition is as a medium of cultural exchange. However, sport can also serve as a vehicle of international prestige, for individual and team championships at the international level can improve the prestige a nation feels on the international front. Competition can also serve as political propaganda. While winning is related to international prestige, tours by national teams can be used not only to impress other nations with one's prowess in sport, but also to show one nation's regard for the esteem of another nation, or the desire for good relations with that nation. For example, the first improvement in relations between communist China and the United States was the so-called Ping Pong diplomacy. When the Americans were invited to send their best table tennis players to meet the Chinese in a series of matches, the invitation served notice that China was ready to improve relations with the United States in other areas as well.

International sports competition can also be used to bolster national pride. The success of a nation's athletes in international competition can develop a strong feeling of pride among the nation's citizens, especially the smaller nations and the newly emerging nations. This national pride in the success of their athletes can be seen in the reactions to the success of the athletes of the newly emerging African nations in the 1968 Olympic games in Mexico City and the successes of the Kenyan and Finnish athletes in the 1972 Games in Munich.

## International Organizations

A major international organization in the area of education is the World Confederation of Organizations of the Teaching Profession (WCOTP), founded in 1952. It works to organize teachers around the world to promote education for the purposes of international understanding; it also looks after the interests of teachers and tries to improve the training of teachers and the programs they teach. With headquarters in Washington, D.C., WCOTP works with the United Nations in some areas of international educational concerns and holds regular conferences

around the world.  One of its members is ICHPER, the physical education group.

The International Council on Health, Physical Education, and Recreation (ICHPER) was founded in 1959 at a meeting of the WCOTP.
With headquarters in Washington, D.C., it assists the WCOTP in fulfilling its goal by working with organizations concerned with the broader
aspects of physical education, including health and recreation, internationally.  It works in the areas of studying the preparation of teachers,
exchanging information on national programs, promoting exchange
programs in physical education, and conducting special international
studies and holding international conferences concerned with international problems in physical education.  It holds a world conference
every year.

The International Federation of Physical Education (FIEP) was
begun in 1923 and has its headquarters in Lisbon, Portugal.  Its object
is to promote physical education for all people, regardless of sex or
age.  It promotes research and the exchange of ideas between nations
by sponsoring exchanges of teachers and scholars between interested
nations.  It holds regular international meetings.

The International Council of Sport and Physical Education
(ICSPE) was established in 1960 and has its headquarters in Munich,
West Germany.  Its primary goals are to improve cooperation between
all groups interested in physical education and sport and to interpret
the cultural values of physical education and sport.  It has regular international meetings every two years.

The International Olympic Academy was established in 1961 to
promote and maintain the ideals of the original Olympic games.  Its
headquarters are in Athens, and it is connected to both the Hellenic
Olympic Committee and the International Olympic Committee.  The
International Olympic Academy conducts annual summer sessions at
the site of ancient Olympia as one way of achieving its objectives.

The International Association of Physical Education and Sport for
Girls and Women was begun in 1953 to bring together women around
the world who were working in physical education and sport.  It also
cooperates with other organizations that promote sports activities.  The
IAPESGW tries to improve school programs by international exchanges
of people and ideas.  It has a world meeting every four years.

Some organizations are concerned purely with sports, unlike the
above groups that are concerned with education or physical education
and include sports primarily as an added area.  The major sport organization is the International Olympic Committee (IOC), established in
1894 to revive the ancient Olympic games.  It has conducted the
Olympic games every fourth year since the first modern games in 1896,

and it tries to encourage sports competitions that are in keeping with the ideals of the ancient Olympic games. It deals strictly with the Olympic Committees of the member nations, such as the United States Olympic Committee (USOC), rather than with the national governments, for it seeks to keep all political considerations out of the Olympic games. Some of its intended patriotic moves have gradually led the modern Olympics closer toward an international political contest; for example, the use of national anthems and flags at awards sessions and recognizing the athletes' home nations as much as their individual skills.

The International Amateur Athletic Federation (IAAF) was begun in 1912 to promote friendly sports competition between nations without any type of discrimination on any grounds. Its emphasis on fair competition has resulted in its being the body that makes and revises the rules and regulations governing international and Olympic track and field athletics (simply called *athletics* in most nations outside the United States). It also is the agency that approves world records. The rules are revised at its international meetings, held every two years. Membership of a nation depends on that nation's chosen representatives being accepted into what amounts to a "gentleman's club" composed primarily of rich, elderly men, much in the tradition of nineteenth-century British athletics, where it was considered unseemly for the common people to be permitted to compete in sports. This attitude can be seen in many of the organization's regulations relating to amateurism that make it difficult for anyone but the relatively wealthy to be "pure" amateurs. Consequently, most nations interpret the rules in this area with considerable latitude, while the IAAF and IOC studiously attempt to look the other way.

The International University Sports Federation (FISU), with headquarters in Louvain, Belgium, was founded in 1948. It tries to promote international physical education among students by sponsoring international sports conferences and contests for university students (the World Student Games or Universiades, every two years). It has regular international meetings every other year.

The International Military Sports Council, also begun in 1948, tries to promote equality within the various armies of the world, while it encourages friendly relations and sports ties among the world's armies. With headquarters in Brussels, Belgium, it promotes international championships in many sports and also holds an annual meeting.

Besides these organizations that are oriented primarily toward sports, there are many international organizations whose goals are related to physical education or sport, but whose primary goals are more specialized than the above groups. One such group is the International Federation of Sport Medicine (IFSP), established in 1928 and headquartered in Brussels. Its goals are to develop physical and moral health through physical education and sports activities. It also makes scientific studies in this area; these are concerned with sport's effects on healthy people and the problems of injuries and disabilities in sport. It has regular conventions every four years.

The International Recreation Association was begun in 1956 and has its headquarters in New York City. Its goals are to promote recreation and to provide international recreational services. It is a consultant to the United Nations and conducts exchange programs to study recreational programs around the world.

The International Union for Health Education was begun in 1951 and has its headquarters in Paris. Its objects are to promote better health through educational means and to promote the exchange of current information in health education. It has a regular convention every third year.

The International Youth Hostel Federation, which stems from an organization begun in 1932, is located in Copenhagen, Denmark, and tries to promote cooperation between national organizations while promoting international understanding among young people. Its primary mode of improving international understanding is to make inexpensive travel possible by providing places around the world where traveling youth can stay at minimal expense. This organization is most active in Europe.

The People-to-People Sports Committee was started privately in 1956 to promote international understanding and sports competition. It does so by sponsoring touring teams in many sports and by working in other ways to promote international sports.

UNESCO, the United Nations Educational, Scientific and Cultural Organization, was established in 1945 and has its headquarters in Paris. Its goals are to contribute to peace and security in the world by promoting cooperation among the nations in improving education, science, and culture, while stressing a basic respect for justice and individual human rights. It has an international meeting every two years.

The World Alliance of Young Men's Christian Associations, with headquarters in Geneva, Switzerland, was first begun in 1844. Its goal is to help YMCAs around the world. Its sister organization is the World Young Women's Christian Association, located at the same address, which was begun in 1848. Its more broadly based work includes the goals of international understanding, basic human rights, and improved social and economic conditions for all people. It has a large world meeting every four years.

The World Health Organization (WHO) was organized in 1948 as an agency of the United Nations, with headquarters in Geneva. Its ultimate goal is to help all people attain a high level of health, which it has defined as "a state of complete physical, mental, and social well-being and not merely the absence of disease or infirmity." It meets annually and provides assistance to any world government that requests it.

In addition to these specialized international bodies, which represent only a small number of the many international organizations, there are many international sports organizations. Almost every sport that has participants in many countries has at least one international organization that keeps its rules updated, verifies world records (if the sport has such records), and provides for international competition and world championships. These organizations are too numerous to list in a short chapter, but some examples are the International Amateur Basketball Federation, headquartered in Munich, for basketball; the International Gymnastics Federation (FIG), located in Geneva, for gymnastics; and the International Amateur Swimming Federation, located in Jenkintown, Pennsylvania, for swimming.

## International Competitions

There are many international sports competitions, but the most important is the Olympic games. Although the ancient Greek games were dissolved in A.D. 394, they often attracted scholars' attention over the next fifteen centuries. The most prominent among the number of people who worked to revive the ancient Greek competition was Baron *Pierre de Coubertin* (1822–1908) of France.

The International Olympic Committee was formed in the 1500th anniversary year of the abolition of the Greek Olympic games, with the revival of the games as its goal. Two years later, in 1896 in Athens, the first modern Olympic competition was held. The games now meet every fourth year, or Olympiad, as did the ancient games, though the world wars caused their cancellation in 1916, 1940, and 1944. A decision was made to add winter sporting events in 1908, but the now-separate winter Olympic games were not held until 1924. More nations now take part in the Olympic games than in any other internationally organized program except the United Nations.

The competition is open to both men and women in a large number of sports, but the number of activities has become so large and unwieldy that suggestions have begun appearing for the summer games to be separated into several parts by different sports and placed at different sites around the world. The primary reasons for this suggestion are: (1) the games are a tremendous expense for any city to face; (2) the large number of competitors and visitors puts an almost impossible strain upon the facilities, housing, traffic, and police work of all except a few of the world's largest cities; and (3) the extreme visibility of such a concentrated sports event has made it seem an ideal place for political demonstrations and possible terrorism, such as the political demonstrations in

The Olympic games are not always above political interference, as shown in this cartoon about the 1976 Olympics. The Montreal Olympics were marked by a walkout by over two dozen nations who were trying to bring pressure in a non-Olympic sport, by the attempts of an organized group to get athletes from Communist nations to defect, and by Canada's breaking Olympic tradition in refusing to permit a country (Taiwan) to participate for political reasons. (Courtesy Doug Marlette and the Charlotte, N.C., *Observer*)

Mexico City in 1968 and the murder of Israeli athletes by terrorists in Munich in 1972. The modern Olympic games are currently facing perhaps the most difficult period of their survival; the danger is that their very popularity will destroy them.

A second major world championship event is the World Student games (Universiade) of the FISU. The first competition was held in 1947, and the event is now held every odd-numbered year. Multitudes of university students from around the world take part in these games, which include a number of sports.

A third world meet, though one of more limited entry standards, is the World Maccabiah games, patterned after the Olympic games, but limited to Jewish athletes. First held in 1931, the competition in many sports is held every fourth year in Israel.

Many area championships that are held regularly involve only a portion of the world's nations. These contests are frequently patterned after the Olympic games, though they may not include so many different sports within their competitive structures. The oldest example is the Asian games, first held in 1913. Although the competition has changed its frequency and the nations involved in the competition a number of times since then, it is now essentially a sports competition for nations in continental Asia, ranging from Turkey to China, but not including Russia (much of which is in Asia). These games now meet every four years; the next competition is scheduled for 1978.

Another major competition is the Commonwealth games, sometimes called the British Empire and Commonwealth games. Begun in 1950, it also meets every fourth year, midway between Olympic games. It is limited to the past and present members of the British Empire and the countries in the British Commonwealth.

The Pan-American games are a multisports championship for nations of the Western Hemisphere (North, Central, and South America). First begun in 1951, the Pan-American games are held every four years, during the year before the Olympic games.

Various European championships, usually involving single sports, are also held at varying intervals. The European nations, as well as Russia, are the participants. Most commonly a European championship is held every fourth year, usually between the Olympics like the Commonwealth games. In track and field athletics an annual meet called the European Cup, which has qualifying meets to cut down the number of contestants, has been added in recent years.

Other competitions represent many smaller regions, while some represent individual sports. An example in team sports is the World Cup, the championships in soccer (football). The final playoffs involving a small number of national teams are held every four years, between the Olympic years, but the national teams qualify for the World Cup Final through a series of playoffs spread over the two years prior to the final.

World championships are held at some regular interval for most separate sports, though not all world championships are designated as such. The rules of the IAAF state that the Olympic games will also serve as the world championship event for track and field athletics, though it is rarely referred to in that way. There are, however, dozens of world championships held during the period of every Olympiad, some of which are connected to the Olympic games and some of which have no connection to the Olympic movement at all.

## Orientations of Physical Education Programs

Physical education programs can vary greatly from nation to nation, for each nation has its own goals and orientation for the program. One of the traditional orientations for several thousand years has been toward *military fitness*. This major objective of physical education programs in the past can still be seen today, to some degree. As we have seen in our historical review, it becomes important during times of war, when national goals are to produce healthy young people who will be physically ready for military service. Military fitness is perhaps the most limited goal of a physical education program.

A second program orientation is toward *competitive sports training.* While the objective of these programs is partially to develop the skills and fitness of all the students by providing basic training in the techniques of competitive sports, they can also be used as "talent hunts"—that is, used to locate students with the potential to become outstanding athletes. In the past, programs of this nature that have been seen in the United States were community programs used to locate athletic talent for school teams. Today when such programs appear, they are more often on a national scale and are used to locate students who have the potential to become national or world class athletes; the athletes are then given training on a higher level in the hope that they will ultimately bring athletic prestige to the nation.

The third orientation, that of the *lifetime sports* program, is seen primarily in the more affluent nations. In a program of this nature, the objective is to teach the students skills in sports that can be enjoyed throughout life, almost regardless of age, in the hope that they will take part in physical activities and maintain at least minimal fitness throughout their lifetimes. This approach is seen more frequently in nations where the people have more money and leisure time, for a citizen in a poverty-stricken nation generally will not have the time (or the facilities or inclination) for such activities.

A fourth orientation might be called *cultural fitness,* for it places much emphasis on activities that are rooted in the culture of the nation. For example, the country stresses only its traditional activities, such as national dances and sports, and puts very little emphasis on activities used in other nations, regardless of their world popularity. This type of program is more likely to be seen in the smaller nations or in nations that have been ruled by other countries and are striving to develop a national consciousness or self-image.

A fifth orientation, *total fitness for life,* is sometimes tied into the program as part of the total educational process. We refer to this approach when we speak of education both of and through the physical. The emphasis is not on any single area of fitness or training; the concern is for the final outcomes of the educational process, whether physical, social, mental, or moral.

## Some National Physical Education Programs

Because we have space to describe only a limited number of national programs of physical education, we will discuss the programs of England, West Germany, the Soviet Union, Japan, and Kenya. Each of

these systems was chosen for a particular reason: The English educational system has been copied around the world (a result of England's
former position as the world's foremost colonial power); West Germany's system is representative of the European programs of physical
education; the Soviet Union provides an example of a system in a totalitarian state; Japan is to some degree a representative of a modern
Asian system (though it has limitations that we will discuss later), and
Kenya serves as an example of the newly emerging Third World nations.
Thus each nation serves as an example of a particular political or
geographical system.

**England.** We will discuss some of the practices of physical education
around the world by looking at programs in several countries, each of
which can represent a number of other countries of a regional or ideo-
logical type. The first example is England. This system was in many
respects copied around the world, for at one time the British Empire
encircled the globe, and when educational systems were developed in
the British colonies, they were for the most part copies of the traditional
English system of education.

The system in England was composed largely of privately run,
elitist institutions that catered primarily to the upper classes. But during
the twentieth century many changes have occurred in British education
as the emphasis has shifted more toward mass education. The total
fitness concept is the basic emphasis of the English physical education
program, which is used as one more phase of an educational process
aimed toward the ideals of social democracy.

England has long been a citadel of games and sports, but these
activities, which have long been part of the life of the people, are used
in an extremely independent way. There is little reliance on coaches or
formal organizations. The activities are self-organized and controlled
by the participants, much like U.S. sport in its developmental stages in
the nineteenth century before the schools took control away from the
students. In England the tradition is sport, as opposed to the emphasis
on competition in the United States which is not entirely the same. The
primary emphasis of English sport is the fun of the competition.

While the English educational pattern in the past was largely
upper-class education in private schools (referred to as "public
schools"), that tradition has largely passed from common practice, for
most English children are now educated in free, genuinely public
schools. All children are required to attend school from the ages of five
to fifteen. There is considerable variety available in English education,
for the English are trying to adapt their educational practices to the
many differences in ability and aptitudes that can be found among the
students.

The English public (private) schools are run privately, are often quite expensive, and cater to the upper classes. As the English free schools have improved in quality, the proportion of students in the private schools has dropped to about 10 percent of the student population. In the private school pattern students attend kindergarten from about the ages of five to eight, then a preparatory school from the ages of eight to thirteen, and finally a private secondary school from the ages of thirteen to anywhere between sixteen and eighteen. Attendance at these schools is followed by education at the university level. Some but not many preparatory schools are boarding schools, while most secondary private schools are. Most schools have required games or sports activities on at least four afternoons weekly. Frequently physical education specialists are available, though their functions are often less authoritarian than in the U.S. schools.

In the free public schools the students at the lower levels are usually taught physical education by their classroom teachers. In the first several years of school the emphasis is on movement education activities, with two short lessons daily between the ages of five and seven; later the daily lessons include some sports activities. As the students get older, more sports activities are added. At the secondary level much of the instruction is by trained specialists. The girls have activities such as "educational gymnastics," dance, and games and sports, while for boys emphasis is put on strength and mobility activities in the games and sports. At the secondary level physical activity is commonly scheduled for four class periods per week, two of which are games and sports. During the last year or so of secondary school, the number of class periods may be decreased as the student prepares for university entrance examinations.

For the secondary students, choosing which of the three types of secondary schools to attend depends on their career plans or occupational directions. Students are given standardized intelligence and achievement tests before entrance to the secondary schools as an aid in determining what type of school they should attend, but there is still considerable controversy regarding this testing practice.

The most common school today is the modern school, which is designed to meet the needs of most of the students. The second type is the grammar school, which emphasizes the academic areas of the humanities and sciences, and which is preferred by the parents as the best route to the university. The third type of school is the technical school, which emphasizes training in trades or industrial work, similar to U.S. technical schools. Another type of school, which is commonly called the comprehensive school and which is similar to U.S. high schools, combines all three of the basic types of English schools into a single school.

At the university level physical education activities usually are not required; they are most commonly voluntary activities oriented toward recreational games and sports. Although most universities have physical education personnel, this staff assists students, but does not plan their programs. Sports organizations are usually organized, financed, and often coached by the students, who may occasionally hire a professional coach.

The teacher of physical education must be certified and approved as a qualified teacher by a governmental educational authority. Certification can be achieved by taking a three- or four-year teacher-training course at a teacher-training college or university. Some colleges specialize in preparing teachers of physical education, though they are of recent origin. A university graduate in another field can take a one-year course of specialization in physical education to become a certified physical education teacher.

Professional coaching has not been a prestigious career in England, and the coaches in the past were athletes who had no educational training. Most sports competition is through clubs, which may or may not hire coaches. A number of sports organizations have developed systems of coaching examinations that are used to certify coaches in a single sport on the local, regional, or national level. Because the overwhelming emphasis of sports competition in England has been the fun of sport, rather than the success of competition, the coach has not been lifted to the exalted status sometimes seen in the United States.

**West Germany.** An example of European programs of physical education is the program of the Federal Republic of Germany (West Germany). The basic emphasis of the West German program lies somewhere between the total fitness concept and that of developing competitive sports. The physical education program is tied strongly to national sports bodies, which have strong national organizations to push sports competition among the youth of the nation. The government sponsors many competitive events for the students.

The educational program is now a decentralized one, with each of the eleven states directing the physical education program in its area. (This arrangement is similar to the state-oriented organization in the United States.) Although the centralized structure of education was broken up after the fall of the Nazi government, the federal government of West Germany still issues guidelines with suggestions for school requirements.

Daily play and instruction are recommended during the first two years at the elementary or primary level. Thereafter the recommendations call for three hours weekly of gymnastics and play activities, with an additional two hours weekly of games and sports, either in the form of competition or of sports clinics. The two types of secondary schools include the professional schools, which basically provide an academic preparation for university training, and the vocational school. Although the same suggestions are made for physical education in both types of secondary schools, the vocational schools allot very little time to physical education, and the actual number of class hours of activity in the professional schools is sometimes less than the recommendations because of the time needed for academic studies.

The greatest emphasis in the curriculum is upon gymnastics, which is largely an outgrowth of Jahn's work in the early 1800s. Much work is also done with games and play activities during the early years of school, while in the later years the program moves into a heavily sports-oriented emphasis. Physical education is not a major part of the curriculum at the university level; it is geared primarily toward voluntary recreational activities, similar to the English system.

Teachers at the intermediate or secondary level must be certified as teachers in two subjects, one of which is physical education. The process is usually satisfied by a three-year teacher-training program in the universities. There are also one- and two-year teacher-training programs available, partially in response to the shortage of physical education teachers in the West German schools. During the last two decades the great national emphasis on developing facilities for play, recreation, and sport has been accompanied by the development of many sports training centers.

**Soviet Union.** An example of physical education in a totalitarian system is the program of the Union of Soviet Socialist Republics (Soviet Union, or Russia). No single emphasis exists in the Russian program—unless the improvement of the physical health and condition of the state might be described as one—but several emphases are evident. First is the total fitness concept, which is used to develop a social-minded, healthy citizen. Mixed in are both the military fitness emphasis, stressed through a concern for defense (Russia has very long national borders and lost many millions of its strongest youths during World War II), and sports training orientation, which is stressed for the attendant national prestige achieved through sports successes.

The educational system has been slightly decentralized, but the programs throughout the nation follow governmental guidelines. Daily activity requirements in the schools include ten minutes of in-place exercises at the start of every school day, in addition to the required physical education classes. The required class activities are split between (1) exercises and sport-type activities and (2) special technique work in a single sport. This second part is organized a bit like the lifetime sports idea in the United States, for it is designed in part to develop a level of skill and appreciation that will encourage the student to continue participation in the activity long after leaving school.

The school physical education program is strongly supplemented by other governmental programs. Summer camps, which are made available for most age groups, stress physical activities, though many nonphysical activities are included. The Sport Badge awards are used to reflect achievement levels in activities and lead up to the highest level, the Master of Sport. These awards are very prestigious, for they require increasing levels of physical fitness in addition to the advanced sports tests. The *Spartakiadas* are regular national sports competitions that are used both to promote physical education and to locate and develop athletes to the highest levels of achievement. These events are promoted through a huge system of local sports clubs.

The high status of physical education in the Soviet Union has resulted in many candidates for admission to the teacher-training programs, which in turn has resulted in higher admissions standards. The entrance examinations that a prospect must pass include tests of intellectual ability, physical fitness, degree of social adjustment, and leadership abilities. Limited class space has created keen competition among quality students.

There are three levels of teacher training in the Soviet Union. The lowest level requires a five-year course that follows eight years of primary school. Its graduates are assistant instructors who usually continue their studies in night classes. The second level is more academic and usually operates through a Department of Physical Education at a teacher-training institute. Its graduates teach at the primary or secondary level, depending on the level of their academic training.

The highest level of training is in the physical education institutes, which offer both undergraduate and graduate instruction. These institutes usually include departments to train sports coaches, for official coaches must be graduates of a physical education institute. Much scientific research is carried on in sport in the Soviet Union, so the prospective coach needs special training to be able to interpret and apply the results of the research. The graduates of the institutes teach and administer programs at the highest levels. There has been a trend toward upgrading the lowest level program to the middle level in recent years. The basic education of the prospective teacher is a rough balance among three areas: (1) the physical fitness of the prospective teacher, (2) a high level of theoretical knowledge, and (3) the knowledge and skills of teaching theory and techniques.

**Japan.** Japan is a representative of the Asian countries to some degree, even though many aspects of its school programs have been built on the model of the United States' school system. This U.S. influence is a result of the U.S. military control and intervention into the life of the Japanese after World War II. The basic emphasis of the Japanese program of physical education is total fitness—the education of the whole child—including physical development, citizenship, and healthful leisure activities. Physical education is required in the schools from elementary school through the university.

Students are required to attend school for nine years (six years of elementary school and three years of junior high school), which may be followed by three years of senior high school and four years of university training. A multitude of activities are used in the school physical education program to meet the broad emphasis of the program.

During the elementary school years the students have forty-five minutes of activity three times each week under the direction of their classroom teachers. At the junior and senior high school level, two or three classes of fifty minutes each per week are allotted to teaching more advanced skills. Traditional Japanese sports and activities are also added at this level. Some theoretical studies are provided to show the benefits of exercise and its place in the individual's life.

At the university level four credits are required in physical education, though two of them may be lecture-type courses in areas such as health education. The course offerings are diverse, in the tradition of the U.S. system. While sports are first offered at the junior high school level, there has been an attempt to organize national programs of competitive sports under educational auspices to avoid the effects of competition that might be considered harmful or might not contribute to educational ends.

Teachers must be certified, which requires completion of either a two-year or four-year program of professional preparation; the four-year graduates teach at the higher school levels. At this time there are only a few graduate programs in physical education in Japan, so many students undertake graduate studies in universities in other countries, such as in the United States. The teacher-training programs are modeled largely on the U.S. system of teacher preparation.

**Kenya.** Kenya represents the newly emerging, underdeveloped nations of the world, sometimes referred to as the Third World. Kenya was once a colony in the British Empire and is now a member of the British Commonwealth. Consequently, many aspects of its physical education program have developed from programs begun by the British. The program was formerly one of physical training (primarily calisthenics), but the primary emphasis today is to develop the individual character. The broad program stresses total fitness and the development of the whole child.

Kenya is still in the process of developing its own national identity in its program of physical education and its requirements. Physical

Abebe Bikila of Ethiopia, shown here winning his second Olympic marathon in Tokyo in 1964, was one of the first prominent African athletes to receive world attention. Since his time, many other and newer African nations have increased their international prestige by their successes in sport. (Courtesy Wide World Photos)

educators are faced with the problem of very limited facilities for physical education activities, which hampers many of the efforts for a broadly based program. At the secondary school level each student must take two periods per week of physical education, though other games and swimming are also provided. Activities are generally in three areas: (1) games (including team sports), (2) dancing activities, and (3) swimming and athletics (track and field).

As is the case in many of the newly emerging nations that are seeking to establish national and international identities, Kenya is striving to develop a competitive international sports program. Much work is done to attract students and adults to sports, both to provide recreational activities and to serve as an athletic talent hunt. Kenya suffers from the shortage of facilities and a lack of national and especially international competition. The nation is seeking to develop its full potential in sport, for much national pride has resulted from its successes in Olympic competition.

All teacher-training programs in the universities require some work in physical education, and all teachers are considered qualified to teach physical education, since they have at least a minimal background. Teacher-training programs are still being developed, and Kenya is appreciative of the benefits it can receive from international exchanges of teachers and from opportunities for its students to be trained in the universities of other countries. Although Kenya still has many problems in its developing educational system, as the nation develops, so its system progresses continually.

By studying the physical education programs and patterns of teacher preparation in other nations, we can broaden our understanding of those nations and of physical education, for we begin to see physical education through many other eyes. International studies can be one more link toward world understanding.

## Suggested Readings

Bennett, Bruce L., Maxwell L. Howell, and Uriel Simri. *Comparative Physical Education and Sport.* Lea and Febiger, Philadelphia, 1975.

Bray, Maureen Clifton. *The History of the Canadian Association for Health, Physical Education, and Recreation, Inc.* Microcarded M.S. thesis, University of Oregon, 1957.

*A Decade of Progress: ICHPER, 1958–1967.* International Council on Health, Physical Education and Recreation, Washington, 1967.

Hall, Sydney Owen. *The Role of Physical Education and Sport in the Nation-Building Process in Kenya.* Microfiched Ph.D. dissertation, Ohio State University, 1973.

Herndon, Myrtis E. *Comparative Physical Education and International Sport, Vols. I and II.* AAHPER, Washington, D.C., 1972.

————. *Theses and Dissertations Related to Comparative/International Education, Physical Education, Sport, and Dance.* Published by the author, Hiram, Ohio, 1973.

Johnson, William, ed. *Physical Education Around the World.* Phi Epsilon Kappa, Indianapolis, Ind. A series of monographs with writings on the programs in a number of nations. Monograph 1 appeared in 1966.

Ndulue, John Chika. *Selected Aspects of Physical Education in Advanced Countries Around the World With Implications for the Developing Areas, Especially Africa.* Microcarded M.S. thesis, University of Illinois, 1974.

*Physical Education in the School Curriculum.* ICHPER, Washington, D.C., 1969.

Putnam, Betty Jean. *A Study of National and International Physical Education Associations.* Microfiched M. S. thesis, Smith College, 1956.

*Sports and Education in Schools: A Working Paper.* ICHPER, Washington, D.C., 1968.

# III The Evolution of Philosophies of Physical Education

# 6  *The Physical Educator and Philosophy*

The study of philosophy is important to physical educators, for in keeping with our whole-person concept of physical education, it helps us to develop personal philosophies that affect every area of our actions as we go about our daily lives. To realize why we need to understand philosophy and the uses of philosophy, we need to look at three areas of philosophy: (1) the definition and application of philosophy, (2) the major philosophical teachings, and (3) how these philosophies have come into being. These major topics are the subjects of the next three chapters.

## Why Have a Personal Philosophy?

At this point you might be wondering: "Why do I need to have a *personal* philosophy? What does it matter? What purposes would it serve?" Davis and Miller have made several observations regarding the value of having a philosophy and the functions it can serve.[1]

***A Common Language.*** The development of a personal philosophy around common philosophical ideas helps members of fields develop a common bond. We are facing what C. P. Snow referred to as the "two cultures"; the sciences and the arts or humanities are gradually growing farther apart and losing their former sense of a common tie. A common language is needed to tie all the diverse educational areas together, and the most common bond can be found in philosophy. Further, the development of the theoretical and philosophical areas of disciplines

---

[1] Elwood Craig Davis and Donna Mae Miller, *The Philosophic Process in Physical Education,* 2d ed., Lae and Febiger, Philadelphia, 1967, pp. 169–176.

and professions helps greatly in explaining the fields to the public, in addition to increasing public acceptance of the fields.

**Professions Move Beyond Isolated Concerns.**  Physical educators need to work more to show that the field contributes to society and its values in broad terms.  Physical educators have traditionally been concerned with short-term, practical goals rather than the study of physical education's contribution to culture as a whole.  In essence we are beginning to move in this direction as we begin to expand the study of physical education and sport to include fields such as philosophy, sociology, psychology, anthropology, and history.  The field is undergoing a necessary diversification as it seeks to broaden its area of interest beyond its earlier narrow concern with limited aspects of exercise and hygiene.

**Highlighted Professional Purpose.**  As physical educators begin to develop individual philosophies, they will gradually begin to clarify their vision of the purposes of physical education.  They will work more to fill the needs that they see as areas where physical education can make a vital contribution. Davis and Miller suggest that one reason for the low quality of many programs designed to prepare physical educators is that no basic purpose or purposes of the programs have been developed either by the institutions or by physical educators as a body.  As personal philosophies develop, major purposes should clarify themselves in the minds of educators.

**Examination of Basic Assumptions.**  Simply put, as philosophical studies are pursued and personal philosophies are developed, the basic assumptions, principles, or theories upon which physical education practices have been based will begin to be examined more closely.  Often we fail to look at accepted theories and practices to see whether they still stand up before the light of current knowledge and experimentation.  If ideas are no longer in line with the present state of knowledge, the pursuit of philosophical studies is likely to expose the problem.  It is hoped that such an examination would result in the development of new theories or the discovery of new principles and thus lead to an improvement in theory and practice of physical education.

**Self-Examination and Independent Work.**  As students become educated, they must learn to expand the horizons of their minds by seeking to develop their own minds and ideas rather than depending wholly on learning the ideas and theories of other people, as is common in most current systems of education.  Students must learn to look inward, to look at themselves for more answers.  The process of education that begins with the examination of what earlier students have learned must be carried to a logical extension as students try to go beyond what earlier students were able to learn. The desire to take part in creative, independent work throughout the professional life should be a natural outgrowth of the development of a personal philosophy.

## What Is Philosophy?

Philosophy has long been a nebulous concept to students. It is difficult to define clearly, for historically the definitions may seem to be in conflict. Zeigler defines philosophy as "a science which investigates the facts, principles, and problems of reality in an attempt to describe, analyze, and evaluate them." [2] One problem is evident in this definition—that is, philosophy's function today is not the same as science's function, for philosophy observes what we might consider the "unobservable": ideas, concepts, and feelings.

Barrow, who suggests that philosophy can be viewed several ways, presents three concepts of philosophy: (1) philosophy as "a study of the truth or the principles underlying all knowledge," (2) philosophy as "a study of the most general causes and principles of the universe," and (3) philosophy as "a system for guiding life." [3] As you can see, philosophy is not a small area of interest; it is so broad as to be almost impossible either to define or to comprehend. Barrow views philosophy as both a process and its resultant product. The process is a route used to establish a system of values, while the product is the system of values that eventually is produced by that process.

Webster notes that the original meaning of philosophy was a "love of truth" or "love of wisdom." [4] It was viewed as a search for both facts and values that are to be studied without any bias or prejudice. As he points out:

> Philosophy is concerned with questions of right and wrong, justice, freedom, and discretion. Though there is a distinction between philosophy and science, philosophy can be said to be a science since it organizes knowledge about man and the universe for the purpose of evaluation and comprehension. . . . Philosophy criticizes, evaluates the worth of things, and synthesizes facts; while science describes, discovers, and analyzes facts . . . . [Scientists]

[2] Earle F. Zeigler, *Philosophical Foundations for Physical, Health, and Recreation Education,* Prentice-Hall, Englewood Cliffs, N.J., 1964, p. 322.

[3] Harold M. Barrow, *Man and His Movement: Principles of His Physical Education,* Lea and Febiger, Philadelphia, 1971, p. 18.

[4] Randolph W. Webster, *Philosophy of Physical Education,* Wm. C. Brown, Dubuque, Ia., 1965, pp. 3–4.

know how [atomic energy] works and how to use it, but only philosophers deliberate about where and for what purpose it should be used. Both processes are essential.

Philosophy originally included the physical and social sciences, but as knowledge expanded and specialized disciplines developed, philosophy was eventually left with meaning, value, appreciation, interpretation, and evaluation as its subject matter.

Davis states that philosophy includes both *process,* or the search for truth or wisdom, and *content,* or what has been learned or decided by using the process.[5] Davis and Miller discuss philosophy as a process by showing as some of its processes the pursuit of philosophical truths, the attitude of reflective thinking (speculative, or looking beyond what is obvious and known or understood), and an attempt to understand the problems of life.[6] They point out that two contrasting processes are involved in philosophy: *analysis,* which is closely studying many things, and *synthesis,* which is trying to see how the things blend together, or indeed *if* they can be blended together.

Davis and Miller summarize philosophy as having four different elements or facets. It begins with *heritage,* or the background of philosophical thought and theory that has been developed over the past centuries. It also includes *action,* or the actual process of building a personal philosophy. This process includes both thinking and synthesis. A third element of philosophy is the *quest,* or the search for new meaning. This element can include using philosophy as a basis for judging the worth of things and as an indicator of directions that should be followed. The fourth element they mention is *discovery,* for the philosophical process is an ongoing search that leads to new discoveries.

Philosophy studies things such as the ultimate meaning of life. We might say that science studies what can be proved, while philosophy studies what cannot be proved. Philosophy is an attempt to extend meanings far beyond known facts to provide directions for each person's life. While an earlier definition spoke of philosophy as a science, philosophy is not a science in the sense that we commonly think of science in the modern world; it tries to go far beyond science's cold facts. We need to consider the relationship between philosophy and some other broad areas of life.

Some of the relationships between philosophy and science were discussed by Davis and Miller.[7] They first noted that science is a precise area that seeks to learn what can be proved with concrete facts,

---

[5] Elwood Craig Davis, ed., *Philosophies Fashion Physical Education,* Wm. C. Brown, Dubuque, Ia., 1963, pp. 4–5.
[6] Davis and Miller, pp. 18–22.
[7] Ibid., pp. 23–29.

Ceremonial dances of primitive societies are an example of man's search for a supreme being. This photograph shows a public ceremonial dance about the creation, given at the circumcision ceremony of young boys in an aborigine tribe in Australia. (Courtesy Australian News and Information Bureau)

whereas philosophy goes beyond the facts and into areas of speculation that probably can never be proved. Actually the scientific method of research is very similar to the methods used in philosophy to gain knowledge. However, science requires observable data, while philosophy does not; philosophy is concerned largely with meanings and values, while science is concerned with provable facts. Science is still close to philosophy in many respects, however, for it developed from philosophy, as we will see in Chapter 8.

Religion is closely related to philosophy, for religion is by its nature very philosophical. Religion is concerned with the idea of God and the relationship between God and people; it also is very concerned with ethics and ethical practices. Religion is concerned with many areas of meaning in life for which there can be no scientific proof. Religion is often self-conscious about the lack of scientifically provable ideas, but that makes it no less valid an area of life or of concern than philosophy. Both seek to go beyond the known and into the unknown, and each seeks to answer questions that science can never answer.

Art is also closely related to philosophy, for no scientific judgment or process can be involved in art. Art is an area of values, where people seek to express, fulfill, and understand themselves, which is a complex process that goes beyond the limitations of science.  Art is by its nature subjective; it is concerned with an inner self that is beyond the bounds of science.

History is also related to philosophy.  Although historians follow scientific methods in studying history, their most vital concern is not the scientific process they follow or their use of provable fact, but the subjective process by which they decide what is important, what facts they will use, what each one means, how it fits together with their other facts, and how they will present and interpret the chosen collection of facts.  Although the process of history is in many respects scientific and objective, the result is largely subjective, for each person's interpretation of a fact may be different.  Each historian has a philosophy that is reflected in the way he or she works and the conclusions he or she draws, which helps tie history closely to philosophy in many respects.

### Philosophical Approaches and Methods

VanderZwaag discusses three approaches to philosophical studies.[8]  In the *speculative* approach, the philosopher tries to answer questions by suggesting possible answers, many of which may be incorrect.  He is speculating, or thinking in a way that will produce suggested experimental answers to questions or solutions to problems.

In the *normative* approach, the philosopher tries to develop guidelines or set standards most often in some area regarding people's conduct or relationships toward other people.  The suggested results would be "norms," or standards considered typical for people.

The *analytical* approach is often a study, or critical evaluation, of the ideas of others.  The philosopher analyzes other people's ideas to determine whether they are true and whether they are clearly understood and then seeks to explain the ideas more clearly.  Vanderzwaag points out that writers in philosophy have never contended that there is a clear line dividing these approaches, which do overlap in many areas.

VanderZwaag presents philosophical methodology as having five areas or "methods" of study for the student.  The first area or method is the *historical background* of philosophy.  Our philosophical concepts have come to us through a long process of historical evolution, and by studying the historical background of the various philosophies, we begin to see how philosophy has been used and how it has been influenced by the times.

The second area or method, *varied interpretation,* is the process of studying areas of philosophy upon which there is little agreement

---

[8] Harold J. VanderZwaag, *Toward a Philosophy of Sport,* Addison-Wesley, Reading, Mass., 1972, pp. 9–14.

among philosophers. Many of our basic concepts are subject to considerable disagreement among people. The philosopher needs to analyze the different interpretations of such concepts and thus clarify the issues to see whether some common ground or truth can be discovered from them.

The *value judgment* method is essentially a form of evaluation. A value judgment is not like scientific assessment, for there may be no available facts upon which a value judgment may be based. Value judgments still have an important place in education, however. Educators are considered the teachers of values as much as facts, and in many cases, the teaching of values might be considered more important than the teaching of facts, though one should not replace the other.

The fourth area or method is discovering and *clarifying the main issues.* Many times people will argue about or study many questions or issues that actually are aspects of a single overlooked problem or issue. One task of the philosopher is to discover and direct attention toward the main issues so they can be studied more clearly. The philosopher will try to direct attention toward the forest and away from the individual trees that are portions of that forest.

The fifth area or method is *determining relationships to similar concepts.* When we are studying various problems or ideas, we need to see more clearly how one relates to another. What is the relationship between the concepts of education, physical education, and liberal education? These are actually philosophical concepts, and they are related to each other, but how are they related? How similar or dissimilar are they? By studying the various concepts we can begin to see these relationships more clearly.

## The Branches of Philosophy

Several branches of philosophy form the field. When we think of philosophy, we usually think of *metaphysics,* which is concerned with the nature of reality and being. Will Durant described metaphysics as a study of the "ultimate reality" of everything, for it tries to answer questions about what is real and what really exists.[9] It is concerned with questions of reality that cannot be answered scientifically.

A second branch of philosophy is *epistemology,* which is the study of the theory of knowledge. It is a study of how to obtain knowledge and what kinds of knowledge can be obtained, or what can be learned and how it can be determined. It considers the processes of perception (how we see things) and knowledge, including the process of learning, which we sometimes call the "scientific method."

---

[9] Will Durant, *The Story of Philosophy,* Pocketbooks, New York, 1954, p. xxviii.

The branches of philosophy. (From Earle F. Zeigler, *Philosophical Foundations in Physical, Health, and Recreation Educa-* *tion,* Prentice-Hall, Englewood Cliffs, N.J., 1964).

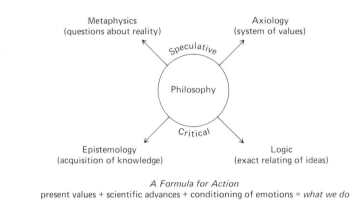

Metaphysics
(questions about reality)

Axiology
(system of values)

Speculative

Philosophy

Critical

Epistemology
(acquisition of knowledge)

Logic
(exact relating of ideas)

*A Formula for Action*
present values + scientific advances + conditioning of emotions = *what we do*

A third branch of philosophy, *logic,* is concerned with the relationship of ideas to each other. It is interested in the ideal method used for thought and research, the steps that should be followed in relating one idea to another, or in proceeding from one idea to another more advanced one. For many people logic is considered the most important area of philosophy.

A fourth branch of philosophy is *axiology,* which is the study of values in general terms; it considers the nature and kinds of values. Rather than studying axiology itself, we are more concerned with two of its subdivisions, ethics and aesthetics, which are more specific areas that study more specific questions.

*Ethics* is concerned with morals and conduct, with trying to decide upon proper rules of conduct. It is a study of ideal conduct and the knowledge of good and evil. It seeks to determine what actions are right and wrong, or what should and should not be done.

*Aesthetics,* which deals with the nature of beauty, is very subjective. Earle Zeigler has defined aesthetics as the "theory or philosophy of taste," for what does and does not constitute beauty is a very subjective question.[10]

## The Levels of Discussion

We can get some idea of where philosophy fits into the search for knowledge by looking at the four levels of discussion that Harry S.

[10] Zeigler, p. 22.

Broudy has given to be used in solving educational problems.[11] They are presented in order from the lowest, or least reliable level, to the highest, or most reliable level.

The lowest level of discussion is the *emotional* or uncritical level. At this level people are usually giving arguments or ideas based only on their personal experiences, which may be quite limited. The arguments are based primarily on emotional feelings or personal prejudices, with little or no thought given to whether further study proves the views to be reasonably accurate. Only the personal opinion is used at this level.

A more objective level of discussion is the *factual* or informational level. At this level people seek facts to prove their arguments or make their points. Opinions cannot stand unless factual support can be provided at this level, but there are still inherent weaknesses in the factual level of discussion. Much depends on which facts are used and which are not, as well as how the facts that are used are interpreted.

A third level of discussion, a step higher than the factual level, is the *theoretical* or explanatory level. In this case the facts that have been gathered are organized as proof of a more general theory that is more broadly applicable—for example, facts proved by research into teaching methods to suggest a theory about how things should be taught.

The fourth and highest level is the *philosophical* level of discussion; the issue has gone beyond the level of facts and theories to become concerned with questions of a more general and philosophical nature about the values, uses, and outcomes of the problem. This level is difficult to reach with satisfactory results, for as we have pointed out, philosophy goes beyond the provable and into the eternal truths of what is real and what is right.

## The Hierarchy of Philosophical Ideas

We need to be acquainted also with the hierarchy of philosophical ideas, as they are explained by Davis and Miller.[12] Essentially they proceed from the lowest level of idea, which is any person's opinion, to the highest level of idea, which is that of a law.

Davis and Miller move first from the level of *anyone's opinion,* which may or may not be valid, up to the level of *authoritative opinion,* the views of people considered to be at least a little bit informed about the area being studied. One level higher is the *agreement of experts,* which is a higher form of opinion, and which is topped by the next level of *proven facts.* Facts are one step removed from the experts' agree-

---

[11] Harry S. Broudy, *Building a Philosophy of Education,* Prentice-Hall, Englewood Cliffs, N.J., 1954, pp. 20–24.

[12] Davis and Miller, pp. 181–183.

ment, for we have moved from *opinions* of what is true to *proof* of what is true.

As we get closer to the philosophical areas of concern, according to Davis and Miller, we move toward *hypothesis,* which is a low-level generalization. When generalizing we are trying to take a small number of facts and explain them or show where they are leading. The hypothesis is a step beyond the fact, for it tries to suggest which direction should be taken in seeking more facts or in learning more about a question.

A *theory* is one step beyond the hypothesis; it tries to determine something that is more probable or more likely to be true than the hypothesis, which is considered to be only a low probability of truth. The theory will often have one or more hypotheses that have been shown to be true, but it will have others that are not yet proved. Thus a theory is an attempt to explain some phenomenon or occurrence, but the attempted theory has not yet been completely proved true.

A *principle* is higher than a theory in philosophy; it is a fundamental, proven truth and the result of philosophical thought. A principle is a generalization based on facts and determined and proved through the philosophic process.

The highest level, however, is the *law,* which is "a generalization of wide application and high probability." [13] The law describes relationships that are always present, by saying that if certain conditions are present, such-and-such will always be the result. The laws that have been determined are the bedrock of knowledge, for everything else, including the process of seeking more or higher knowledge, is built upon the foundation of the laws that have been determined.

We have discussed what philosophy is, and what its branches are, and we have considered other levels and hierarchies that exist in the field of philosophy. We now need to look more precisely at the major questions philosophy seeks to answer; we can then develop a clearer perception of the directions that philosophical studies take.

## The Questions of Philosophy

The major questions or concerns of philosophy are classified by Baley and Field as falling into nine areas:[14]

1    *Nature of the universe:* Historically philosophical discussion concerned the origin and nature of the earth and what basic materials

---

[13] Ibid., p. 182.

[14] James A. Baley and David A. Field, *Physical Education and the Physical Educator,* 2d ed., Allyn and Bacon, Boston, 1976, pp. 227–232.

had been used in its development. Today this issue is of little concern to philosophers, for it has been largely taken over by the scientists.

2   *People's place in the universe:* Are human beings just other animals, or are they supreme creatures? Are they important or unimportant? Are they the masters of their own destinies, or is their fate controlled by higher forces?

3   *Determination of good and evil:* Are there any absolute measures for determining good and evil, right and wrong? Do such standards vary according to the situation involved? What constitutes "the good life"? These questions are still considered very important today, and in many respects it is of great concern to physical educators in their teaching and their practices.

4   *Nature of God:* Is there a God, or do gods exist? Is there some supreme being, and if so, what are his characteristics? Where do we find God, and what is his relationship to people? These are some of the important questions involved in the philosophy of religion.

5   *Soul and immortality:* This area of concern may be related to the previous issue, depending on the philosophy and beliefs of the person involved. Does a human being possess a soul—that is, some inner part that is intangible, has no parts that can be seen, or felt? When the human body dies, does the soul die also, or does it continue to live on in some other place or some other form? This area of philosophy goes into the age-old religious questions regarding life after death: Is there life after death, and if so, what is it like?

6   *People's relationship to the state:* This area becomes an increasing concern as the rapid expansion of the world's population brings on increased governmental regulation and monitoring of people's lives. What is the best form of government? Who should reign supreme: people or the state? Is the answer to the question of supremacy an absolute, or can it change as circumstances change?

7   *Role of education:* What is the role of education in the social structure? What part does it play, and what should be its goals? These questions are crucial, for they determine how a civilization reproduces itself or fails to do so. What should be taught in education, and how should it be taught?

8   *Relationship between mind and matter:* How do people affect, and how are they affected by, their environment and surroundings? Which is superior, mind or matter, or is one superior to the other? How do they relate to each other?

**9**    *Implications of philosophy for physical education:* This area of
concern refers to physical education in the broad sense, including
such related areas as health and recreation.  How do the answers
—those we have determined for ourselves as being the best—to
the questions in the first eight areas affect our program of physical
education?

As Baley and Field point out:

> Philosophy is man's effort to see the universe in a coherent, sys-
> tematic, and meaningful way.  It gives our actions direction.  If our
> objectives, principles, and methods are to be consistent we must
> possess a reasonably well thought-out philosophic position.
> Otherwise, we are likely to be like the horseman who tried to run
> off in all directions at once.[15]

The questions that we seek to answer by our study of philosophy are
used to help clarify our ideas and beliefs regarding life and how it
should be lived.  They make our purposes and goals clearer.  By doing
so, they play a major role in determining how we will view physical
education and its function in society, what our feelings about it will be,
and what we will try to do with it.

## Thought and the Philosophical Process

We often think of philosophy as being related only to the mind, a purely
mental or thought process.  To see how we should use philosophy, we
need to understand how to use the thinking processes.  In discussing
the part thinking plays in the philosophical process, Davis and Miller
present five necessary aspects of the satisfactory use of the thinking
processes in philosophy.[16]

They first refer to *intelligent striving,* which is applying intelligent
thought over a length of time.  The philosophical process is not a short
one.  Evaluation and reevaluation of ideas is a constant necessity.  The
philosopher must never quit attacking a problem simply because it
appears to defy analysis or understanding, but must continue to make
the effort to understand and clarify the questions of philosophy.

The philosopher must also *meet the challenge.*  A challenge provides a goal or purpose for philosophical inquiry.  Just as we need
goals or challenges to make life meaningful and enjoyable, we need

---

[15] Ibid., p. 23.
[16] Davis and Miller, pp. 217–220.

challenges in philosophy, for the mind expands when faced by such challenges.

The *ability to discriminate* is also vitally necessary. A student of philosophy needs to be able to evaluate the relative worth of ideas and theories, for they are not all of equal importance. Unless we can discriminate in judging issues and problems, we may waste much time on questions or problems of little importance and thus become slaves to the philosophical version of "busy work."

The philosopher must be able to *draw reasonable generalizations.* We must be able to determine when we have enough information to defend our conclusions as being reasonable. Too often we see situations where leaders accept ideas that have not been proved and then develop ideas or programs that are of questionable value because they were based on premature assumptions.

Finally, *generalizations should be studied carefully.* A generalization should not be accepted as proven without considerable study by a number of people. Instead, we should consider generalizations to be tentative answers and subject to further study. Just as people may fail to draw reasonable generalizations, so they may also fail to study those generalizations enough to see whether they are really justified.

## What Are the Different Types of Thinking?

As we attempt to utilize the philosophical process in developing our personal philosophies, we need to understand the different types and levels of thinking. The thought processes are inseparable from the practice of philosophy, and the types of thought, as well as the levels of thought, affect the quality of the philosophical process that we use. Through the use of our thought processes we are continually building our philosophy, then reviewing it, testing it, and synthesizing it into a more coherent, clear, and meaningful interpretation of our personal philosophy. Davis and Miller have discussed the different types of thinking at some length and have categorized at least nine types of thought processes.[17]

*Mental wandering* is not an orderly process; it is not planned and may not even be conscious. Undirected thoughts simply wander from one area to another. Although good ideas may result from this process, many persons might not consider it a true process of thought.

As with mental wandering, many persons do not consider *intuitive thinking* a thought process. Knowledge seems to come immediately, with no real thought process involved in developing an idea or in lead-

---

[17] Ibid., pp. 203–216.

ing to a particular conclusion. Some persons would categorize this as unconscious thought, since it seems to follow no conscious patterns of rational thinking processes.

*Creative thinking* might be termed "inspirational thought," though this process, which uses total absorption in a problem to lead to new ideas, might be termed "inspiration" by others. Creative thinking depends on broad experience or contact with other ideas and thoughts, and its success depends heavily on how widely the individual has pursued his or her interests or curiosity. As Davis and Miller point out, ideas generally will not develop from nothing; there must have been exposure to old ideas or facts upon which the creative thought processes may be based.[18] Although a new idea may be a great breakthrough in theory, it often will have come from some earlier ideas; it does not spring full-grown from an empty mind.

The necessity of contact with other ideas, which is vital to creative thinking, emphasizes the importance of the physical educator's being interested in many other fields. Although specialization is spreading rapidly, the generalist with a broad base of experience and interests is vital to the field of physical education, for the generalists will have to show the worth of the field *as a whole.*

*Problem solving* is a type of thinking concerned with finding solutions to problems. The basic steps are essentially the same as those often referred to as the "scientific method":

**1**   A problem occurs (problem stage).
**2**   The problem is identified and defined (identification stage).
**3**   Possible solutions are suggested (theory stage).
**4**   The possible solutions are developed further (projection stage).
**5**   The idea is tested and accepted or rejected (trial and decision stage).

While variations have of course been suggested by many scholars, this basic list is the essence of the process. The primary difference between problem solving in philosophy and problem solving in science is that in science we deal with tangible or observable data or subjects, while in philosophy our experiments and tests are all in the realms of thought and theory. The basic process concerns realizing and defining philosophical problems and then trying to find an acceptable solution through a rational process.

One type of thinking has been classified by a number of different names, such as *reverie, musing, contemplation,* and *meditation.* It is a

---

[18] Ibid., p. 210.

process of deep thought that may go beyond creative thinking. The thinkers review everything they know about a subject, and by scrutinizing or examining the subject carefully, they try to consider all possible combinations of ideas, both new and old. This type of thinking is a deeper form of reviewing our thoughts and philosophy, and it might be considered a self-study of what we really know and believe, or what really constitutes our beliefs and philosophy.

*Comprehensive thinking* is another type of thought that tries to comprehend or to fully understand something that may be known by ourselves, or by someone else, but that is not yet clearly understood. True comprehension of the ideas of other people can assist us in understanding not merely *what* people believe, but *why* they believe it. The more we can understand of the ideas of other people, the more we will be able to use their knowledge and expand our own knowledge.

*Trying to recall* is another type of thought. We still do not clearly understand the workings of the memory. The product of memory is often unreliable, though it is very necessary to thought. People have devised many ways of trying to improve the memory, for a good memory is a vital necessity to every type of thinking.

*Responsiveness* might be a term for another type of thought, a type that Davis and Miller found difficult to categorize clearly. This type of thinking is triggered by one's response to something else; for example, a sight, something heard, or almost any type of sensory experience to which there might be an appreciative reaction. This might be considered the aesthetic side of thinking, for it is concerned with the thought responses or processes that result from pleasing aesthetic experiences, such as seeing a beautiful movement or reacting to a beautiful phrase in someone's writing.

*Rationalizing* is the last type of thinking suggested by Davis and Miller. This type of thinking is used primarily to remove ourselves from embarrassing situations or to provide ourselves with excuses for actions that we do not really consider good actions. We may rationalize simply for the benefit of our egos, so we can still consider ourselves "honorable" or "important" or whatever might be the problem to which we reacted by rationalizing. The idea that "everyone else does it, so there is nothing wrong with me doing it, too" is a typical example of rationalizing.

## How Do We Apply Philosophy in Physical Education?

Philosophy is a vital part of the process of developing physical education programs, for it is a major influence on the early stages of program planning. The figure illustrates roughly the steps leading from what we already know (facts) through what we theorize and believe (our personal philosophy) through the various stages of development until we arrive at the actual policies and procedures that we will use in administering the physical education program.

We begin at the lowest level with *facts,* or the base of information that has been conclusively proved. If there is no base of proven fact at the roots of the physical education program, the program will simply be an experimental vehicle of questionable value. In a time of increasing demand for accountability, the chances of success for such a program are slight.

We next apply our personal *philosophy* to the facts we have at our disposal. In essence, we are taking what we *know* and adding to it what we *believe.* We use our philosophy to try to determine fundamental *principles* upon which we will base our program. Webster has defined the principle as "a fundamental truth or cause . . . which serves as a guide for conduct and procedure . . . a guide which is used in the attainment of an aim or objective." [19] Principles are viewed as fundamental laws, though they are closer to universally accepted hypotheses or theories, for principles *can* change.

When the principles that apply to the program are determined, the next step is determining the *needs* of the program—that is, for what purpose is the program being designed? Blending the needs of the program with the principles that are involved then produces the *goals* of the program.

The goals may include a number of closely related aims and objectives, which are simply more specific aspects of the overall goals of the program. The goals of the program may be expressed in terms of gaining or developing knowledge (cognitive goals); attitudes, appreciations, and a sense of values (affective goals); and skills (primarily psychomotor goals in physical education).

When the goals of the program have been determined, the *standards* that will be used in evaluating the goals must next be developed. The standards are evaluative criteria that set the *level* of the desired outcomes. For example, if a certain skill is to be developed, how thoroughly must it be developed to satisfy the goals of the program?

The program will be administered by the *policies and procedures* that result from the combination of desired goals and suggested standards for the program. The policies and procedures state how the actual program will be run in terms of administration, requirements, and application of the curriculum.

---

[19] Webster, p. 148.

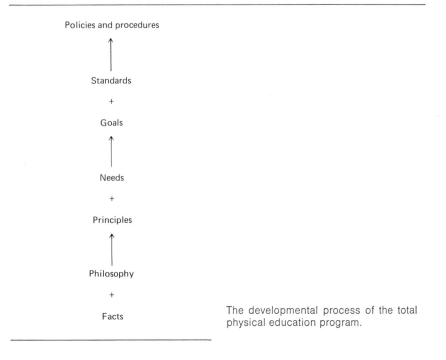

Policies and procedures

↑

Standards

+

Goals

↑

Needs

+

Principles

↑

Philosophy

+

Facts

The developmental process of the total physical education program.

At the heart of the entire resulting physical education program is the philosophy of the program, for philosophy enters the planning process in developing a program at the earliest stages and thus determines the areas that will be emphasized within a particular program. Because of the crucial part philosophy plays in planning the program, the personal philosophy of each person involved should be as clearly thought out as possible, for philosophy's ultimate effect on the program is considerable.

## A Summary and the Next Step

This chapter has attempted to explain the *why* of philosophy, rather than the *what*. Although we have discussed briefly what the study or process of philosophy is, we have also discussed its value to physical educators, or why we study philosophy. In an age increasingly concerned with science, we tend to forget the importance of things that cannot be tested against concrete facts.

As science has made rapid advances, many scientists have become concerned with how their discoveries will be applied and have thus moved from science into philosophy. Science developed theories that led to the first nuclear weapons, but many scientists then moved into the area of philosophy, because they were concerned not with whether such weapons were possible or practical, but with the *morality* of the weapons. Do human beings have a moral right to develop such weapons? To use them? Questions such as these are philosophical, for they cannot be answered with simple facts.

The rise of questions of this nature has shown us repeatedly that while we are moving toward the "two cultures" of C. P. Snow, both cultures are still tied to the realm of philosophy. Unanswerable or untestable questions exist in every discipline and field of learning, and if answers to such increasingly difficult questions are to be found, all fields of learning must be familiar with the nature and uses of philosophy. The concept of the ultimate value of all learning will come to us from our studies in philosophy, not solely from those in our separate fields.

Now that we have discussed what philosophy is, what its purposes are, and why we study it, we are prepared to move to the second of the three steps in studying philosophy: What are the current philosophies and concepts of physical education, and what effect do they have on the physical education program? We will discuss those questions in Chapter 7, for it is upon that base that we will build our future practices.

## Suggested Readings

Broudy, Harry S. *Building a Philosophy of Education.* Prentice-Hall, Englewood Cliffs, N.J., 1954.

Davis, Elwood Craig, and Donna Mae Miller. *The Philosophic Process in Physical Education,* 2d ed. Lea and Febiger, Philadelphia, 1967.

Durant, Will C. *The Story of Philosophy.* Pocketbooks, New York, 1954.

Fahey, Brian William. *Women and Sport: An Existential Analysis.* Microfiched Ph.D. dissertation, Ohio State University, 1973.

Ferm, Vergilius, ed. *History of Philosophical Systems.* Philosophical Library, New York, 1950.

Frost, S. E., Jr. *Historical and Philosophical Foundations of Western Education.* Charles E. Merrill, Columbus, Ohio, 1966.

"The Language of Movement." *Quest,* 23 (January 1975), entire issue.

Magill, Frank N. *Masterpieces of World Philosophies in Summary Form.* Salem Press, New York, 1961.

Runes, Dagobert D. *Dictionary of Philosophy.* Littlefield, Adams, and Company, Paterson, N.J., 1962.

Russell, Bertrand. *A History of Western Philosophy.* Simon and Schuster, New York, 1945.

Snow, C. P. *The Two Cultures: and A Second Look.* University Press, Cambridge, England, 1964.

Thomas, Carolyn Elise. *The Perfect Moment: An Aesthetic Perspective of the Sport Experience.* Microfiched Ph.D. dissertation, Ohio State University, 1972.

Zeigler, Earle F. *Philosophical Foundations for Physical, Health, and Recreation Education.* Prentice-Hall, Englewood Cliffs, N.J., 1964.

# 7

## Contemporary Philosophies of Education and Physical Education

The purpose of this chapter is to summarize the basic concepts of the major philosophies and to show how the concepts are interpreted and applied in education and physical education. We will then see what effect the different philosophies have on the physical education curriculum. We will discuss the major philosophies and approaches (naturalism, idealism, realism, pragmatism, and existentialism) as well as some newer philosophies or approaches coming into common use. We will conclude with the eclectic approach to philosophy and educational practices. By that point we should have a reasonably clear understanding of the nature and use of philosophy as well as its place in and effect on the physical education program.

### The Philosophy of Naturalism

***Basic Concepts of Naturalism.*** Naturalism is in many respects a simple philosophy, and its basic concepts are few:

1   Nature is the only real thing. Nature is the key to life, for everything we experience is a part of nature. Everything in life moves according to the laws of nature.
2   Nature is reliable and dependable. Because it does not change, anything that is of value will always work.
3   Each person is more important than society. Social goals are secondary to individual goals. We accept a social system because some system is needed to prevent chaos, not because the system is good.

***Naturalism Applied to Educational Practices.*** We can see the basic concepts of naturalism reflected in its application to the educational process; the emphasis remains on the processes of nature and the value of the individual:

1    Education is more than just mental. The educational process must include both the mental and the physical, neither of which is considered superior to the other. The education of each person must be a balanced concern.

2    Education is by natural means. The rate of the educational process is governed by the rate of each person's mental and physical development. The "natural process" of education governs when the person is ready to learn.

3    Education must satisfy each person's needs. Because each person is more important than society, education should be more in terms of the individual person's needs than those of society.

4    The students teach themselves. Education is an active process, not a passive one, and the student should thus be in primary control of the learning process, which is the normal procedure for learning from nature. The teacher is nature, rather than a person, and the student actively controls the educational experience.

5    The teacher guides the educational process. The teacher helps the students see how to learn, but does not necessarily teach in the traditional way.

6    Punishment and reward are a part of the learning process and should be in the form of a mild system of natural consequences. For example, if a student is late for class, the student misses something good.

**Naturalism Applied to Physical Education Practices.** The naturalistic program of physical education is simpler than the traditional one. It is a less formal system than physical educators are accustomed to:

1    Physical activities are more than just physical in nature. Physical activity is a major source of the overall development of the student (especially with young children, as suggested by Rousseau's *Emile*). Students can learn values, social patterns, and develop mental processes, as well as improve physical development.

2    Students learn through self-activity. This idea naturally fits physical education, for one cannot be a passive participant in a physical activity. This type of activity encourages self-expression and internal motivation.

3    Play is an important part of the educational process. This idea is a cardinal principle of the naturalistic process and was a major theory behind the founding of the first kindergarten.

4    There is little emphasis upon competition between individual people or between groups. Although competition is natural,

naturalism emphasizes the person alone rather than as part of society. Hence competition is more inward; people compete against themselves.

5    Physical education is concerned with the development of the whole person, not just the physical aspect of the person's development. The naturalist's concept of physical education is broader than the idealist's.

6    Teaching methods are often informal. The learning process, which is in keeping with the ways of nature, is reasonably democratic. Each student is supposed to learn and develop at his or her own rate.

7    The teacher must know the students' needs and processes of development. If nature is to be assisted in educating the student, the teacher must understand how nature works and what the processes and rates of change are for the student.

**Strengths and Weaknesses of Naturalism.** Zeigler suggests that naturalism has one strength and one weakness, and that they are the same: The philosophical practice is extremely simple.[1] This simplicity is an advantage, for most people find a simple education a relaxing change. On the other hand, it may be a disadvantage, because the approach of naturalism may be too shallow and simple to prepare the student to cope with an increasingly complex world. A simple education may be a handicap, rather than an asset, in an advanced, scientifically oriented civilization.

## The Philosophy of Idealism

**Basic Concepts of Idealism.** Bucher gives a good synopsis of the major points of the philosophies and how they are interpreted in practice in education and physical education,[2] and we will summarize and discuss some of his points not only on idealism but on the next three philosophies and approaches as well.

We can make four points in our synopsis of the beliefs of the idealists:

1    The focus of our being is the mind. All things that are real essentially come from the mind, which is more real than anything else. We interpret everything in terms of the mind.

---

[1] Earle F. Zeigler, *Philosophical Foundations for Physical, Health, and Recreation Education,* Prentice-Hall, Englewood Cliffs, N.J., 1964, pp. 65–66.

[2] Charles A. Bucher, *Foundations of Physical Education,* 7th ed., C. V. Mosby, St. Louis, 1975, pp. 29–41.

**2**   People are more important than Nature. The physical world is not as important to us as people are, because we interpret everything in it in terms of the mind.

**3**   Moral values are permanent and are not affected by people. This idea comes from the belief that ideas are true, so they never change. People have free will; they can choose between right and wrong.

**4**   Our rational (reasoning) powers help us to find the truth. The mind is the primary force that helps us learn about the world, though we may use scientific methods to help us in the discovery.

*Idealism Applied to Educational Practices.* We can summarize the basic educational ideas of the idealists with the following concepts:

**1**   The teacher creates a learning environment and is the student's primary inspiration. While the student is responsible for the actual motivation, the teacher is expected to do much to create this motivation in the less-interested student.

**2**   The process of education comes from within the student. Self-direction is essential; if the student relies on the teacher for motivation, the student may never learn very much. Although the teacher may help to give direction, much of the learning process should be initiated by the student.

**3**   Since idealism is concerned with the mind, developing both the rational powers and the mind is important. Most of the learning process passes through the mind, which must be developed to benefit from the traffic. Education should contain much objective content.

**4**   Education develops the individual personality and should thus be concerned with the development of moral and spiritual values. The educational process involves the whole personality, not just a small segment of it.

**5**   A variety of teaching methods can be used, though all should cause the student to want to actively pursue knowledge. Although the teacher can work to motivate the student, education is an active process for the student, rather than a passive one. A passive student will not become educated.

*Idealism Applied to Physical Education Practices.* Now that we have summarized the idealists' basic ideas for education, we need to determine what ideas the idealists have about the physical education program. Their major ideas are:

**1**   Physical education is both *of* and *through* the physical. It can assist in the more complete development of the individual, but it is less important than the more thought-oriented educational activities. It can make a major contribution to the development of the intellect.

2   Strength and fitness activities help to develop the personality, but play and recreation are also very important in developing the well-balanced personality.

3   The program is based on known principles, truths, and ideas. These known things are relatively fixed and unchanging, which can result in a formal program that can be planned ahead of time, for few necessary changes will appear. However, a true idealist would not use a program that was too rigidly fixed; the idealist prefers to use a variety of techniques.

4   The teacher is a model for the students. Part of the educational process is involved in teaching ideas and values. A teacher acts as an important example for the students in demonstrating the actual use of these values.

5   The teacher is responsible for the effectiveness of the program. Although much of the motivation for the learning process must come from the student, the teacher's role is important, for the program must be planned to grasp the interest of the student.

**The Strengths and Weaknesses of Idealism.**   Zeigler discusses a number of strengths and weaknesses of the philosophy of idealism, particularly as it is applied to education and physical education.[3]

1   The philosophy is well-developed and all-inclusive. It is attractive because it gives each person a strong place in the universe and thus helps develop a feeling of individual importance.

2   The philosophy of idealism gives a single concept of the student. The students are presented as unified individuals, but each one's potential for educational development varies.

3   The student can gain *broad* educational development in the physical education program, which is more than just physical education. It allows room for education both of and through the physical and helps in the mental, social, and moral development of the student.

4   The values and processes learned in physical education can be applied to other areas in life. Physical education develops broader abilities and processes than simply those closely tied to the physical.

5   Play and recreation are important. They contribute to the all-

[3] Zeigler, pp. 241–244.

around development of each person. The result is a broader concept of physical education.

Zeigler also suggests some weaknesses of idealism as a philosophy of education and physical education:

1    The idea of the soul is difficult to comprehend. It is a very complex problem to approach and one that is difficult to interpret and apply to the program.
2    Some people disagree with the idea of teaching values that have been established by past experience. The past experiences might have been inadequate to prove the values to be true.
3    The program is likely to give little attention to the body, for its primary concern is with the mind and its development.
4    There is less interest today in the idea of dedication and sacrifice for older ideals that may be called for in an idealist's program. Idealism is less in tune with the present day than some other philosophies.
5    Some teachers' actions often run counter to the very values of idealism despite their claiming to support and wanting to teach these values—as in the saying that "actions speak louder than words."
6    People's conflicting ideas of work and play make the application of physical education difficult to explain at times. Some people often have difficulty in accepting or getting others to accept that play can in many ways have values as great as those of work.

### The Philosophy of Realism

***Basic Concepts of Realism.*** Bucher discusses a number of concepts basic to realism.[4] He suggests that the major concepts of the realist are the following:

1    The physical world is real. This idea means that our world is one of nature and that we learn to understand it by the use of our senses and experiences.
2    The physical things that happen result from the laws of nature. Physical laws govern the actions of the universe, and everything conforms to those laws of nature.
3    We find the truth by using the scientific method. Experimental means will help us to discover and interpret truth, though we are not able to know everything.
4    There is a close, harmonious relationship between the mind and

---

[4] Bucher, pp. 31–33.

the body. They cannot be separated, and neither is superior to the other.

5 Religion and philosophy can coexist. Idealism permits religion, but naturalism does not, for naturalism puts nature over everything else. Realism permits the individual to go either way in determining individual beliefs.

**Realism Applied to Educational Practices.** When we apply realism to the process of education, we are using a system that is far more concerned with science than most philosophies. The basic concepts of realism as applied to education are the following:

1 Education develops the reasoning power. This goal is a major aim of the educational process, for the reasoning power is extremely important in the realist's scheme of things.
2 Education is for life. Because it is basic to life, the educational process should have useful purposes. This concept is common to most philosophies.
3 Education is objective. The realist wants to use scientific, objective standards for everything. There is no place for the subjective or interpretive approach in education for a realist.
4 The educational process is orderly. It follows scientific rules and procedures; it is not subjectively organized by each individual teacher.
5 The curriculum is scientifically oriented. The major emphases of the educational process are toward research and the scientific method, for that is how knowledge is discovered and proven.
6 Educational measurement techniques should be standardized. An attempt to set objective performance standards in education requires the development of scientifically objective techniques of measurement.

**Realism Applied to Physical Education Practices.** Physical education can play a good, specific role in the realist's program of education. The basic concepts of physical education as seen by the realist are:

1 Education is for life. Physical education is a valuable part of the educational curriculum, for it permits life to be lived more fully.
2 Physical fitness results in greater productivity. A healthier person will be more productive in society simply because the person is better prepared to lead a full life.
3 The program is based on scientific knowledge. It utilizes only proven principles, based on facts rather than on experimental theories.

**4**    Drills are an important part of learning.  The realist breaks units of work or learning down into scientific or organized progressions.

**5**    Sports programs can lead to desirable social behaviors.  The individual can learn good behavioral traits and learn to adjust to the pressures and requirements of the real world.  The realists emphasize this aspect of athletics rather than stressing winning as the primary goal.

**6**    Play and recreation assist in life adjustment.  These activities help make each person better able to function in society, because they bring each person more into contact with the real world.

***Strengths and Weaknesses of Realism.***  Zeigler suggests three strengths and four weaknesses of the philosophy of realism:[5]

**1**    It encourages us to accept the world as we find it.  We live in a world of cause and effect, and in many respects we can do nothing to change a given situation.

**2**    Realism suggests that cultural traditions are what we have discovered to be true, and the educational material we thus transmit has been proved true.

**3**    Realism gives physical education a unique function to fulfill: to develop an adequate physical basis for the body in order to permit the intellectual life to function.  One of these areas cannot succeed without the other, which makes the claim of physical education more clear-cut.

However, the weaknesses of the realistic philosophy must also be considered:

**1**    Zeigler speaks of its educational philosophy as "academic artificiality," or an overemphasis upon the cultural traditions of the society.  We master known facts at the expense of further developing our problem-solving abilities that permit us to cope with the future.

**2**    Realism interprets physical education in the very narrow sense of "education of the physical," whereas physical education offers many broad educational advantages when it is interpreted in its broadest sense, as we have tried to do in this book.

**3**    The authoritarianism found in the realist educational process is not consistent with the goals of education in democratic societies.  Less authoritarianism is necessary if the students are to learn to function in a democracy.

---

[5] Zeigler, pp. 162–164.

**4**    The realists put insufficient emphasis upon society and the social implications of the educational process.  They need to place more emphasis upon relating the learning process to societal needs and trends.

## The Philosophy of Pragmatism

***Basic Concepts of Pragmatism.***  Zeigler refers to pragmatism by its older, sometimes used name of "experimentalism," because it is based on experiences or experimenting to learn.[6]  The basic concepts of pragmatism are the following:

**1**    The basic reality is change.  The belief that change is the characteristic common to everything in life is reminiscent of the saying that "the only things that are certain are death and taxes."
**2**    Success is the only judge of the truth or value of a theory.  Truth and reality are the same thing.  If a theory is true, it can be proved.
**3**    Each person is a part of society.  Each person plays a role in society, and the actions of each person reflect that society.  People and society must be able to live together in harmony.

***Pragmatism Applied to Educational Practices.***  Pragmatism has played a major role in the development of U.S. education.  Some of the basic pragmatic concepts of education are:

**1**    Each person learns through experience.  This idea relates to Dewey's idea of "learning by doing," which we discussed earlier.  Only through experience do we gain knowledge.
**2**    Education is for social efficiency.  Pragmatism is very social-minded; its major orientation in education is toward society.  It teaches that the major role of education is to prepare people to take their place in society.  Social aims are very important in pragmatic education.
**3**    Education is child-centered rather than subject-centered.  The differences from one person to another are very important, for all people should be permitted to progress at their own speed.  Everyone should not be forced into the same mold.
**4**    Problem solving is necessary in a world of change.  The idea of the importance of problem solving as a part of the educational process has also come down to us from Dewey.  This type of learning is both purposeful and creative.
**5**    Evaluation is in terms of adjustment to the environment.  When the

---

[6] Ibid., p. 69.

Several philosophies, particularly pragmatism, stress the importance of learning
through actual experience and experimentation. (Courtesy Julie O'Neil, Stock,
Boston)

primary goals of education are to make each person a productive
member of society, this approach to evaluation might be considered a natural result.

**6**   Education is to develop the *total* person: mind, body, and soul.
Education is a very broad process rather than one with a narrow
focus.

***Pragmatism Applied to Physical Education Practices.*** The pragmatic
physical education teacher will recognize these as the primary concepts
of the pragmatic teacher:

**1**   When many kinds of activities are available, more meaningful experiences result. This concept is understandably true, since the
basic idea of the pragmatist is learning through experience.

**2**   Physical activities have a social value in that the student learns
how to act and react with other people. The activities thus help to
integrate each person into society.

**3**   The curriculum is determined by the needs and interests of the
student. Since the process is child-centered and the goal is the
development of the whole person, the necessity for this approach
to curriculum-planning can be seen.

**4**    The student should learn the problem-solving method. One goal of the problem-solving method of education is the development of creativity in each person.

**5**    The teacher is a motivator. Since the student is learning by doing, the teacher must play a motivational role most of the time, rather than actively leading or pushing the student.

**6**    Standardization is not a part of the program. The stress is upon the individual and individual differences, even though a major goal is to get the individual integrated into society.

***Strengths and Weaknesses of Pragmatism.***    Zeigler discusses the strengths of pragmatism by noting the following points:[7]

**1**    Pragmatism is a practical approach to life. It encourages each of us to meet daily life head-on and to experience it fully.

**2**    Pragmatism breaks down the distinction between life in school and life out in the real world, which helps make education more realistic and more applicable to life.

**3**    Pragmatism is good for developing political democracy, for it teaches people how to work together in society.

**4**    The pragmatist's educational program is based on pupil interest, which makes the task of the teacher easier. Teaching an interested student requires much less effort than teaching one who is not motivated.

**5**    Physical education can be an important part of the curriculum because of its broad educational applications and its social uses.

**6**    Pragmatism encourages the unity of the many areas comprising physical education, since it does seek the broad goals that can be gained more easily through a broadly based study.

On the other hand, Zeigler also cites a number of weaknesses of pragmatism, for while it may be one of the most widely followed philosophies of education, it may also be one of the most controversial:

**1**    Pragmatism does not provide the stability and direction that many students need. It has no fixed aims or values. Young people in school need stability and definite goals and values.

**2**    It is not yet an all-inclusive philosophy. While some argue that pragmatism has not completely developed, others claim that its time of value to the educational program has passed and it is no longer needed.

**3**    The experimental approach may spread us too thin in physical

---

[7] Ibid., pp. 109–110.

education. A program can have too many goals just as it can have too few. Only so many goals can be pursued at a given time.

4    Children need strong direction and a good basic education, regardless of whether they want it or not. How can immature children evaluate their educational experiences? The students need decision and direction provided from the leaders of the educational process. Pragmatism suffers from a lack of such unified direction and decision.

## The Philosophy of Existentialism

*Basic Concepts of Existentialism.* As we have shown earlier, the chief concern of the existentialist is the individual person. The basic concepts of existentialism are these:

1    Human existence is the only true reality. We interpret all of our experiences in terms of ourselves.
2    Each person must determine his or her own system of values. If students do not develop their own particular systems of values, the teacher is not emphasizing the individual person as existentialism does.
3    Each person is more important than society. Because of this belief, each person's search for a role as an individual member of society is a critical one. Existentialism is not concerned with whether the individual person fits into society.
4    The existentialist belief that nothing can be done to change things may seem to be a negative philosophy, for it teaches that there can be no real progress. For this reason some people may view the future as hopeless.

*Existentialism Applied to Educational Practices.* As Butler suggests, no one has tried to apply existentialism formally to either education or physical education.[8] We can suggest several ideas that form a basis for existentialist educational practices, however:

1    Education is a process of learning about oneself and one's own beliefs. People must develop their beliefs from themselves rather than from other people's ideas or beliefs.
2    Education is an individual process. The school is used only to provide a learning environment, for education is not group-oriented. Each person is the center of the educational process.

[8] J. Donald Butler, *Four Philosophies and Their Practice in Education and Religion*, 3d ed., Harper & Row, New York, 1968, p. 462.

**3**    The curriculum is centered on the individual student. The student selects the subject matter and learning methods, for each person should control his or her own learning process.

**4**    The teacher acts as a stimulator. The task of the teacher is to encourage the students to learn their own truths and to encourage creativity and individuality.

**5**    Education should teach responsibility. This is not responsibility in the usual sense of responsibility toward others or to society but rather in the sense of responsibility toward oneself. The students must be made aware that they have to bear full responsibility for the consequences of their decisions.

**6**    The educational process is heavily affective in its approach. Because it is more oriented to the affective domain (attitudes and appreciations), it does not lend itself well to measurement.[9]

***Existentialism Applied to Physical Education Practices.***  Again, existentialism has no real approach to physical education. We can suggest some basic ideas, though:

**1**    The program allows freedom of choice. The program is not a fixed, unchanging process. Because each person has the freedom to determine his or her own program, the program may take almost any form and cannot be planned far ahead of time by the teacher.

**2**    A variety of activities are used. Because existentialism emphasizes individuality, physical education has no single program of activities. The program is as diverse as the students who are involved in it.

**3**    Play results in the development of creativity. This idea recognizes the value of physical education–type activities in the educational process at all ages.

**4**    Students learn to know themselves. The students should learn to know what they need, to understand themselves, for education is a process of self-discovery.

**5**    The teacher is a counselor. Because the student in essence directs the educational process, the role of the teacher changes to that of a counselor who shows students the various available educational options. The students are made to feel more responsible for their education.

***Strengths and Weaknesses of Existentialism.***  We suggest that existentialism has only one real strength, if we can really consider this

---

[9] Van Cleve Morris, *Existentialism in Education: What It Means,* Harper & Row, New York, 1966.

aspect a strength: The emphasis on individuality makes each student very important in education. Each student has a status that is not found in any other philosophical approach; the existentialist educational process revolves totally around each student's needs and wishes.

This strength of existentialism is also its greatest weakness, because each student becomes more of a center of everything in school than is the case in real life. The student who is taught to create his or her own values and ideals may be very uncooperative in society, for he or she is prepared to work only outside society. The student is not concerned with learning to work with other people. Existentialism suggests that society is unnecessary to each person, which is an approach better suited to anarchy. This overriding flaw makes existentialism seem an unlikely choice for the sole basis of a successful program of mass education.

## New Variations of Educational Philosophy

A number of new philosophies of education have appeared over the last few decades. Although they are not always well-developed philosophies, and although they may apply primarily to education rather than physical education, we need at least a passing acquaintance with them. We will discuss four of these newer philosophies: perennialism, essentialism, progressivism, and reconstructionism. After discussing each of these approaches, we will consider briefly the growth of humanism in education and the eclectic approach to philosophy.

***The Philosophy of Perennialism.*** One explanation of the educational views of the perennialists is that "learning is accomplished through mental discipline, which will bring out the rational character of man." [10] Perennialism is a conservative philosophy; the perennialist believes the curriculum is more important than the interests of the students. The rigid, formal system emphasizes discipline, and character training is considered important as a part of the education. The program can be planned ahead of time, for few changes occur in the system, which is rooted in the past.

The teacher is thoroughly in control in a perennialistic program; the teacher acts as the ultimate authority in all cases. Physical education is considered unimportant as a part of the educational process,[11] and it usually is not mentioned in discussions of the curriculum of

---

[10] Karl W. Bookwalter and Harold J. VanderZwaag, *Foundations and Principles of Physical Education,* W. B. Saunders, Philadelphia, 1969, p. 35.
[11] Zeigler, pp. 146–147.

perennialism. This type of educational system can be included in the philosophy of essentialism also.

**The Philosophy of Essentialism.**  Essentialism is defined by Zeigler as "The educational belief . . . that there is a fundamental core of knowledge and ideals that should be transmitted to all students while maintaining high achievement standards; individual freedom is seen as a goal rather than a means." [12] This philosophy basically preserves society's cultural heritage by passing it on to the next generation. An essentialist may be an idealist, a realist, a rational humanist, or a Catholic realist.[13]

Essentialism is at heart a very conservative approach to education. Education is not considered "fun" or even necessarily "interesting"; it is simply necessary. The process requires well-disciplined procedures. No choice is allowed for the students, as the entire program is required. The teacher is firmly in control of the educational process, for the system is governed by authority from the top levels.

Zeigler contends that physical education can be an important part of the educational curriculum, though it is a more rigidly formal, drill-oriented version of physical education than we are accustomed to today.[14] Students have little choice of what activities they will have. Zeigler suggests that few physical educators believe in the essentialist philosophy.

**The Philosophy of Progressivism.**  Frost refers to progressivism as "a modern-day version of pragmatism integrated with some newer elements to make it more encompassing and relevant." [15] Progressivist education emphasizes the development of the "whole child"—that is, the student's mind, body, and soul. The progressivists are the opposites of the essentialists (see the figure). The essentialists are oriented toward the past, while the progressivists are oriented toward the future.

The progressivists use social emphasis to prepare the student to cope with society and the future. The emphasis is on total learning—that is, *all* experiences contribute to the student's education. They believe that change will and should come and that the schools should help to bring about social change.

The educational program is less structured, with more student

[12] Ibid., p. 319.
[13] Earle F. Zeigler and Harold J. VanderZwaag, *Physical Education: Progressivism or Essentialism?*, rev. ed., Stipes Publishing Company, Champaign, Ill., 1968, p. 67.
[14] Zeigler, pp. 71–76.
[15] Reuben B. Frost, *Physical Education: Foundations, Practices, Principles*, Addison-Wesley, Reading, Mass., 1975, p. 123.

The spectrum of educational philosophy.
(Adapted from Earle F. Zeigler, *Philosophical Foundations for Physical, Health, and Recreation Education,* Prentice-Hall, Englewood Cliffs, 1964, p. 252)

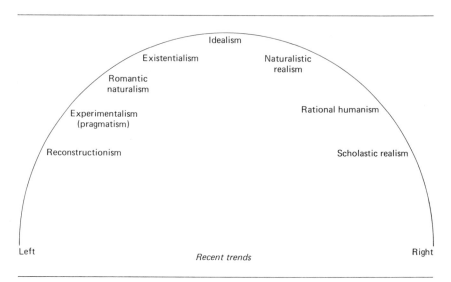

In reconstructionism physical education is important insofar as it can contribute to the goal of social self-realization. Because the physical education program seeks the *total* development of each person, its extracurricular activities may help the educational process as much as the regular curricular activities.

involvement in planning the program. There are fewer distinctions between school and nonschool activities. Frost suggests that the key words in progressivist education are "diversity" and "flexibility." [16] Progressivism calls for few specific requirements in the physical education program, but the progressivist program is broader in scope and offers many more electives to provide wide possibilities of experience.

**The Philosophy of Reconstructionism.** This philosophy might be considered a logical result of progressivist teachings, but its orientation is entirely toward the future. The educational idea of reconstructionism is to prepare the students to build a future society that is different from the present one. The major educational goal of reconstructionism is "social self-realization." [17]

In reconstructionism physical education is important insofar as it can contribute to the goal of social self-realization. Because the physical education program seeks the *total* development of each person, its extracurricular activities may help the educational process as much as the regular curricular activities.

[16] Ibid., p. 124.
[17] Zeigler and VanderZwaag, p. 62.

The process of education in reconstructionism is elective through group-process, and the emphasis is on group-centered activities, with heavy student involvement in the planning process. The educator and the students plan programs for a changing society and hope to speed the change.

**The Humanistic Approach to Education.** Zeigler defines humanism as "a position in which concern for man's welfare is central; stresses the importance of man in working out his own destiny." [18] Bucher gets closer to the heart of the current educational concept of humanism as he defines it as "a revolt against depersonalization and . . . the emergence of the belief that every human being is an individual and should be treated as an individual rather than as part of a larger group." [19] Frost speaks of the "humanization of education" that is needed.[20]

The humanistic approach attempts to counter the effects of the depersonalization that is a natural outgrowth of crowded societies by attempting to show concern for every person. It encourages the involvement of everyone in the educational process, not just some of the members of a class.

The humanistic approach in education is an attempt by educators to return to a basic concern for each person. It is not an attempt to make each person the center of everything in education; it simply attempts to assure that each person retains his or her personal identity in society. The approach tries to maximize students' potential contributions to society, while it tries at the same time to develop maximum student self-respect. Physical education can play a major role in the trend toward humanism, for its activities include very close primary contact between individuals and groups.

**The Eclectic Approach to Philosophy.** We have now studied the major philosophies and approaches to philosophy that affect our practices in and concepts of physical education. Each student must develop a personal philosophy of life, of education, and of physical education. The last approach for the student to consider in developing a personal philosophy is the eclectic approach to philosophy. Zeigler defines eclecticism as "the practice of combining a variety of theories from different philosophical schools into a body of fairly compatible beliefs." [21]

---

[18] Zeigler, p. 320.
[19] Bucher, pp. 41–42.
[20] Frost, p. 24.
[21] Zeigler, p. 319.

We might view the eclectic approach as a supermarket, "pick-and-choose" development of a personal philosophy; each student takes whatever he or she agrees with from the different philosophies and gradually constructs a personal philosophy that may bear no resemblance to any single philosophy of physical education. Although Zeigler suggests that the eclectic approach is an immature stage in the development of a philosophy,[22] it is very common among educators, for few of us are philosophers.

We have discussed the meaning and use of philosophies as well as their basic teachings regarding education and physical education. You can now study the philosophies and decide what your own personal philosophy of education and physical education will be as you lead the life of a physical educator. For those of you who want to understand how the different philosophies developed, we discuss the origins and evolution of the major philosophies in the next chapter.

## Suggested Readings

Brubacher, John S. *Modern Philosophies of Education,* 4th ed. McGraw-Hill, New York, 1968.

Butler, J. Donald. *Four Philosophies and Their Practice in Education and Religion,* 3d ed. Harper & Row, New York, 1969.

Clark, Gordon H. *Thales to Dewey, A History of Philosophy.* Houghton Mifflin, Boston, 1957.

Cobb, Robert A., and Paul M. Lepley, eds. *Contemporary Philosophies of Physical Education and Athletics.* Charles E. Merrill, Columbus, O., 1973.

Davis, Elwood Craig, ed. *Philosophies Fashion Physical Education.* Wm. C. Brown, Dubuque, Ia., 1963.

Fraleigh, Warren P. "Meanings of the Human Body in Modern Christian Theology." *Research Quarterly,* 39 (May 1968), 265–277.

Gerber, Ellen W. "Identity, Relation and Sport." *Quest,* 8 (May 1967), 90–97.

————, ed. *Sport and the Body: A Philosophical Symposium.* Lea and Febiger, Philadelphia, 1972.

Harper, Ralph. *Existentialism: A Theory of Man.* Doubleday, Garden City, N.Y., 1958.

Hellison, Donald R. *Humanistic Physical Education.* Prentice-Hall, Englewood Cliffs, N.J., 1973.

Hileman, Betty J. *Emerging Patterns of Thought in Physical Education*

---

[22] Ibid., p. 292.

*in the United States, 1956–1966.* Unpublished Ph.D. dissertation, University of Southern California, 1967.

Holbrook, Leona. "A Teleological Concept of the Physical Qualities of Man." *Quest,* 1 (December 1963), 13–17.

Jarrett, James L. *The Humanities and Humanistic Education.* Addison-Wesley, Reading, Mass., 1973.

Keenan, Francis Wilson. *A Delineation of Deweyan Progressivism for Physical Education.* Microfiched Ph.D. dissertation, University of Illinois, 1971.

Kneller, George. *Existentialism and Education.* Philosophical Library, New York, 1958.

Lockhart, Aileene S., and Howard S. Slusher, eds. *Contemporary Readings in Physical Education,* 3d ed. Wm. C. Brown, Dubuque, Ia., 1975.

McGlynn, George H., ed. *Issues in Physical Education and Sports.* National Press Books, Palo Alto, Calif., 1974.

Martin, Wm. Oliver. *Realism in Education.* Harper & Row, New York, 1969.

Morris, Van Cleve. *Existentialism in Education: What It Means.* Harper & Row, New York, 1966.

Neff, Frederick C. *Philosophy and American Education.* The Center for Applied Research, New York, 1966.

Osterhoudt, Robert Gerald. *A Descriptive Analysis of Research Concerning the Philosophy of Physical Education and Sport.* Microfiched Ph.D. dissertation, University of Illinois, 1971.

————. "A Taxonomy for Research Concerning the Philosophy of Physical Education and Sport." *Quest,* 20 (June 1973), 87–91.

Russell, Bertrand. *On Education.* George Allen and Unwin, London, 1926.

————. *Wisdom of the West.* Edited by Paul Foulkes. Fawcett World Library, New York, 1964.

Sakomizu, Sachiko. *An Analysis of the Philosophical Concepts in Recreation.* Unpublished M.S. thesis, University of California at Los Angeles, 1962.

Siedentop, Daryl. "The Humanistic Education Movement: Some Questions." In *Issues in Physical Education and Sports,* edited by George H. McGlynn, National Press Books, Palo Alto, Calif., 1974.

VanderZwaag, Harold J. *Delineation of an Essentialistic Philosophy of Physical Education.* Microcarded Ph.D. dissertation, University of Michigan, 1962.

Wahl, Jean. *A Short History of Existentialism.* Philosophical Library, New York, 1949.

Warren, William E. *An Application of Existentialism to Physical Education.* Unpublished Ed.D. dissertation, University of Georgia, 1970.

Webster, Randolph W. *Philosophy of Physical Education.* Wm. C. Brown, Dubuque, Ia., 1965.

Weinberg, Carl, ed. *Humanistic Foundations of Education.* Prentice-Hall, Englewood Cliffs, N.J., 1972.

Weinstein, Gerald, and Mario D. Fantini, eds. *Toward Humanistic Education.* Praeger Publishers, New York, 1970.

Williams, Jesse Feiring. "The Destiny of Man." *Quest,* 4 (April 1965), 17–21.

Zeigler, Earle F. *Philosophical Foundations for Physical, Health, and Recreation Education.* Prentice-Hall, Englewood Cliffs, N.J., 1964.

———. *Problems in the History and Philosophy of Physical Education and Sport.* Prentice-Hall, Englewood Cliffs, N.J., 1968.

———, and Harold J. VanderZwaag. *Physical Education: Progressivism or Essentialism?,* rev. ed. Stipes Publishing Company, Champaign, Ill., 1968.

# 8 The Historical Development of Western Philosophy

We trace the beginnings of our concept of philosophy back to the time of the ancient Greeks, over two thousand years ago. To have a better understanding of the major philosophies, we need to understand how they developed. If we learn the sources of our philosophies, we are more likely to understand the directions they are taking today.

Rather than try to summarize the entire history of philosophy in the Western world, we will make a survey of five of the most influential philosophies of the past and present: naturalism, idealism, realism, pragmatism, and existentialism. Although there are other important philosophies today, these have been the most influential ones in the development of most later philosophies. Rather than try to study the history of these five philosophies in one chronological mass, we will study each one separately; we will still proceed chronologically, but within each separate philosophy. We begin with the oldest of the major philosophies, naturalism.

## The Development of Naturalism

If we think of the schools or theories of philosophy as a tree, we would probably see naturalism as the roots of the tree; most other major philosophies have developed from naturalism, or they include some elements of naturalism in their basic ideas. The strain of naturalism flows throughout philosophy, for it is concerned in many ways with human ties to Nature.

We can trace the first crude roots of naturalism to the *Milesian* philosophers who lived in Miletus in western Turkey during the sixth century B.C. They were the first to try to seek ultimate realities purely in terms of Nature. Their leader, *Thales*, declared that water was necessary to all things in nature, because it was the one ingredient shared by all things. Although we trace the beginnings of formal philosophy to his successful prediction of an eclipse in 585 B.C., we must remember that in ancient times there was little difference between the fields of philosophy and science.

A fuller development of naturalism began with *Leucippus* and *Democritus,* two philosophers who lived in Thrace, a northeastern area of the Greek peninsula, in the fifth century B.C. Because they theorized that everything could be reduced to small parts, or atoms, that could be reduced no further, these two philosophers are sometimes referred to as "atomists." They did not believe in chance, but believed that Nature came from atoms by design and that people should try to live in harmony with nature. They taught that people should live a peaceful life, simple and close to nature, and should try to balance work and pleasure. When we think of "getting back to nature," we are expressing an idea that is thousands of years old.

We might say that ancient naturalism reached a peak with the teachings of *Epicurus* (342–270 B.C.). Namesake of the Epicurean philosophers, his ideas are commonly thought to represent the ultimate in sensuality, but in reality they are almost the opposite. Epicurus wanted to have the greatest possible pleasure throughout his life, but he defined pleasure in the negative sense: the absence of pain and fear. As a result he simply tried to avoid pain by living such a simple life that pain would not be possible, and rather than concern himself with the theories of reality, he sought a code of conduct. He taught that people should seek serenity by trying to find peace of both mind and body and that people could best accomplish this goal by having extremely simple needs or desires and by retreating from the affairs of the world.

Epicurus' ideas of philosophy did develop beyond the theories of Democritus. He was able to see that there could be some element of chance in the actions of Democritus' atoms, but he did not feel that this possibility of chance actually changed the ultimate determination of things to any real extent. Epicurus' ideas were promoted by *Lucretius* (96–55 B.C.). Lucretius made few changes in the ideas of Democritus or Epicurus; he is known primarily for promoting naturalism and the Epicurean ideas by praising them in his poetry. He was also the last solid link with the naturalistic philosophy until relatively modern times, when Hobbes appeared.

Although traces of naturalistic philosophy can be seen over the intervening years, the next important philosopher of naturalism was *Thomas Hobbes* (1588–1679) of England. He was not a pure naturalist, for he did not include religion or theology within the scope of his interpretation of philosophy. His definition of philosophy was not limited simply to the realm of Nature; it included real matter within Nature. For this reason he is sometimes referred to as the "first modern materialist." Although he did not place religion in the realm of philosophy, he wrote of God as the original cause of all things.

Hobbes saw Nature as bodies moving in space, and his suggestion of three kinds of reality—space, body, and motion—was very similar to the earlier teachings of Leucippus and Democritus. He also suggested that things are real in themselves, that people do not need to be aware of them for them to exist. Despite his writings in other areas, Hobbes is best known for his philosophy in the areas of politics and society, particularly for the "social contract."

Hobbes was concerned with the questions of each person's ultimate freedom and control over his or her own fate. He tried to mix a view of the liberty of the individual with the necessities of Nature. He suggested that a human being basically has free will, but because his or her actions occur within a context of cause and effect, each person's life was a mixture of liberty affected by necessity. He was pessimistic about the native human condition, for he considered it to be warfare against all other human beings.

Hobbes stated that humans have survived because of the "social contract" (which idea was later repeated by Rousseau in his book, *Social Contract*). If people want to save themselves from continuous war and find any peace, Hobbes believed, they need some political organization. Each person therefore delegates authority to one person or a group of people, who in turn makes laws governing the actions of all people, so each person can live in harmony. This concept of people being basically free and giving their authority to others to use for the benefit of all figured prominently in the philosophy that ultimately led to the concept of government in the early United States.

Hobbes was primarily a naturalist, for he saw human beings as a part of Nature and interpreted all things in the context of Nature. He believed that humans gain knowledge through their senses and that they live with free will in a universe governed by the cause-and-effect process found in Nature. He led the way to the theories of one of the best known philosophers of naturalism, Rousseau.

Although we class *Jean Jacques Rousseau* (1712–1778), the French writer and philosopher, as a naturalist, we must stretch a point to do so, for he did not consider himself to fall in that category. Since we have already described the ideas expressed in two of his major works, *Social Contract* and *Emile,* in Chapter 3, we will simply summarize his major philosophical ideas here.

Rousseau believed life had been spoiled by civilization. He agreed with the popular belief of his time that concerned the "noble savage," or the idea that in primitive societies people lived beautiful and free lives, shared their property, and found peace of mind. He liked

Today's "noble savage" is still trying to escape the ills of modern society by returning to nature. More and more people are taking up backpacking and other wilderness activities, and many are even leaving the cities and suburbs to start new lives in rural areas. (Courtesy George Bellerose, Stock, Boston)

Hobbes's idea of government as a society joined freely by the people, who kept their own political powers.

He expressed a strong preference for the peaceful, simple life, and like other philosophers we have cited, he thought this type of life could be found by living close to Nature. He believed that people are good, so long as they are close to Nature; when they join human society, they become ruined by civilization, which is evil and corrupt. He shared the desire of the earlier naturalists to remain apart from the ambitions and conflicts of society and to stay close to Nature. He wanted children to be educated as naturally as possible—that is, by being led rather than pushed into learning.

He also revolted against the ways of society because he considered society artificial and evil. He glorified Nature as an ever-dependable "order" that was more stable and preferable than the so-called civilized human society. An unfortunate aspect of his philosophy was that its followers had to be reasonably wealthy to be able to get back to Nature.

The most recent major philosopher of naturalism was *Herbert Spencer* (1820–1903) of England. He was an engineer who became a writer and philosopher after being influenced by reading Charles Darwin's *Origin of the Species* (1859). He was very struck by the theory of evolution, though he misinterpreted it into what we now refer to as "social Darwinism." He thought that because the strongest *individuals* (rather than species) were most fit to meet the challenge of survival, the strong ones could justify using force to overcome the others. (This idea reappeared with vigor under Hitler, who was not a naturalist.)

Spencer referred to his philosophy as the "Synthetic Philosophy." He considered everything to be a process of evolution and dissolution, or continually forming, then gradually weakening, and finally breaking up. Nature was always changing because of these forces of evolution and dissolution. He did not believe that the ultimate reality could be known by human beings. He believed that people could not comprehend God and defined the power of God as a force or energy. Because he viewed energy as the ultimate being, he is sometimes referred to as an "energist." Although Spencer was a major force in nineteenth-century philosophy, his influence has faded considerably today.

While naturalism is not as prominent in the twentieth century as it was in the past, its influence has not disappeared. We see the effects of naturalism in our other philosophies, particularly realism and pragmatism, which we discussed in Chapter 7.

## The Development of Idealism

Idealism as a philosophy is almost as old as naturalism, for we trace its origins to ancient Greece. Idealism teaches that ultimate reality is found in ideas or the mind; idealism interprets everything in terms of the mind. Because the term "ideal-ism" makes us think of "ideals," we are often confused about the theories of idealism. We can clarify our thoughts, however, if we think of "idea-ism," for ideas lie at the heart of idealism. Rather than interpret everything in terms of Nature, the idealist interprets everything in mental terms, as ideas.

Although we think of *Socrates* as the first prominent idealist, most historians of philosophy begin with *Plato* (c. 427–347 B.C.), for everything we know about Socrates we have received from Plato's writings. Plato wrote in the form of dialogues or conversations between two or more people; we might say his style of writing was similar to the process of thinking by carrying on a conversation with yourself.

In idealism the mind and reason stand out above everything else. Each person has his or her own ideas. When people share their ideas with a group of people, they can then discuss all of the ideas and thus make the discussion a form of experimentation that can result in learning. The idealist teaches that people see everything in terms of ideas, so reality is a mental concept. Plato believed that ideas endure. A person's focus should be a life of reason, for everything comes from reason.

Physical educators have considered Plato to be the first prominent scholar-philosopher to express the importance of physical education in people's lives, but in recent years there have been arguments about whether the claims of Plato's support for physical education are justified. Kleinman summarized the arguments against using Plato as a proponent or supporter of physical education.[1]

The original idea was that Plato taught that the body and mind should be developed equally, which is in line with the current concept of training the "whole person." Scholars have pointed out, however, that Plato was really a dualist—that is, he considered the mind and body two separate things. While he was concerned with the body's effect upon the mind, he apparently still considered the mind more important than the body. However, as Kleinman points out, Plato did *not* make the body unimportant.

Plato did stress the importance of physical activity throughout the lifetime; he felt that the overdevelopment of either body or mind, without similar attention to the development of the other, was not beneficial to a person. The key to Plato's philosophy is a *balanced* development of the mind and the body. He did consider the mind more important than the body, which was not a radical idea for a man who saw ideas and the mind as the ultimate reality, but he realized and taught that the mind would function better if the body was also highly developed.

According to such evidence, we do not need to abandon Plato as a champion of physical education because he considered the mind superior to the body, for he did not neglect the importance of the body. As physical educators, we do need to avoid placing the body and its development over the mind, which then would make us dualists—with a very unsupportable position. Like Plato, we want to teach the balanced, harmonious development of both mind and body.

Although we could discuss how idealism evolved, we will pass through time to the modern philosophers and to the next important idealist, *Rene Descartes* (1596–1650) of France. He had two major ideas that contributed to his importance as a philosopher. First, he considered the self the most immediate reality in the experience of each person. His belief in the reality of the self was expressed by the statement, "I think; therefore I am." (To which some people replied, "I am; therefore I think.") Like the saying at the Delphic oracle, "Know thyself," Descartes believed that the path to knowledge began with the self and self-knowledge.

His second idea was his argument for the existence of God. He stated that people are imperfect and therefore cannot form the idea of a perfect being: Since people cannot form such an idea, God, as a perfect being, must have caused them to have the idea; therefore God

---

[1] Seymour Kleinman, "Will the Real Plato Please Stand Up?" *Quest,* 14 (June 1970), 73–75.

exists. Descartes also had ideas that tie him to the realists, as did two of his followers we mention below.

Feibleman marks the philosophy of Descartes as the time of the split between science and philosophy,[2] for Descartes suggested that people should investigate mind or matter. The philosophers took the area of the mind, and the scientists took the area of matter, which gradually led them far apart. Descartes was the first philosopher to draw this important distinction between mind and matter.

*Baruch Spinoza* (1632–1677), a Spanish Jew who lived in Holland, was a follower of Descartes. His philosophy, like Descartes's, is also tied to the realists as well as the idealists. We think of Spinoza particularly in the area of ethics, for his ideas were basically God-centered. He suggested that a single, eternal substance underlies the universe and that this substance is God. He stressed God as a thinking being, and although each person is only a small part of the universe, he or she is a part of God. Spinoza saw the mind and body as having only one reality, which is God: If God is the significant fact in the universe, then moral and religious values are important to our existence.

*Gottfried Wilhelm von Liebniz* (1646–1716) was a German philosopher who, like Spinoza, was a successor to the ideas of Descartes. In trying to solve the dilemma of the relationship of mind and matter, he formed a theory that recalled the atoms of Democritus; he said that everything, both mind and matter, was formed of small units, which he called monads. Liebniz' thinking was somewhat in the realm of the idealists, for he believed that these monads were not physical units, but were points of mental force. He suggested that since both mind and matter are formed of monads, all things, whether they are different or the same, have a pre-existing harmony.

He gave an example of two clocks: Although the clocks are not connected in any way; they are set and wound to run on the same schedule. Neither clock has any effect upon the actions of the other, yet they are running in a pre-established harmony. The action of the clocks is an example of the mind-body relationship, because both parts work in coordination (like the two clocks keeping the same time), but neither is dependent on the other and neither affected by the other.

Liebniz taught that the monads had been combined in only one of many possible ways to form the world, but many other arrangements were possible. He suggested that the world as we know it was the best of all possible worlds, however, for it had the least amount of evil necessary to produce the greatest amount of good. This theory was

---

[2] James K. Feibleman, *Understanding Philosophy, A History of Ideas*, Dell, New York, 1973, p. 104.

severely ridiculed by Voltaire in his parody *Candide,* which is probably better known than the philosophy or philosopher on whose ideas it was based.

*George Berkeley* (1685–1753) was an English bishop and philosopher. He felt that the true reality was the mind or spirit; things were perceived by the senses. He was sometimes called an "empiricist," because he based his thinking on what he learned empirically, or through experience. His philosophy was developed in reaction to the increasing emphasis given by scientists in his time to the importance of matter and the material rather than the mind. He suggested that matter was seen by the mind, rather than experienced.

Berkeley taught that nothing exists if there is no mind to perceive it, and his philosophy was based on the existence of God, for if God did not exist, things that were not seen by people would not exist. He taught that God created each thing, and because God's mind perceives each thing, it exists: What we perceive is what God's mind has created.

Another prominent idealist was the German philosopher *Immanuel Kant* (1724–1804), who combined aspects of idealism and realism in his philosophy. His first major book was the *Critique of Pure Reason.* He viewed conscious reason as the unifying center for all human experience. His basic idea was that each person has a unified point of view and observes the world from the viewpoint of his or her own personal beliefs. Kant had several important beliefs in the area of ethics. He believed in universal moral laws: No person has the moral right to do anything that cannot justifiably be done by anyone else. He taught that people feel obligated to obey these moral laws, and this sense of duty, in his view, was based on human reason rather than human experiences. He further believed that all people are free.

In Kant's ethical rationale the soul was believed immortal: People cannot follow moral law perfectly; therefore, to reach perfection of the soul, which requires more than any person's lifetime, the soul must be immortal. Kant finally taught that God exists; he saw God as a supreme intelligence. Kant believed that people feel some moral imperative or duty within themselves, which had to come from somewhere, and he theorized that God was the source of this sense of duty to moral laws.

The last of the major idealists we will discuss is *Georg Wilhelm Friedrich Hegel* (1770–1831), another German philosopher. He taught that value and meaning are found by relating the parts and wholes of things. As an example, if we wish to see meaning in our life, we must relate our life to the totality of all things, the Absolute Idea. Parts of anything must always be seen in their connection to the whole, if the meaning and place of each thing in the scheme of life is to be understood.

Reality, which Hegel saw as a process similar to a debate or dialectic, moved with its own logic through three stages: the first is the thesis, or a beginning idea; the second stage is the antithesis, or an argument or idea that is the opposite; and the final stage is the synthesis, or a compromise solution in which the thesis and antithesis are resolved. This process is ongoing, for the synthesis then becomes a new thesis. Hegel was considered an idealist because he defined reality and being in terms of reason, which comes from the mind.

We have now reviewed the major parts of the historical development of idealism, and we have discussed the current concepts of idealism and how they are interpreted and applied in education and physical education in Chapter 7.

## The Development of Realism

Realism, the third of the major philosophies, is in contrast to idealism because it teaches that people live in a *real* world. The things we experience are real and do not depend on our minds or our perceptions to exist. As we study the development of the realist philosophy, we will see that the path to tracing its evolution is rocky, for there is scarcely a succession of realist philosophers, as such. Most of the realist philosophy has come from the last century.

We trace elements of the philosophy of realism to *Aristotle* (384–322 B.C.), who was Plato's contemporary in ancient Greece. Aristotle was not necessarily a realist as we think of realists today, but his philosophy did have realist elements to it. We might think of him as a practical version of Plato and the idealists; while Plato was interested in ideas, Aristotle was interested in specific things, or in reality.

Rather than argue about the reality of Nature, Aristotle stated that its existence is evident and need not be proven. Instead, he considered Nature the starting point of philosophy and attempted to describe and interpret as many areas of Nature as he could. He tried to analyze what was behind Nature, because he was always interested in the causes of things. Aristotle saw God as the prime mover or first cause of all things, and this idea—that God is responsible for all of existence—appears repeatedly with the earlier realists.

*Thomas Aquinas* (c. 1225–1274) was an Italian churchman who is often considered a major religious philosopher. As is true with a number of the philosophers we discuss, Aquinas was not necessarily a realist, but he did share some of the ideas of the realists. He followed Aristotle in his idea of God as the prime mover. He taught that God created matter, and he believed in the reality of that matter. He theorized that the world was made by God and that the world is a combination of matter and universals, or we might say of matter and ideas.

Several of the idealist philosophers we discussed earlier are also known for ideas that fit into the realist scheme of things. They are Descartes, Spinoza, and Kant. Descartes showed realist tendencies when he said that the world is real because it has been created by God, who is perfect and would not deceive people. He taught that the basis of the world is substance, of which there are two kinds: mind (or ideas) and matter (or the body). While each substance is independent of the other, he believed, both depend on an absolute substance, God. Matter is physical, and it operates according to mechanical laws.

Spinoza taught that there is a substance that exists eternally and infinitely: an ever-present, unchanging reality. Like Descartes, he gives the substance two characteristics or parts: mind and matter. Kant taught that we learn by experience, which we obtain from the sensations our minds receive from the external or real world, and although our mind converts these sensations to ideas, they represent a real world.

*John Locke* (1632–1704) was an English philosopher whose ideas on education were discussed in Chapter 3. His basic philosophical idea, which placed him with the realists, was that the mind is a blank tablet at birth: Nothing is in the mind at birth—neither present ideas nor ideas that can be discovered by reasoning power after the person matures.

Locke believed that the world makes impressions on the blank tablet of the mind, which is not active; the mind passively receives the impressions given by the real world; and everything that enters the mind must come from experience (through sensation and reason). Because Locke believed the mind was acted upon by a real, material world, his philosophy was another step in the development of realism.

*Johann Friedrich Herbart* (1776–1841) was a German philosopher, though he is better known as an educator who also attempted to estab-lish psychology as a science. His contribution to philosophy was to distinguish the soul from the mind by defining the mind in terms of its content: The mind is not an active agent that causes changes; instead, it is the total of all of the impressions that have been made on the soul. In Herbart's view, neither matter nor the soul can be known or defined, but both do exist; the mind is gradually built up by the soul's contacts with the physical or real world.

The last major realist philosopher we will discuss is *William James* (1842–1910), an American philosopher who is more commonly con-nected with pragmatism than with realism. However, he had a direct connection to the birth of both realistic and pragmatic thought in the United States. In realist philosophy, he defined consciousness as a function, rather than as a substance; he saw consciousness as an awareness of experience. This theory ran counter to the idea that both matter and spirit or consciousness have substance.

James said that consciousness has no reality of its own. He

suggested that experience is not limited merely to each person's own personal experiences; it includes all of human experience, and the world of human experience is a real world. James found no single common substance, but instead multitudes of substances. His theories had a great impact on both philosophy and psychology.

As the world entered the twentieth century, other American realists were reacting to James's philosophical ideas and trying to tie realism more closely to the sciences. Realism is still one of the more popular philosophies at the present time.

## The Development of Pragmatism

Although we will discuss several early philosophers who expressed ideas that we consider pragmatic, pragmatism is basically a modern American philosophy, for most of its development took place in the United States within the last century. The term *pragmatism* comes from a Greek word that means "practice." The essential claim of pragmatism is expressed in the phrase "what is true works": ideas are tested and proven through actual experience.

*Heraclitus* (c. 540–470 B.C.) was a philosopher from Ephesus, in ancient Greece. We have only a few fragments of his philosophy, but he does show clear elements of pragmatic ideas. He placed great stress on the fact of change in the world, which is an idea common to modern pragmatism. Although he saw many opposites in nature and life, he did not consider them to be separate or different things; he viewed them as appearances that gradually change and become their opposites. Change is the key to everything in his philosophy: Reality is not a substance; instead, reality is constant change.

The ideas of Heraclitus were expanded by wandering teachers called *Sophists,* who flourished in fifth century B.C. in Greece. Because they agreed with Heraclitus that everything changes, they defined knowledge as sense perception: Nature produces a stimulus, a person responds to that stimulus, and the result is sense perception. If separated, none of the three elements in this definition is reality; instead each is a part or stage of the constant change they saw. The sense perception comes close to genuine knowledge, as expressed in Protagoras' saying that "man is the measure of all things." This idea means that each thing a person perceives is at least true for that person, for each person measures knowledge against his or her own sense perception.

The next major philosophical influence upon pragmatic thought came from *Francis Bacon* (1561–1626), an English philosopher and statesman. Several of his writings were important in their expression of ideas accepted by the pragmatists. His first book, *Novum Organum,*

The ancient Greeks tried not only to appreciate beauty but also to define it in their philosophies. Myron's famous "Discobolus" (discus thrower) is a classic example of the physical beauty the Greeks often portrayed in sculpture and other art forms. (Courtesy The Bettmann Archive)

was an attempt to change the basis for human knowledge. In it he charged that most of human knowledge was simply the acceptance of earlier ideas, many of which had almost no relation to reality. Rather than use the ancient Greek philosophers' deductive reasoning, he suggested the use of inductive reasoning to gain knowledge, for it was the process of observing things to gain knowledge, as in the scientific method. He called for the use of the scientific method—that is, using research and investigation to gain new knowledge.

Because Bacon taught that people created ideas from their own minds rather than from the real world, most of his ideas have no basis of reality. He also wrote *New Atlantis,* which dealt with the use of science as a means of pursuing social goals or improving the state of society. He believed that science could make great changes in the development of society and he called for all scientists to work together to help society solve its problems.

*Auguste Comte* (1798–1857) was a French philosopher who suggested that there were three stages of growth to history. These stages might also be viewed as three levels of intellectual insight in the development of human thinking. The earliest level was religious, for people thought first in theological or religious terms. This stage was helpful to society in bringing about order and civilization. The effect of the second, or philosophical, stage was difficult to show clearly. It was primarily a transitional stage leading to the third, and highest, stage, the scientific stage, which could replace the other two stages.

Comte saw order among the sciences and did much to suggest how the sciences as a whole could be ordered and structured. He believed that science could answer all questions; that science could be used to form a new society; and that society could be studied by a new branch of science, which he referred to as the "social sciences." Comte had a positive social interest, for like Bacon he believed that science could be used to benefit society. He taught that ideas arise from a social context, and if they are important, then they will have social significance.

As we have pointed out, while these early ideas—from Heraclitus' stress of change, to Bacon's evolution and promotion of inductive reasoning, to Comte's suggested social significance—laid the foundation for pragmatism, pragmatism was highly developed and defined by American philosophers. The originator of the single idea that we consider the basis of modern pragmatism was *Charles Sanders Peirce* (1839–1914). His basic idea was somewhat misinterpreted by *William James* (1842–1910), who made pragmatism widely known and very popular. Pragmatic thought was carried to its most widely known level by *John Dewey* (1859–1952), who had an immense impact upon twentieth-century education in the United States.

Peirce was actually a realist, but at one point in his early philosophical development he coined the term *pragmatism*. Like the realists, he wanted to be very objective about everything. He tried to define reality and knowledge by following Kant's philosophy, but he had a difficult time. His idea, which James adopted, was phrased by Butler in this way: "In order to determine the meaning of an idea, it must be put into practice; the consequences which follow constitute the meaning of the idea." [3] In short, if you have an idea and want to know whether it is true, the only way to know is to try it. Feibleman phrased this concept more succinctly as "what is true will work." [4]

William James made Peirce's idea known, and he did so with a passion. However, he misinterpreted Peirce's idea and changed the meaning to "what works is true," [5] which is not quite the same thing as the earlier statement, for anything at all might work on some occasion. James did not suggest how long something had to work before it could safely be considered true. Since we have already included James's philosophy in our discussion of the realists, we will only consider here the way his views helped to popularize pragmatism.

James's practical view of life was popular in turn-of-the-century America. People accepted the new philosophy as the national philoso-

---

[3] J. Donald Butler, *Four Philosophies and Their Practice in Education and Religion,* 3d ed., Harper & Row, New York, 1968, p. 375.

[4] Feibleman, p. 180.

[5] Ibid., p. 181.

phy, for it was closest to what they were already doing—that is, if it works, go ahead and do it, and don't worry about the results. The greatest problem with James's pragmatism was that it might be called "short-run" pragmatism: It was concerned with today's needs, rather than with long-term needs or problems. It showed practical truths that would be used immediately, so long as they appeared to work. James set the stage beautifully for the appearance of John Dewey, who really used pragmatism to make an impact on educational practices.

Dewey was one of the greatest American philosophers and educators. He was undoubtedly the greatest single individual influence upon twentieth-century education in the United States. Although he began as an idealist, Dewey moved toward empiricism, which is sometimes called "experimentalism." Like Heraclitus, he believed that things are always changing: We cannot gain knowledge of the ultimate reality, and the closest things we have to absolute truth or knowledge are those hypotheses that have been tested and proven true by experience.

According to Dewey, people have to take their ideas and test them, if they are to determine their true meaning. He wanted science to study social problems and try to find solutions for them, just as Bacon had suggested. In his advanced concept of social education, the educational process was used to bring about social changes. His leading work, *Democracy and Education* (1916), stressed the idea of learning through experience, which is often referred to as "learn by doing" and which is among his educational ideas that we have already discussed in Chapter 4.

Pragmatism is often considered the "American philosophy," for it seems to fit the practices of U.S. citizens so well. While it has had a vast influence upon twentieth-century American education, largely because of the work and influence of Dewey, it is not the only currently popular major philosophy. We need to consider the development of one other major viewpoint that has appeared entirely within the last century: existentialism.

## The Development of Existentialism

We need to remember that, as Davis points out, existentialism is an *approach* of philosophy, rather than a separate school of philosophy itself.[6] The basis of this approach was first suggested by *Sören Kierkegaard* (1813–1855), a Danish philosopher. His idea that the only true

---

[6] Elwood Craig Davis, ed., *Philosophies Fashion Physical Education,* Wm. C. Brown, Dubuque, Ia., 1963, p. 109.

existence is individual existence led to the term *existentialism*. The approach stresses individuality and the individual person above all else, but Feibleman notes that some critics refer to existentialism as a "crybaby philosophy,"[7] for it seems to hinge on a person's discomfort and agonized reaction to the discomfort.

Some of the ideas of existentialism have been expressed by the German poet and philosopher *Friedrich Nietzsche* (1844–1900), though some scholars have argued over whether he should be considered an existentialist. He stressed individuality by teaching that instead of giving in to their environment, people should struggle to overcome it and influence and control their own destiny. His teachings were a call for the individual to stand and face life, rather than meet it passively.

*Martin Heidegger* (1889–1976) was a German philosopher who combined aspects of the philosophies of Kierkegaard with those of Edmund Husserl to form an existential philosophy. Heidegger studied the problem of existence by starting with the individual and his or her personal experiences and consciousness. He tried to analyze the nature and content of an individual's experiences. Heidegger taught that people learn about the nature of all existence by coming to understand their own existence and that the center of knowledge and understanding is the individual rather than some outside universal.

The best known proponent of existentialism is the French playwright and novelist *Jean-Paul Sartre* (b. 1905). The negative side of existentialism was suggested by one of his books, *Being and Nothingness.* However, his writings have made existentialism famous in the mid-twentieth century. He interprets reality wholly in terms of the individual. Each person is ultimately responsible for himself or herself alone and thus also responsible *to* himself or herself alone; the individual is essentially separated from society and has no genuine ties or duty to it. Sartre teaches that each person stands alone and controls his or her own destiny. What you make of your life, in other words, ultimately depends solely on you.

The biggest difficulty with existentialism as a philosophical stance is its extreme subjectivity. As we have noticed, the history of philosophy is an attempt to gain knowledge of ultimate things. As time has progressed, philosophers have attempted to make philosophy more objective. While philosophy cannot be considered a science, it has increasingly attempted to use many aspects of the scientific method to gain more reliable or objective information. Existentialism goes counter to this development: The philosophical process or viewpoint is very personal; each person interprets existentialism differently; and none of the

---

[7] Feibleman, p. 203.

viewpoints can be easily proved.  Davis and Miller point out this impre-
cision in existentialism by noting that "existentialism lends itself better
to literary than to philosophic treatment."[8]  Because of its subjectivity,
existentialism is very difficult to develop or explain precisely.

## The Next Step

So far we have discussed the meaning and use of philosophy, the major
schools of philosophy, and the historical development of philosophical
thought.  At this point you might try to set your philosophy down on
paper, so that you can see whether it is clear.  We have discussed the
essential elements needed for developing and interpreting a philosophy,
and it is up to you to clarify your own philosophy of education and
physical education.

## Suggested Readings

Blau, Joseph L.  *Men and Movements in American Philosophy.*  Pren-
    tice-Hall, Englewood Cliffs, N.J., 1952.
Butler, J. Donald.  *Four Philosophies and Their Practice in Education
    and Religion,* 3d ed.  Harper & Row, New York, 1968.
Clark, Gordon H.  *Thales to Dewey, A History of Philosophy.*  Houghton
    Mifflin, Boston, 1957.
Durant, Will.  *The Story of Philosophy.*  Pocketbooks, New York, 1954.
Edmondson, Cornelia.  *A Continuum of Thought on the Value of Health,
    Physical Education, and Recreation from the Time of John Locke
    Through the Early Twentieth Century.*  Microcarded Ph.D. disserta-
    tion, University of Washington, 1966.
Ferm, Vergilius, ed.  *History of Philosophical Systems.*  Philosophical
    Library, New York, 1950.
Gerber, Ellen W.  *Innovators and Institutions in Physical Education.*  Lea
    and Febiger, Philadelphia, 1971.
Gilson, Etienne.  *Reason and Revelation in the Middle Ages.*  Charles
    Scribner's Sons, New York, 1938.
Huelster, Laura J.  "The Body of Knowledge in Physical Education—
    Philosophical."  *The Physical Educator,* 22 (March 1965), 6–8.
Lamprecht, Sterling P.  *Our Philosophical Traditions.*  Appleton-Century-
    Crofts, New York, 1955.
Magill, Frank N.  *Masterpieces of World Philosophies in Summary Form.*
    Salem Press, New York, 1961.

---

[8] Elwood Craig Davis and Donna Mae Miller, *The Philosophic Process in Physical
Education,* 2d ed., Lea and Febiger, Philadelphia, 1967, p. 149.

Medlin, William K. *The History of Educational Ideas in the West.* Center for Applied Research in Education, New York, 1964.

Neff, Frederick C. *Philosophy and American Education.* Center for Applied Research, New York, 1966.

Perelman, Ch. *An Historical Introduction to Philosophical Thinking.* Trans. by Kenneth A. Brown. Random House, New York, 1965.

Runes, Dagobert D. *Dictionary of Philosophy.* Littlefield, Adams and Company, Paterson, N.J., 1962.

Rusk, Robert R. *Doctrines of the Great Educators,* 3d ed., rev. St. Martin's Press, New York, 1967.

Russell, Bertrand. *A History of Western Philosophy.* Simon and Schuster, New York, 1945.

————. *Wisdom of the West.* Edited by Paul Foulkes. Fawcett World Library, New York, 1964.

Shvartz, Esar. "Nietzsche—Philosopher of Fitness." *Quest,* 8 (May 1967), 83–89.

Stumpf, Samuel Enoch. *Socrates to Sartre, A History of Philosophy.* McGraw-Hill, New York, 1966.

Ulich, Robert. *History of Educational Thought,* rev. ed. American Book Company, New York, 1968.

Ward, Keith. *Fifty Key Words in Philosophy.* John Knox Press, Richmond, Virginia, 1968.

Woodward, William Harrison. *Vittorino da Feltre and Other Humanist Educators.* Teachers College, Columbia University, New York, 1963 (1897 ed.).

Zeigler, Earle F. *Philosophical Foundations for Physical, Health, and Recreation Education.* Prentice-Hall, Englewood Cliffs, N.J., 1964.

# IV The Rise of Sports in America

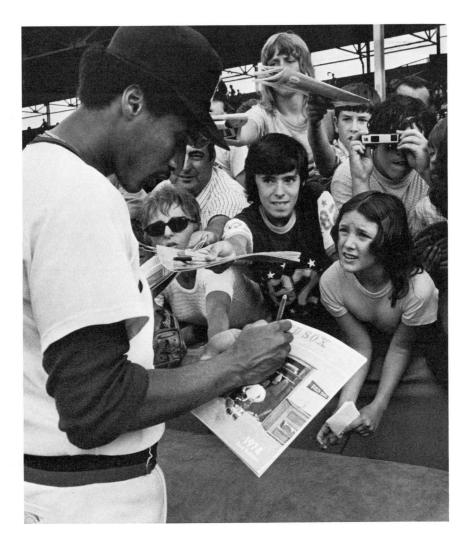

# 9 The Background and Development of American Sport

We have discussed the historical development of physical education, but we have not yet considered the history of sport itself. We will discuss aspects of the history of sport in the United States to show not only its effects on the development of physical education, but the resulting effects on school physical education programs and public attitudes toward physical education, as well. While in recent years interest has risen in studying sport as separate from physical education, we do not wish to separate physical education and sport entirely, for that is one cause of the problems physical educators are now trying to resolve.

To understand American sport we cannot start in the United States, for sport did not appear as some fully developed area of interest that originated in North America. The United States is a nation of immigrants, and its sporting heritage is also immigrant, though sport in the United States has developed independently for many decades now. We need to understand the sporting experiences of our ancestors if we are to understand how today's sports picture came to be. To explain the development of sport in the United States more fully, we will go back to the roots of Western history and study sport in Europe from early times through the nineteenth century.

We defined sport in Chapter 1 as an organized, competitive form of play. As we study the history of sport, we will see how it has developed away from the play aspect and toward an emphasis upon the aspects of organization and competition. When we think of organized sport today, we think of an extremely intense competitive system.

In this chapter we will try to show the roots of the system in Europe and the United States until approximately 1900. The emphasis in Chapter 10 will shift slightly, for we will be concerned not merely with the continued development of sport, but with its clash with physical education, and how each affected the other. When you have completed the next two chapters, you should understand more clearly how we arrived at both our present systems of physical education and of sport, and you should comprehend more fully the sometimes delicate relationship between the two. In the minds of most people physical education and sport cannot be separated, so a deeper understanding of the relationship is critical.

### Survival Sport: Prehistoric Times

We have already discussed the physical activities of primitive people in Chapter 2, though in a context of educational activities. The essential characteristic of primitive physical activities was a base of survival skills: The physical activities provided practice in the skills primitive people needed for survival and defense against natural enemies. We might view sport in the same way—that is, as "survival sports," or "natural sports,"—for many of the sporting activities had their source in the same basic skills.

Sporting activities of primitive people can be viewed in the categories of games and sports, or they might also include dance activities, which were very important to primitive cultures. Hackensmith refers to three types of primitive games: games of chance, games of dexterity and skill, and children's games.[1] We will view sport primarily in the area of the games of dexterity and skill. These activities included ball games and games such as archery, hoop and pole, and snow snake. While the competitive sports were often between two or more people in a village or tribe, some competitions were held between different villages and tribes. Most often these were ball games similar to forms of today's lacrosse or soccer contests.

When we look at the early forms of sports used by primitive people in Western culture (European prehistory), we often see a warlike basis for the activities. The sports involved basic skills of war if the contestant was to be successful. While we have traditionally considered this warlike basis of sport to be a common trait of primitive societies, evidence suggests that this idea is untrue.[2] While primitive sport was not always warlike or war-oriented, it was taken seriously.

### The Golden Age of "Pure" Sport: Ancient Greece

We feel close to the ancient Greeks for many reasons. We see the Greeks as the first people to express our modern concept of democracy,

---

[1] C. W. Hackensmith, *History of Physical Education,* Harper & Row, New York, 1966, p. 7.

[2] Maxwell L. Howell, Charles Dodge, and Reet A. Howell, "Generalizations on Play in 'Primitive' Societies," *1974 North American Society for Sport History Proceedings,* pp. 18–20.

and we still think of their theoretical educational system as one of the best-balanced systems of all time. Their philosophy of the harmonious relationship between the mind and the body lies at the heart of most contemporary theories of physical education.

The Greeks were similar to modern societies in many respects, but one common link is the similarity of their strong interest in athletic competition. Sport was an important part of life for the Greeks. It was supported by most Athenians as an important part of the educational process, in the sense that it assisted in their search for bodily perfection to accompany their training of the intellect. It was also supported by the government, as in Sparta, for it produced a population that would be better prepared to serve in the army if the need arose.

The Greeks were the founders of the Olympic games, as we discussed in Chapter 2. Because the Greeks held many local games, other than just the Olympic games, interest in athletic competition was widespread. The athletic games had developed from ceremonies to worship the Greek gods and from games that were held in conjunction with funerals. During earlier times the prizes for the games were small, but as time passed the size and nature of the awards changed.

The prize for victory at the Olympic games was traditionally a wreath formed from an olive branch, which was primarily a symbolic prize rather than a valuable one. However, the city-states began to offer additional prizes to their native athletes who won Olympic victories. At the vale of Olympia a man received only an olive wreath, but when he returned home he might be given enough wealth to last out his life. Gifts of money, food, and civic honors were frequent and worth winning, so more competitors entered the games.

As the civic prizes grew, the level of Olympic competition gradually changed. Fewer true amateurs competed, for they could not match the skills of those who had no occupation other than "athlete." As the athletes competed for larger prizes, professionalism grew. As the extent of professionalism spread, the Olympic games began to die. The games faced heavy competition from city-state games that offered large prizes. Men no longer competed for the honor of victory, but for the prizes that were offered.

Although we think of the time of the ancient Greeks as a time of "pure" sport, genuinely amateur competition was not the true state of affairs. Although the number of professionals grew slowly, amateurism was dying even during the Golden Age, for the amateurs had neither the time nor money to permit them to compete on equal terms with the professional athletes. The problems of amateurism versus professionalism with which we are so familiar date not to the Romans but to the Greeks. The Greeks developed a philosophy of "sport for sport's sake," but they were not able to live up to that philosophy. Although the Olympic games continued into Roman times, they had long since lost most of their purity.

The decline of sport came when sport shifted its common emphasis from participation to the winning of prizes and the amusement of spectators. The athletes competed for the prizes offered by the city-states; the city-states offered the prizes to attract athletes; and the games were staged to bring fame and business to their city-states. Sport became more of a business than an amusement, for both the organizers and the competitors.

## The Age of Professionalism: The Roman Empire

A number of advantages aided the survival of sport—particularly track and field—in Greece. The Greeks had centuries of experience in sport; it had religious ties because of its ceremonial uses, it had been a pastime of the wealthy, and it was still a part of the educational experience for Greek youth.[3] Sport did not have the same advantages in the Roman world.

As we discussed earlier, the Greeks were more philosophical than the Romans, who were more practical-minded. The Greeks had a philosophical basis for sport as a cultural activity, but the Romans saw sport only in two ways, both of which were basically practical: as military training and as entertainment. The Romans were not interested in the educational value of sport except in relation to preparation for war.

Two primary differences existed between the Greek and Roman approaches to sports: (1) the Romans were primarily spectators, rather than participants as were the Greeks; and (2) the Romans were more wholehearted in their support of professionalism, which was in contrast to the Greek ideal of amateurism in sport. The Romans for the most part did not compete in sports; they watched *others* take part. Many questions have been raised concerning whether we should call the Roman spectacles "sport," rather than "athletics," or perhaps even "entertainment." This change would also affect our calling the participants "athletes," as opposed to "competitors," or simply "participants." The Romans did not want to see less-skilled amateurs; they preferred highly skilled professionals. The Roman pattern of going to sports events to be entertained is a trend that can be seen in contemporary athletics.

The growth of professionalism under the Romans helped to destroy what strength remained in the Greek sports system. Few amateur

---

[3] H. A. Harris, *Sport in Greece and Rome,* Cornell University Press, Ithaca, N.Y., 1972, pp. 72–74, 184–185.

athletes were interested in the Olympic games, for they could not compete with the professional athletes. The concept of the mind-body balance was lost, as was the idea of all-around bodily development. The age of specialization had hit the ancient world, and we can still see the ill effects in modern sport. The emphasis of sport originally had been the honor of victory and the joy of competition, but over a period of centuries it gradually changed until there was only one real emphasis: victory. The better it paid, the more pleasant it was. The athlete competed for the prize, rather than either the honor or the joy.

This overemphasis and professionalism carried into the early medieval period, when it (and much of sport) lost favor in a Christian reaction against the pagan elements of sport. As the Roman Empire dissolved, the rich prizes were no longer available on a regular basis, and organized sport as known by the Greeks and Romans gradually disappeared.

## Medieval Sport: Source of the Sport Dichotomy?

***The Sport Dichotomy.*** The Sport Dichotomy refers to a characteristic of sport that has been noted back as far as the ancient Greeks: the growth or control of sport by the upper classes of a society.[4] The Homeric games are referred to as involving primarily the upper classes, for the lower classes either were not permitted to compete or had too little time to train for competitive success. Some scholars note that this trait of the Greek games disappeared rather early, however, and they do not consider it a common characteristic of Greek games.

We next see this dichotomy, or class split in sport, during the Middle Ages. As mentioned in Chapter 2, when we think of physical education or sport in the Middle Ages, we usually think of the activities of the upper classes. The age of chivalry, with its tournaments, was an upper-class age only; no chivalric tradition existed for the majority of the people. "Accepted" sports—that is, sports that were considered "worthwhile"—were always sports of the upper classes. This tradition has continued to a marked degree to the present day. Even today the modern Olympic games are completely controlled and dominated by a small group of wealthy people who are self-appointed custodians of the spirit of amateurism. Their requirements still reflect the same upper-class prejudice against allowing the general populace a part in sport that was notable not only in the nineteenth century, but also in the fourteenth century.

---

[4] E. Norman Gardiner, *Greek Athletic Sports and Festivals,* Macmillan, London, 1910, p. 25.

**Knight Sports: The Haves.**  We have already discussed the tradition of chivalry in Chapter 2. Most of what we think of as sport of the medieval upper classes fell into this area. We think commonly of the tournaments at which the knights would fight to prove their strength and prowess.[5] The tournaments are traced back to the tenth century, though elements of their activities go back to Roman times. They originated as military exercises, with some emphasis on the safety of the knights, but over a period of centuries they degenerated until they either were banned by the church or became pointless after gunpowder was invented.

The tournaments, like the tradition of chivalry, were strictly upper-class sport, for while other segments of society could be spectators, only the upper classes were directly involved. However, as the time of the Renaissance drew nearer, other activities were developing that would cut across such class boundaries. Also, the lower and middle classes were developing their own sports activities separately from those of the upper classes.[6]

**Middle-Class and Lower-Class Sport: The Have-Nots.**  The lower classes of the Middle Ages, the vassals and farmers, could almost be described as being outside of society. Although they might be lowly spectators at the tournaments, that was their only involvement in that sort of sport. As a result, they had their own games, most of which harked back to ancient times, and these emphasized running, jumping, and throwing objects. The middle class, which began to develop with the rebirth of the cities after the tenth century, was also interested in sports activities. The people developed their own variations of the knights' tournaments as they trained themselves to defend their cities. They imitated upper-class sport in many respects, but they also were involved in adding democratic elements to sport.

One such influence was a French ball game, similar to rugby, called *soule*. Contests were held between many different competitive units, including cities, and the primary democratizing element was that people from every class—farmer, burgher, clergyman, and nobleman— might be on the same team. After the contest, both teams had a communal meal (which might not be a bad tradition to return to contemporary sport). People were beginning to discover that sports gave them opportunities in equality that were not available anywhere else:

> In his struggle for recognition as an individual, man discovered in sports a meeting ground where he could prove himself under fair

---

[5] Jan Broekhoff, "Chivalric Education in the Middle Ages," *Quest,* 11 (December 1968), 32–43.

[6] Nicolaas J. Moolenijzer, "Our Legacy from the Middle Ages," *Quest,* 11 (December 1968), 32–43.

conditions. The respect for democratic practices and the self-esteem of the burgher combined with the desire for fair-play may well be one of the most important contributions that the Middle Ages made to our heritage.[7]

## Renaissance Sport

We do not find any radical changes in sport as we move from the Middle Ages through the Renaissance period. The Renaissance, which we discussed in Chapter 3, was a period of rebirth of learning and interest in the arts. The classics of the ancient Greeks were imitated, and many of their theories of physical education and sport were also attempted. Further evidence indicates that the Sport Dichotomy—the distinction between the upper classes and the common people in sporting activities—continued in Italy, where the Renaissance originated.[8]

The Renaissance was also the period of expansion of the universities, many of which were founded at the height of the Middle Ages. Considerable evidence has been gathered to suggest that university sports were every bit as popular in the Middle Ages and Renaissance as they are today.[9] However, sport was considered an area of student activity that the school frequently tried to suppress or limit, for often physical activities were considered to interfere with the academic studies. We do not think of student sports of the Renaissance in the sense that we think of them today; the activities were closer to today's intramurals.

The Renaissance concept of the all-around person, developed intellectually and physically, helped contribute to physical training and sport, for sporting skills were considered as important as book skills for the well-rounded person. Team games were continuing to develop, and individual competitive activities, such as competition in the military skills, were also popular.

As we move closer to the modern era, sport was still in a low-level, disorganized state. Games had common forms and rules, but they were not standardized. Many variations of the same basic game could be found across Europe. Although the concept of nationalism was growing, no such thing as national or international sport had emerged. No sporting contests on the scope of the early Greek Olympics had yet appeared in any nation. It is only in relatively recent times that we see the rise of sport as we know it today: a more formal activity with set,

---

[7] Ibid., 42.

[8] Peter C. McIntosh, "Physical Education in Renaissance Italy and Tudor England," in *A History of Sport and Physical Education to 1900,* ed. Earle F. Zeigler, Stipes Publishing Company, Champaign, Ill., 1973, pp. 249–266.

[9] Ray C. Thurmond, "Student Sports in the First Five Centuries of Universities (1150–1650)," *1974 North American Society for Sport History Proceedings,* pp. 9–10.

standardized rules of competition and with competition both within and between nations.

## Early Modern Sport in Europe

To study early modern sport in Europe, we must look at nineteenth-century Europe, for most of what we have come to know as modern sport has developed from the growth of sport in the nineteenth century, primarily in Europe. In studying European sport between 1800 and 1900, we will look at three particular trends or developments: the continuation of the class dichotomy in sport; the origins of organized competitive sport, as opposed to informal or internal sports activities; and the revival of the Olympic games under Baron Pierre de Coubertin in 1896.

*The Dichotomy Continues.* Our best example of the dichotomy in the the sports world comes from the British public (private) schools, for they preserved their traditional educational patterns for centuries, until the mid-nineteenth century. The British public schools had a strong sporting tradition, for sport was considered an activity of the leisured gentleman. The school system that promoted sports was also strongly class conscious. England had very clearly defined classes of citizens, and the upper classes were very hesitant to associate with the other classes.

The graduates of the British public schools were perhaps the major influence on the development of organized sport, for not only were they the primary leaders in organizing sport, but they also organized it within the framework of the public school philosophy: Sport was purely for the sake of the competition and pleasure; winning was at best a secondary interest. This philosophical direction was probably one of the most fortunate aspects of the early development of organized sport, though it created problems both then and now.

Another notable aspect of the British public school influence at this time was the definition of amateurism. The requirements for amateur status, which enabled the athlete to enter organized competition, made participation very difficult for the lower classes, for their jobs did not allow them time to train. The lower classes were discouraged, if not outright barred, from competing with the leisured gentlemen who made the rules. The "accepted" sports were still largely a domain of the upper classes.

*The Birth of Modern Organized Sport.* Organized sport really dates from late in the nineteenth century. During much of the first half of the century wars and national revolutions in Europe created unstable conditions that were not conducive to the development of sport. In the second half of the century, times were more peaceful and nationalism

Baseball has been called the American pastime. An American business-oriented group attributed the game's invention to the American Abner Doubleday, but it really seems to have developed from the English game called "rounders," which was popular in the 1700s. This Currier & Ives lithograph shows an early form of the American game. (Courtesy The Harry T. Peters Collection, Museum of the City of New York)

was growing. Sporting organizations were beginning to develop, along with a consciousness of national pride.

Sports clubs are an easily noticed development of that period. Although there was some mixing of the classes in the membership of the clubs, their policies and practices were dominated by the public (private) school graduates. Local championships were started, playing fields were constructed, and eventually moves were made to form national sporting bodies.

We can see six rough stages of development during the rise of organized sport. The first stage was the growth of university sports, for the early sporting tradition was born in the universities. The second stage was the growth in popularity of sport, as people first became interested as spectators, then as participants. This popularity led to the third stage, the development of sports clubs, as the participants banded together with other people interested in the sport to provide competition and playing facilities that would permit them to follow their sporting interests. (Some sports clubs were oriented toward several sports, while others concentrated on a single sport.) In the fourth stage, national organizations and national championships in sports were developed. The fifth stage, the development of common national and international rules for the sport, was followed by the sixth stage (where it is applicable), the keeping of national and international records. Most of these stages were completed during the nineteenth century, when the emphasis on informal sport ended and the move toward standardized national and international sports competition started. Most of the international organizations were formed in the twentieth century, for the primary emphasis before 1900 was national.

An example of these developmental stages may be seen in the changes in English track and field during this period. Competition within the universities was appearing in the 1850s, though the events were highly variable from one competition to the next. The first interschool meet was between Oxford and Cambridge in 1864. Multitudes of sports clubs were being formed, and the first English championship meet was held in 1866.

The time and place of the meets, which kept most nonuniversity students and citizens who lived any distance from London out of the championships, caused considerable conflict among the sports clubs. After the Amateur Athletic Association, a national track and field body, was formed in 1880, the national meet was changed to a time of year when all athletes could compete, and the site of the meet was changed from year to year as well. The move to develop international rules and records came in the next century with the formation of the International Amateur Athletic Federation in 1912, whose task was revising the international rules and approving world records.

As the nineteenth century came to a close, many changes had taken place in European sport. Sporting organizations had developed to make the rules more consistent. National championships had been started for many sports. The upper classes' influence on sport was beginning to weaken as multitudes of nonaristocrats became sports competitors and spectators. The last stage in the move toward organized sport was coming closer: the development of international sport. This stage appeared as the brain child of Baron Pierre de Coubertin of France, who worked for years to revive the ancient Olympic games.

**The Phoenix Arises: Rebirth of the Olympic Games.** Baron de Coubertin might almost be called the modern Olympics, for the games would not likely have been revived without his long years of work to promote their rebirth. John A. Lucas has studied the work of Coubertin at length, particularly as it relates to the Olympic movement.[10] Born in France in 1863, Coubertin was a well-educated nobleman. He was an ardent supporter of the tradition of the British public schools, especially as the tradition had been developed by the work of Dr. Thomas Arnold

[10] John A. Lucas, "The Genesis of the Modern Olympic Games," in *A History of Sport and Physical Education to 1900*, ed. Earle F. Zeigler, Stipes Publishing Company, Champaign, Ill., 1973, pp. 331–340.

of the Rugby School. This tradition of the English schools, which was considered by Coubertin to be a major reason for the strength of England, stressed character, intellect, and the development of the body. Organized games were required of all students, and sport was thus as important a part of the educational process as intellectual training.

Coubertin was motivated by a desire to help France. Because he believed that lack of exercise had made France a weak nation, he was a major supporter of physical education in the schools. He hoped to develop sport with an international outlook. In 1892 he called for the revival of the Olympic games, but he discovered that no one was really interested. He spent the next three years trying to make people conscious of what he called "Olympism."

At an 1894 congress at the Sorbonne, Coubertin formed the International Olympic Committee, with the purpose of reviving the Olympic games in 1896. One man was elected to represent each nation on the committee. The committee members were required to value internationalism above nationalism. They also set the standards of amateurism. The formation of the committee continued, if it did not magnify, the class dichotomy in sport, for only wealthy men were on the committee. The choice of wealthy men was intentional: They were as independent a body as Coubertin could devise; they were thus more likely to be totally independent and unaffected by political or nationalistic influence. Unfortunately, they also were unlikely to understand the views of the common people and the athletes.

Olympism, as Coubertin called it, was characterized by religion, peace, and beauty. The strong element of character has always been a notable part of the Olympic tradition. The love of beauty, especially as expressed in the beauty of movement, is also still notable. Today we often forget the religious part of the emphasis, but the early games were held to honor the gods; there was a strong religious element in the traditional Olympic games.

Coubertin's experiment was an attempt to blend academic training with moral and physical education. It was designed to promote peace and contribute to international understanding. He hoped to make the competition as close to "pure" amateur athletic competition as was possible. He did not visualize women taking part in the games for two particular reasons: they had not taken part in the original Olympic games, and in his view, competing in sports was undignified for women. His views on sport for women, which were those shared by most men at that time, were not an example of the Olympic ideal carried to its logical conclusion.[11]

---

[11] Mary Leigh, "Pierre de Coubertin: A Man of His Time," *Quest,* 22 (June 1974), 19–24.

Coubertin succeeded in reviving the Olympic games. The first modern Olympic games, held in Athens, began on Easter Sunday, April 5, 1896. The rebirth of the games was the result of Coubertin's dream and was one of the greatest influences on modern sport. Although sport has changed vastly from nineteenth-century Europe, most of our practices and problems can be seen even at that early time.

## The Growth of American Sport

Now that we have seen the development of Western sport until 1900, we are ready to study how sport grew in the United States. We will study the development of American sport by considering three topics. The first topic is sport in colonial and early national America, which was essentially recreational in nature and not too highly organized. We will next look at the rise of organized sports, which came at about the same time as in Europe, yet had some essential differences. Finally, we will look at American sport at the turn of the century: its organization, its emphasis, and the directions it was then taking as it influenced American society.

### Social Sport in Colonial and Early National America (1607–1850).

The primary emphasis of sport in the American colonies and the early United States was largely social. Life was not easy for the early settlers who had few chances to relax and enjoy themselves. On the frontier, people were often widely separated and had few chances to meet other people. They welcomed the chance to get together socially on such occasions as holidays, militia training days, election days, court meeting days, and church revivals.

The religiously-oriented colonies were usually opposed to recreational activities as wasteful idleness and often legislated "blue laws" designed to prevent any irreligious activities on Sundays. They passed other laws against many sporting activities, but they were not very successful in preventing the activities.[12]

As the colonies became more solidly based and the citizens had more free time, more recreational activities sprang up. Sports were not very highly organized at that time; people played games they had learned as children, or they followed the directions for games given in the English sporting magazines and game books. Since most of the earlier settlers were English, most of the early games were of English origin. The English publications, which became widely spread in America during the late 1700s and early 1800s, helped make the de-

---

[12] Donald P. Zingale, "Puritans at Play," *1973 North American Society for Sport History Proceedings,* pp. 13–14.

velopment of English sport a major influence on the later organization of sport in the United States.

As the settlers moved westward, life again became difficult, and the competitions also became much tougher. The most popular competitive activities during early American times were contests such as horseracing, cockfighting, gambling activities, rowing, and baseball. Horseracing, with both open races and match races, was always popular throughout the colonies. Cock-fighting, or matches between specially trained fighting roosters, was also popular, particularly in the southern states. Gambling activities, whether on other sporting events or with games of chance, were popular. Rowing developed in the middle-1800s as one of the first collegiate sports. Baseball gradually evolved from English ball games, until it was considered a native American game. One reason for baseball's popularity was that it was one of the few sporting activities that showed no distinction between the social classes.

Although many sporting activities were popular in early times, the real growth of sport in the United States came only after the nation had become more settled and urbanized. Some stability and a certain level of wealth and leisure time are needed before sport can become highly organized in a society, and these conditions were not that noticeable until after the middle of the nineteenth century.

**The Rise of Organized Sport in America (1850–1906).** During the second half of the nineteenth century, a dual development occurred in the trend toward the organization of sport: Not only were teams being formed in the schools (beginning with the colleges in the northeastern United States), but at the same time athletic clubs were being formed and were working to organize sport. Both played important roles in the organization of sport before 1900.

Betts refers to the period from 1860 to 1890 as "the age of the athletic club." [13] Many athletic clubs were formed in the larger cities. Some clubs concentrated on specific sports, while others emphasized many different sports. Many of the clubs were sponsored by college students, until the colleges permitted them to have school teams. One leading club was the New York Athletic Club. This track and field–oriented club introduced such new developments as the spiked shoe, the cinder track, and standardized track and field rules; it also did much work to promote the sport in general.[14]

---

[13] John Rickards Betts, *America's Sporting Heritage: 1850–1950,* Addison-Wesley, Reading, Mass., 1974, p. 98.

[14] Harry A. Scott, *Competitive Sports in Schools and Colleges,* Harper Brothers, New York, 1951, p. 19.

The athletic clubs promoted the growth of some professional sports, particularly baseball. Eventually they worked to form national organizations to hold national championship competitions. An example is the Amateur Athletic Union, formed in 1888 from an earlier track and field group started by the New York Athletic Club.

Sport was also growing rapidly in the colleges. The earlier school teams were similar to today's extramural or club sports programs, for they were organized and directed by the students themselves.[15] For the most part, the schools made no attempt to control these sporting activities, beyond occasionally banning an activity that was considered dangerous or that was interfering with reasonable scholarly interests. The first competition between two colleges was a rowing match between Harvard and Yale in 1852, and by 1875 intercollegiate contests were held in baseball, football, and track and field.[16] Although no more than two dozen schools had school teams by 1875, they were increasing rapidly in popularity. The faculties of the colleges usually permitted the sports for two reasons: The idea of letting the students direct some of their own activities was coming into fashion, and the school teams made student life more attractive to prospective students.

Gymnasiums were being constructed in many areas by cities, by athletic clubs, and by schools. The addition of year-round athletic facilities helped to promote sports all the more, for activities became less limited by the weather and seasons. Gymnasiums were also being built because of a growing acceptance by the schools of the values of physical education activities for the students. At this time, however, physical education and sport had no real connection. The 1889 conference on physical education, which we discussed in Chapter 4, included practically no mention of sports activities, for physical education was more ritual and calisthenics at that time.

By late in the 1800s many new developments were taking place in collegiate sports. The rowing enthusiasts were the first to use hired coaches.[17] The secondary schools developed sports teams in imitation of the collegiate teams, often for competition against the college teams. Collegiate athletic associations and conferences were also formed to organize and regulate competition. Some examples are the formation of the Intercollegiate Association of Amateur Athletes of America

---

[15] Charles A. Bucher and Ralph K. Dupee, Jr., *Athletics in Schools and Colleges,* Center for Applied Research in Education, New York, 1965, p. 5.

[16] Guy Lewis, "Enterprise on the Campus: Developments in Intercollegiate Sport and Higher Education, 1875–1939," in *Proceedings of the Big Ten Symposium on the History of Physical Education and Sport,* ed. Bruce L. Bennett, Athletic Institute, Chicago, 1972, pp. 53–66.

[17] Betts, p. 102.

(IC4A) for track and field competition in the eastern United States and the American Intercollegiate Football Association, founded in 1876.[18]

Another reason for the growing popularity of sports programs in colleges came from the schools' belief that sports reflected the interests and values of leading businessmen, who often gave financial support as alumni. Many of the problems common to sport—such as professionalization of school sports and excessive outside influence, especially by alumni—date from this era when the schools did not wish to have any official part of school sports. Although football developed late, by the late 1800s it had become one of the most influential sports. It was particularly influential, for many of the problems created by college football led to the start of a struggle in the schools to control school sports and eliminate what they considered harmful outside influences.

**American Sport at the Turn of the Century.** We will consider briefly four areas of sport as of 1900. First is the status of women and blacks in sport. The second concern is the abuses of sport at that time. Third we will consider the progress toward organized sport. Finally, we will look at the relationship between sport and education.

Little time is needed to discuss the part women played, or more correctly, were permitted to play in sporting activities. Women's sporting activities included any activity that did not require the lady (that was the point of it all) to sweat, though phrased more elegantly, or display her body.[19] The activities were those that could be played while fully dressed, which at that time was full indeed. Sports were used primarily for respectable social encounters and were usually individual sports, such as archery and croquet. Women's physical education was becoming accepted in the schools, and interest in sports was also growing. Team sports were coming into women's activities by 1900, particularly basketball, but there was still much suspicion of the idea of women's activities. The women were often quite interested in sports, but the schools and the public tended to disapprove and discourage their competition as unladylike or unsafe.

Blacks had become very involved in sport by 1900, but they were handicapped by a number of developments. During the slavery years the blacks were allowed to participate in boxing and in horseracing, foot racing, and boat racing. After the slaves had been freed, the blacks began to imitate many of the "white" sports, just as the middle and

---

[18] Scott, p. 17.
[19] Ellen Gerber, *The American Woman in Sport,* Addison-Wesley, Reading, Mass., 1974, p. 4.

When women were permitted to participate in sports before 1900, they were
usually forced to dress much more
awkwardly than male athletes; they were
to remain "ladylike" by not revealing
their bodies in any way. (Courtesy State
Historical Society of Wisconsin)

lower classes of the Middle Ages imitated the tournaments of the
nobility. Although blacks were involved in many areas of sport in the
late 1800s, they were most active and successful in baseball (some
blacks were major league players in the early 1880s), horseracing (most
of the top jockeys before 1900 were black), and boxing.

During the 1880s and early 1890s the rising tide of racism resulted
in the Jim Crow laws that called for separation of the blacks and whites
in many areas of life. The laws, which were upheld by the Supreme
Court in 1896, cut blacks off from many of the previously integrated
activities. Baseball barred black players in the 1880s; white players
were pressured to refuse to play if a black was on the team. (This
segregation in baseball lasted until 1946 in the major leagues.) Efforts
to bar black jockeys from horseracing were largely successful by 1900,
and numerous other sports were pressured to do the same because
blacks were considered "uncivilized" and thus should not be allowed to
compete with whites. The racism of the late 1800s was reflected most
vividly in the "great white hope" of boxing, or the long-sought "savior"
of the whites who would defeat the black boxing champion Jack
Johnson, who was an object of white hatred for several years after 1900
when he was the world's best boxer.

By 1900 black athletes were barred from most integrated competition. Black major leagues were formed in baseball, which was perhaps the most popular sport among the blacks at that time, and the
formation of black college sports conferences provided segregated
competition at the college level. In 1900 few sports were integrated,

though occasionally, but not often, black competitors participated in mixed sporting events. Some colleges, notably Harvard, had some blacks on teams, particularly football and baseball, but these schools encountered difficulties in arranging competitions with other colleges. Many schools would not permit a black to compete against their teams, which forced the integrated school team to bench a black athlete. The breakthrough for integrated sport was not to occur until the Depression, and most sports were not to be affected until after World War II.

Sport contained many abuses in its common practices by 1900, some of which we have already discussed. Other examples are the recruitment of athletes by offering them excessive inducements, the methods of recruiting athletes from one college by another college, and the lax concern for safety procedures. Concern about the number of football deaths was growing, as were indications that a class system was present in American sport, just as it was in English sport.[20] The primary difference in American sport was that the upper class was based on wealth, much of which was recent, rather than traditional social standing and noble origins.

Considerable progress had been made toward modern organization in sport, however. The colleges had begun forming competitive conferences as well as associations to set rules of competition and eligibility standards. The colleges made this move to take control of collegiate sport, which until that time had been in the hands of the students or outsiders. The steps the colleges were taking to control intercollegiate sport were imitated at the high school levels, as state athletic associations began to form for essentially the same purpose (the first of these associations was in New York in 1903).[21]

The colleges developed internal athletic associations to control sports in their schools. As physical education had been accepted as having value in the educational program, the faculties added control of athletics as one more area of educational physical activity. National rules were written, and open (not collegiate) national championships were held. By 1900 the organizational level of sport was radically different than in 1850.

The conflict between education and sport was growing rapidly. The formation of the National Collegiate Athletic Association (NCAA), under an earlier name, in 1906 was the first step toward national control of school sports by the schools. The body was formed in reaction to the outcry over the increasing number of deaths in college football. The NCAA had three basic goals: to establish high ethical standards for

---

[20] Richard Wettan, "Sport and Social Stratification in the U.S. 1865–1900," *1974 North American Society for Sport History Proceedings,* pp. 29–30.

[21] Bucher and Dupee, pp. 6–7.

college sports, to develop physical education in the schools, and to promote intramural athletics.[22] The goals were clearly those of a group of people more concerned with the broad goals of education than with narrower sporting goals.

We have now seen how the U.S. sports program developed through the last century. In the next chapter we will continue the history of the growth of sport and physical education in the twentieth century. We will try to see and understand the conflicts between physical education and sport. We hope to see what effect the conflict has had on our physical education and athletics programs as we know them today.

## Suggested Readings

Betts, John Rickards. *America's Sporting Heritage: 1850–1950.* Addison-Wesley, Reading, Mass., 1974.

Cantwell, Robert. " 'America Is Formed for Happiness.' " *Sports Illustrated,* 43 (December 22–29, 1975), 54–59, 62–66, 69, 71.

Eisen, George. "Physical Activity, Physical Education and Sport in the Old Testament." *Canadian Journal,* 6 (December 1975), 44–65.

Eyler, Marvin Howard. *Origins of Some Modern Sports.* Microcarded Ph.D. dissertation, University of Illinois, 1956.

Gerber, Ellen W. *Innovators and Institutions in Physical Education.* Lea and Febiger, Philadelphia, 1971.

Hill, Phyllis Jo. *A Cultural History of Frontier Sport in Illinois, 1673–1820.* Microcarded Ph.D. dissertation, University of Illinois, 1966.

Jable, J. T. "Pennsylvania's Early Blue Laws: A Quaker Experiment in the Suppression of Sport and Amusements, 1682–1740." *Journal of Sport History,* 1 (Fall 1974), 107–121.

Kennard, June A. "Maryland Colonials at Play: Their Sports and Games." *Research Quarterly,* 41 (October 1970), 389–395.

Kleinman, Seymour. "Toward a Non-Theory of Sport." *Quest,* 10 (May 1968), 29–34.

Korsgaard, Robert. *A History of the Amateur Athletic Union of the United States.* Microcarded Ed.D. dissertation, Teachers College, Columbia University, 1952.

Lewis, Guy M. "America's First Intercollegiate Sport: The Regattas from 1852 to 1875." *Research Quarterly,* 38 (December 1967), 637–648.

———. "Enterprise on Campus: Developments in Intercollegiate Sport and Higher Education, 1875–1939." In *Proceedings of the Big Ten Symposium on the History of Physical Education and Sport.*

---

[22] Hackensmith, p. 399.

Edited by Bruce L. Bennett. The Athletic Institute, Chicago, 1972, pp. 53–66.

Lowe, Benjamin. *The Representation of Sports in Painting in the United States, 1865–1965.* Microcarded M.S. thesis, University of Wisconsin, 1968.

Loy, John W. "The Nature of Sport: A Definitional Effort." *Quest,* 10 (May 1968), 1–15.

Lucas, John A. "Pedestrianism and the Struggle for the Sir John Astley Belt, 1878–1879." *Research Quarterly,* 39 (October 1968), 587–594.

Moore, John Hammond. "Football's Ugly Decades, 1893–1913." *Smithsonian Journal of History,* 2 (Fall 1957), 49–68.

Quercetani, Roberto L. *A World History of Track and Field Athletics, 1864–1964.* Oxford University Press, New York, 1964.

Robinson, Rachel Sargent. *Sources for the History of Greek Athletics.* Privately published, Cincinnati, Ohio, 1955.

Sage, George H., ed. *Sport and American Society: Selected Readings,* 2d ed. Addison-Wesley, Reading, Mass., 1974, Chapter 1.

Smith, Michael D. *The Development of Positions Taken by the Faculty Regarding Intercollegiate Athletics at the University of Wisconsin, 1873–1925.* Microcarded M.S. thesis, University of Wisconsin, 1967.

Somers, Dale A. *The Rise of Sports in New Orleans, 1850–1900.* Louisiana State University Press, Baton Rouge, 1972.

Thompson, James G. "Athletics Versus Gymnastics in Classical Antiquity." *Canadian Journal,* 6 (December 1975), 66–74.

Van Dalen, Deobold B., and Bruce L. Bennett. *A World History of Physical Education,* 2d ed. Prentice-Hall, Englewood Cliffs, N.J., 1971.

Voight, David Q. "Reflections of Diamonds: American Baseball and American Culture." *Journal of Sport History,* 1 (Spring 1974), 3–25.

Zeigler, Earle F., ed. *A History of Sport and Physical Education to 1900 (Selected Topics).* Stipes Publishing Company, Champaign, Ill., 1973.

———. "Putting the Greek Ideal in Perspective." In *History of Physical Education and Sport: Research and Studies,* 2 (1974), 13–25. Published for the History Committee of the International Council of Sport and Physical Education (UNESCO), Tokyo.

# 10 Sport and Physical Education Meet in the Twentieth Century

We see the first real meeting of sport (especially as competitive athletics) and physical education during the early years of the twentieth century, especially from 1900 to 1930. Two aspects of this growing relationship (and conflict) are noticeable: (1) the gradual addition of competitive athletics, including intramurals, to the school programs, followed by a boom in popularity after World War I; and (2) the addition of sports and games to the school physical education curricula, the "American system" or "New Physical Education" discussed earlier.

These two developments were separate during the early years of the century, yet they were gradually drawing the areas of athletics and physical education closer together because of their common interest in movement activities. We can see the resulting conflict between athletics and physical education even today. Part of the reason for the conflict was the fear that athletics would be overemphasized, which happened many times, and part of the reason for the conflict was the physical educators' fear that athletics might gain control of the entire program and subvert its goals and objectives. We can see these fears reflected in the conflicts related to women's sports in the 1930s and again in the 1960s and 1970s.

Today physical educators have to work out differences of opinion as school programs are increasingly combined into the field of physical education and sport. As we work to solve the problems and smooth the relationships, we need to understand how the shaky relationship between physical education and athletics developed.

## Sports Comes into the School Program (1900–1930)

As we look at the history of American physical education and sport in the first third of the twentieth century, we can see three rough stages of development. The first stage was the period of student control of the sports programs in the schools, which we date roughly until 1906, when the NCAA was formed. The second stage was the period of increasing control of sports by the schools, which we will set from 1906 to 1922, when the National Federation was formed for high school sports. The third stage, the New Physical Education, lasted from 1922 to 1930 and was the time of the greatest progress in drawing sports into the physical education program.

**The Period of Student Control.**  As the twentieth century began, school sports was still controlled by the students. The common practice was for a group of students to form a team and then choose a team captain and a manager. The manager was the critical decision, for he was responsible for the organizational success of the team. The manager arranged the schedule of contests, arranged for practice facilities and team equipment, raised money from alumni and local supporters, handled the business of the team, and hired the coach, if the team had a coach. This arrangement was the ultimate in student control, for the school had no connection with the team other than the fact that the members of the team were (usually) its students.

The schools were gradually accepting the idea of the values of exercise as a part of the educational process. They were learning that healthier students were more successful students, and they had been adding required physical education classes to the school curriculum. The faculty members were beginning to agree that sport could also be a valuable part of the educational experience, and they were working to bring the control of sports under the protective wing of the schools. This move to control sports was also a reaction to the many abuses of sport at that time, since sports were not really controlled well by any organization. Football, because it had annual fatalities, was the most conspicuous example, but basketball was rapidly becoming a popular school sport.

Basketball had been invented by James Naismith at Springfield College in 1891, with the first official game played there on January 20, 1892.[1] The game spread very rapidly across the country among both men and women students. The women adopted the game so enthusiastically that in some parts of the country it was considered exclusively a women's sport.

Women were getting involved in many sports by this time, especially in the colleges, with participation in sports such as basketball, baseball, rowing, golf, bicycling, aquatics, and winter sports.[2] The

---

[1] Harry A. Scott, *Competitive Sports in Schools and Colleges*, Harper Brothers, New York, 1951, p. 25.

[2] John Rickards Betts, *America's Sporting Heritage: 1850–1950*, Addison-Wesley, Reading, Mass., 1974, pp. 219–220.

women were beginning to get away from the "delicate flower" concept of womanhood, though several more decades would be required to complete the task. The women were making their own basketball rules because no national organizations had been formed for women's sports.

The interest in student sports was shown in informal student-arranged intramurals that were beginning to appear on many campuses. However, the first department of intramurals in a college was not started until 1913, at Michigan,[3] and the real boom in intramurals was not to come until after World War I.

Concern over problems in competitive sports was leading to school interference in the student control of sports as the century began. Student control began to pass from the scene with the founding in March of 1906 of the Intercollegiate Athletic Association, which changed its name to the National Collegiate Athletic Association (NCAA) in 1910. The schools had decided to take control of school sport and were trying to put it to some educational use.

**Increasing Control by the Schools.** During the years from 1906 to 1922 the schools were actively taking control of the interschool sports programs. Six trends can be seen in sports and physical education during this time. The first trend was the gradual assumption of control over intercollegiate sport by the NCAA and the college athletic conferences. The NCAA, whose purposes we discussed in Chapter 9, began to develop rule books to standardize the rules of sports competition. Athletic conferences and associations were springing up and working to standardize sports procedures. They wanted to develop consistent rules, set standards of eligibility for competition, and make fairer competitive matches in their sporting events. Much progress was made in bringing the athletic programs into the schools, though problems continued to develop.

A second, parallel trend was the work by the high schools to control their sports programs. The high school athletic programs were very imitative of the collegiate sports programs, just as the high school academic programs were largely patterned to meet college needs and practices. State associations, followed by some regional associations, were being formed in the hope of equalizing competition, standardizing rules, and setting consistent eligibility requirements. In 1922 a national body was formed, the National Federation of State High School Athletic Associations,[4] which has since broadened its scope of extracurricular activities beyond athletics and changed its title to the National Federation of State High School Associations.

---

[3] Charles A. Bucher and Ralph K. Dupee, Jr., *Athletics in Schools and Colleges,* Center for Applied Research, New York, 1965, p. 8.

[4] Scott, p. 36.

A third trend of the period was the rapid growth of interest in women's athletics. Between 1906 and the end of World War I (1918) supervised athletics was added in many colleges.[5] The women wanted sports competition. Gerber has pointed out that the magazine *Review of Reviews* had a written symposium on women's sports in 1900.[6] Although many women wanted sports, their participation was controversial, as it still is in other respects today. During the 1920s many arguments were expressed both for and against women's sports. Although many women were in favor of competitive athletics for women, many female physical educators spoke out in opposition.[7] The basic reason for opposition to sports for women was a combination of Victorian standards (women must be feminine and delicate)[8] and fear that women's athletics would end up as corrupt or uneducational as men's college athletics seemed to be. For this reason, the period of rapid growth was followed by another period of growth away from the concept of interschool sports for women.

A fourth trend was the boom in intramural sports, or sports involving only the students within the school. The school intramural program as another offshoot from the earlier student-run sports programs.[9] Intramurals had been gaining in popularity in the colleges, and Michigan became the first university to form a department of intramurals to run programs for the student body.[10] The great boom in intramural sports that came after World War I is evident in the slogan of the times: "A sport for every student and every student in a sport." The emphasis was upon numbers of participants, rather than how much they participated, which created a temporary sidetracking of the intramural program goals.[11] Intramurals were to become an important part of the goals of the total physical education program as it evolved toward its present state.

---

[5] Betts, p. 136.

[6] Ellen W. Gerber, *The American Woman in Sport,* Addison-Wesley, Reading, Mass., 1974, p. 12.

[7] For the views of those who favored athletics for women, see Harriet I. Ballintine, "The Value of Athletics to College Girls," in *Chronicle of American Physical Education,* ed. Aileene S. Lockhart and Betty Spears, Wm. C. Brown, Dubuque, Ia., 1972, pp. 196–198; and Celia Duel Mosher, "The Means to the End," in *Chronicle of American Physical Education,* ed. Aileene S. Lockhart and Betty Spears, Wm. C. Brown, Dubuque, Ia., 1972, pp. 402–409. For the opposing view, see Ethel Perrin, "A Crisis in Girls' Athletics," in *Chronicle of American Physical Education,* ed. Aileene S. Lockhart and Betty Spears, Wm. C. Brown, Dubuque, Ia., 1972, pp. 440–443.

[8] Gerber, p. 13.

[9] Scott, p. 419.

[10] Ibid., p. 51.

[11] Ibid., p. 420.

A fifth trend was the addition of games and sports to the physical education curriculum. Although the change was gradually accomplished over three decades, the new programs were a radical departure from the older, formal systems of gymnastics that had been at the heart of American physical education since its early days.[12] Games and sports were more popular with the students, and the acceptance and enthusiasm for physical education improved considerably.

A sixth trend was also visible during this time: The emphasis of physical education gradually changed from medicine to education. This important trend signaled the acceptance of a much broader program of physical education—one that was more in line with the developing philosophy of the American school system—and permitted the use of games and sports in the curriculum, which increased student acceptance of the physical education requirement. It also marked a gradual change in the professional preparation of physical educators, for rather than being products of medical schools and formal gymnastics training courses, they increasingly became graduates of regular college training programs in education and physical education. The eventual results of this trend were a more widely accepted physical education program as well as more and better-trained teachers of physical education.

**The New Physical Education and the Golden Age of Sport.** The period from 1922 to 1930 can be summarized from the viewpoint of either physical education or sport. In physical education it was the time of the New Physical Education, while for the sports-minded person it was the Golden Age of Sport. Athletics had a great boom period in the United States for a decade after World War I. Postwar prosperity had a strong effect on the country: The standards of living were higher, the cities were growing, and the people had more leisure time available.[13]

World War I provided a great impetus to sports, though we are not exactly sure why it had such an effect. Sports activities had been pushed very heavily as a part of the military training, and after the war many men continued to play the new sports activities they had learned.

The boom in sports may have been primarily a relieved reaction to the end of the war. Betts refers to this time as "a decade dedicated to escapism," [14] and thus sport, which is a popular form of escapism, grew rapidly; in fact, football reached a pinnacle in popularity. Football

---

[12] Ibid., pp. 43–44.
[13] Betts, pp. 136–139.
[14] Ibid., p. 250.

games were followed widely on every level of competition, and the sport created much controversy. Just after this peak of "football-mania," a city championship high school game in Chicago drew over 120,000 spectators.[15]

The abuses of sport during this decade were being attacked, and the colleges called for an examination of the college sports scene by the Carnegie Foundation. The year of 1929 was a difficult year for sports, for college sports took two hard blows. The economic collapse of Wall Street started the slide into the Great Depression, and the Carnegie Report (Savage Report)[16] on college athletics was released. This detailed report of the abuses of college athletics showed the problems of professionalism, commercialism, and lack of academic integrity that affected many college athletic programs. It suggested that many colleges were losing sight of their primary purpose.[17] It was used as a weapon to make many changes in college sports programs.

Physical education and sport were beginning to be forced together by the schools during this time. One sign of this growing integration of physical education and sport was the founding of the nation's first School of Physical Education at the University of Oregon in 1920.[18] Led by Dean John F. Bovard, the school organized a unit of four departments that had previously been separate: the Department of Men's Physical Education, the Department of Women's Physical Education, the University Health Service, and the Department of Intercollegiate Athletics. The interest in this unified organization of different departments considered related to physical education spread across the country and was adopted by many other schools.

The rise of the New Physical Education has already been discussed in Chapter 4. It was simply the acceptance of games and sports activities as a legitimate part of the school physical education curriculum. Clark W. Hetherington had been calling for a particularly "American" form of physical education, and Jesse Feiring Williams had been popularizing a broader concept of physical education. Sports activities were creeping slowly into the curriculum until the writings of Thomas D. Wood popularized their use in a well-planned program of physical education activities.[19]

---

[15] Ibid., p. 257.

[16] Howard J. Savage, *American College Athletics,* Bulletin No. 23, Carnegie Foundation for the Advancement of Teaching, New York, 1929.

[17] Betts, p. 255.

[18] Scott, p. 52.

[19] C. W. Hackensmith, *History of Physical Education,* Harper & Row, New York, 1966, pp. 415–418.

## The Great Depression and the School Sports and Physical Education Program

The Depression, which took time to develop fully and affect the entire country, lasted from 1929 into the start of World War II (1941). The lack of money in communities hit physical education and sports very hard. Many moves made to drop physical education from the school curriculum were based on the claim that it was a "frill" course.[20] This attack on the place of physical education in the school program came as a surprise to physical educators. For the first time they became aware of the need for a good program of public relations; they realized that people simply did not understand what the purposes of physical education were and how it contributed to the education of the students.

The school athletic programs were also hurt, for the combination of the embarrassing revelations of the Carnegie Report and the lack of many sports fans with spending money was a difficult blow. The programs depended heavily on gate receipts, which were dwindling; they also needed public support, which had been hurt by the Carnegie Report. Interscholastic sports were reaching all the way down to the junior high school level by this time, but were facing much criticism. The suggestion that intramurals be used instead of interschool competition at that level (since intramurals would involve more students, yet cost less money) led to an increase in the number of junior high school intramural programs.

The small colleges, which were hurt more by the Depression than the larger schools, were forced to drop sports in many cases. The small colleges were becoming increasingly critical of the NCAA, for they thought the NCAA had been founded by and thus favored the larger schools. During the late 1930s and early 1940s moves were made to found national organizations similar to the NCAA for the small senior colleges and for the junior colleges.[21]

The big boom during the Depression was in recreation, for two reasons. First, unemployment gave many people much more leisure time for recreational activities, and the unemployed wanted something to do. Second, the government tried to fight unemployment by creating jobs; many workers were hired to build recreational facilities, playing fields, hiking trails, park areas, and so forth. The large growth in available recreational facilities also acted to increase the extent of public recreation.

Women's sports during the 1920s were being held back primarily

---

[20] Ibid., pp. 439–442.
[21] Ibid., pp. 455–456.

by the efforts of the leading women physical educators.[22] One reason for this opposition had been an effort by the Amateur Athletic Union (AAU) to take over control of women's track and field in the United States. The women educators believed that women should control and direct women's sports. They were irritated as much by the administrative procedures of the AAU as by their ambition to control women's track and field. Until that time the women had made no effort to organize sport.

The women created a Women's Division of the National Amateur Athletic Federation to control women's sports. It was a well-organized body of women who not only ran the college programs for women, but also trained the teachers, which extended their influence out into the nation. They could influence both the present and future practices.

As we have mentioned before, the women leaders had several fears that limited their support for women's competitive sports on a grand scale. While they continued the Victorian image of women as frail creatures who might suffer serious physiological harm from competing in sports, they also had a far more legitimate concern: They feared that a fully developed program of interschool athletics for women would end up suffering from the same excesses that plagued men's athletics. The poor example created by men's sports may have done more to hold back women's athletics during the 1930s than any other factor, though this would be difficult to substantiate.

Some of the arguments against sports for women that appeared during the 1920s and 1930s were merely old fashioned, while others bordered on the ridiculous, particularly the writings of John R. Tunis, a widely-quoted writer of sports and fiction (which is a close description for some of his comments on women's athletics). As the 1930s drew to a close, the emphasis in women's sports was moving away from the idea of interschool athletic competition; the programs were becoming centered on a "play day" emphasis more similar to intramurals. These play days were low-keyed sporting activities, in which large numbers of people were involved, and in which teams were formed by mixing players in attendance from the various schools. Play days were organized with the basic concept of "education for all," with the education coming through physical activities and an attempt made to reach as many people as possible with those activities.

As the 1940s drew closer, both physical education and athletics had come through a difficult decade. The Depression had forced both to give up ground in terms of the scope of their programs as well as

---

[22] Ellen Gerber, "The Controlled Development of Collegiate Sport for Women, 1923–1936," *Journal of Sport History,* 2 (Spring 1975), 1–28.

public acceptance. The next decade would bring a radical reversal of that trend, as war again clarified a need for both in the school program.

## The Effects of War on American Physical Education (1941–1953)

The coming of World War II cut out the arguments over whether physical education and sport belong in the educational program. Of the first two million people examined for military service at the start of the war, 45 percent were rejected for mental or physical reasons. Little of this excessive rate could be blamed on the school programs, but extensive publicity began to make the public aware of the fitness problem.[23] The government saw a great need to improve the health and fitness of all the people.

During World War II the government formed a series of organizations to work to improve the health and fitness level of the citizens. A Division of Physical Fitness was formed that worked first under the Office of Civilian Defense and later under the Office of Defense. It had an advisory board to help develop community fitness programs, and a sports board of celebrities and sports authorities was appointed to try to reach the public with a message of the need for fitness.

The physical education programs were facing a struggle to keep from being forced back to the old concept of physical training, for the war-need emphasis was for fitness only, with little interest in broader goals. Many physical educators were involved in devising fitness tests to assess the results of armed forces training programs. Fitness tests, which had been available for boys, were also constructed for school-girls. One wartime plus for physical education was that many states replaced their older laws recommending physical education in the school program with laws that required the teaching of physical education.

During the war, sports activities continued with few limitations. Although many young athletes were in the armed forces and gasoline rationing hampered travel, sports was considered a positive influence on national spirit and was thus highly encouraged. Many of the sports teams that were formed on military bases competed against college teams. Intramural sports were encouraged in the armed forces, and sports activities were used as a part of basic training. An unfortunate side effect was the tendency to limit the objectives of physical education to fitness for military needs alone.

The end of the war started another sports boom similar to the one in the 1920s, as competition and sports facilities underwent great ex-

---

[23] Hackensmith, pp. 467–474.

pansions.[24] The people developed a greater feeling of world unity, as seen in the formation of the United Nations, and they became more conscious of international competition as the postwar Olympic games were revived in London in 1948. Many international cooperative sports programs were founded to foster peaceful competitions and to help nations meet each other and come to know each other on the field of sport.

## The Emphasis on Fitness in the Cold War and on the New Frontier (1953–1968)

The results of the Kraus-Weber Test of minimal fitness of elementary school children appeared in the United States late in 1953. As we described in Chapter 4, these results hit the American public with explosive force. The test found U.S. children were far less fit than European children. President Eisenhower reacted to this massive blow to American egos by forming the Council on Youth Fitness in 1956.[25] The purpose of the council was to promote fitness on the local level, but it primarily served the purpose of publicity for the administration. The programs never really got off the ground.

AAHPER reacted to the study by working to develop tests of fitness that could be used in the public schools and finally published the battery of tests forming the AAHPER Youth Fitness Test in 1958. Despite complaints that the Kraus-Weber Test was not a genuine fitness test, the Youth Fitness Test bore essentially the same results: U.S. children were less fit than their European counterparts.

The Council on Youth Fitness was revived in 1961 by President Kennedy as the President's Council on Youth Fitness. Kennedy was a sports enthusiast who was very concerned with the fitness of the country's youth. His influence and example brought on a rash of fitness-oriented activities, such as the fads of touch football and fifty-mile hikes. He started a concentrated push toward school fitness activities, which was the first such nonwar effort to come from the upper levels of the government. The United States was becoming much more sports-conscious as the decade passed.

The rapid growth of professional sports activities was also having an impact on the nation. Sporting activities as public entertainment had begun to team with television to start the nation on its way to becoming a society of spectators. Professional sports efforts to influence the lower-level amateur sports to imitate their practices affected football

---

[24] Scott, pp. 76, 78–82.
[25] Hackensmith, pp. 485–505.

and basketball practices most heavily. Amateur sports was threatened at the grass-roots level with losing its throng of local fans by desertion to the nearest television, which was sure to have a contest featuring more talented athletes. The professional "sport ethic," which seemed to be reaching down to the level of amateur athletics, promised many changes in sport in the years to come.

Sport was becoming an international concern in a world shrunk by communications satellites. Nations were sending sports teams to other nations for friendly competitions as a sign of mutual trust and friendship, and increasingly as a means to open the way to more political concerns. Sport was becoming a political tool to a greater degree than ever before. A time of rapid, radical change was about to begin.

## Changing Emphases in Physical Education and Sport (since 1968)

The years around 1968 were a time of attack upon many traditions in many nations. United States involvement in war in Southeast Asia carried over into many areas of American life; many people felt that the country had lost its ideals, while others felt that the traditional ideals were under attack. During this period of confrontation, everything seemed to be argued in political terms. Sport and physical education were attacked from numerous sides.

The attack on the physical education requirement as a part of the curriculum was renewed at many levels. The basic argument was that while physical activity is beneficial, the student should be allowed more freedom in deciding what activities to take, or even *if* activities would be taken. We might view this attack on the physical education requirement as a small part of a larger educational move of the time, which was a general attack on all school course requirements. Physical education was considered by many opponents of school structure as the weak link in the requirement system and thus the most logical place for an initial attack. Because of this movement, some required programs of physical education at the college level were changed to elective programs.

A concurrent trend was toward a recreational emphasis in the program of physical education activities, or what was called "lifetime sports." This trend is continuing, as more students still choose electives, such as tennis and bowling instead of the traditional fitness and competitive sports-oriented activities.

The call for educational accountability also developed at this time. Citizens wanted the schools to show that their programs were of value and that the students were genuinely making progress. This issue had important implications both in the area of the required physical education program and in the sports program, as justification was required for their inclusion in the school program.

Athletics faced many problems during this period. As a well-publicized area of American life, athletics became an excellent target for publicity seekers. Athletics was becoming increasingly politicized and brought many of its problems upon itself. Coaches claimed sports were what kept America a democracy, while Russians argued that it helped keep their nation communist. Sports leaders tried to wrap themselves in the cloaks of patriotism and religion by staging militaristic shows at football games and adding religiously oriented shows at the beginning of the festivities. The unfortunate result of these excesses was to widen the split between those who thought politics and religion were compatible with athletics and those who did not think so; both sides were convinced they were morally right.

The ultimate results of these excesses in sport may be seen in the riots and demonstrations at the 1968 Olympic games in Mexico City and the murder of the Israeli athletes by Arab extremists at the 1972 Olympic games in Munich. The games themselves had become a political symbol, and because of the intense worldwide publicity they generated, they were a perfect target for any group wanting instant, worldwide publicity.

The "big-time" college sports programs were attacked as an example of highly financed programs of "sports for the few." Student groups worked to limit student funds allocated to athletic departments; they preferred to have the money put into programs of intramurals, extramurals, and club sports that would reach more of the students. The students put increasing emphasis on a program of more sports for all rather than the existing system of limiting competition to a narrow segment of the student population.

At the same time there was a move to return sports more closely to the original traditions of student control. Students were agitating to run their own intramural and extramural programs, and they were increasingly starting club sports. Students were showing greater interest in less formal types of intramurals, such as drop-in, coeducational intramurals in which the competitive units were always changing. They wanted sports competition for the fun, not the honor.

Women's athletics was undergoing radical changes at this time. The women's liberation movement was gaining strength and pushing for fairer treatment of women in all areas of life, including sport, for women had been given few opportunities for competition. Although women had competed in some sports to some degree since at least the 1860s, women's sports programs had been relatively unpopular with administrators and had only marginal educational support.

Women's sports had been controlled by the Women's Division of the NAAF, then by the Division of Girls and Women's Sports (DGWS) of AAHPER, which did not accept the idea of intercollegiate sport

Women are participating in sports more and more, including sports that were once considered "male" sports because of the intense training and strenuous physical activity involved. These women are members of Boston College's crew team. (Courtesy Ellis Herwig, Stock, Boston)

until 1963.[26] Control of women's sports in the colleges eventually was passed to the AIAW (Association of Intercollegiate Athletics for Women), which was begun in 1972.[27] It promoted sport on the national and international level. The National Federation of State High School Associations also became more active in girls' sports and began to develop rule books and statewide competitions at the high school level.

Unfortunately, even with these changes, most of the opportunities for the women were as competitors or chaperones, for on the higher levels of administration and coaching, men continued to run the women's programs. The basic argument for this practice has been that the women lacked experience, but they were not given any opportunities to gain the necessary experience.[28] This problem still exists in women's sports programs across the nation.

The last decade has seen massive changes in women's athletics, both in practice and in public attitudes toward the programs. Most arguments against the programs are no longer based on whether sport is safe for women or whether they have a right to equal competition. Most opponents now are concerned primarily with the economic aspect of women's sports. To be more exact, do more women's programs mean that less money will be spent on the men's programs? The next decade will most likely see even more massive changes in the programs of sports for women.

Many changes have also taken place to promote racial integration

[26] Gerber, *The American Woman in Sport,* p. 75.

[27] Ibid., p. 84.

[28] Ibid., pp. 43–47.

Branch Rickey hired Jackie Robinson as a member of the Brooklyn Dodgers in 1946 in order to initiate the integration of major league professional baseball. Though black athletes had played in the major leagues in the 1800s, since about 1900 they had been forced to form their own segregated baseball leagues. (Courtesy Wide World Photos)

in sports. The segregation of black athletes was largely continued until after World War II. But there were exceptions: The first black American had competed in an Olympic game shortly after 1900, numbers of blacks began to appear in the Olympics in track and field competition after World War I, and whites began to notice the abilities of top black athletes in the late 1930s. Even as Hitler proclaimed his doctrine of the Aryan's racial superiority, a black American, Jesse Owens, won four gold medals in the 1936 Berlin Olympics and Joe Louis, the "Brown Bomber," fought the German world boxing champion. Finally, in 1946 Jackie Robinson became the first black athlete in professional baseball in over sixty years in the major leagues, as a result of Branch Rickey's deliberate attempt to integrate baseball. Robinson's obvious athletic skills—combined with his ability to withstand player and fan hostility—were convincing enough to lead to integrating professional sports. These achievements helped pave the way for integration of college sports in the 1960s, as did the early leadership of a small number of collegiate teams, such as those at Harvard, who insisted on playing with integrated teams. The Supreme Court decision in 1954 that reversed the tradition of "separate but equal" schooling led to integrated sports in the public schools over the next two decades. Although there were many abuses of the athletes in the schools, by the 1970s American sports were for the most part integrated.

## Problems in Physical Education and Sport Today

We will look briefly at four areas of problems in physical education and sport today. The first problem area is the *abuses of sport.* One writer listed some of these abuses:[29] direct or indirect payments to students for athletic services, encouragement of students to migrate from college to college for athletic purposes, lack of faculty control in games and grounds, coaches of questionable morals and influence, and bad moral effects of games when rules are broken or evaded. This last abuse, incidentally, was subject of a complaint made in 1903; thus while the abuses of sport may be more intricate today, they are not new. Many of the problems of abuses in sport need to be corrected, and while the educators must show leadership in this area, there seems to be no sign of interest in an investigation such as the one conducted by the Carnegie Foundation in the 1920s.

A second problem area is the question of *overemphasis on sports in the schools:* Are sports overemphasized? If we consider sports to be a genuine contribution to the educational process, which most physical educators do, then we would expect it to be important. In many cases, though, sports seem to be overemphasized—that is, pushed not for lessons, but promoted simply for the victories and fame that can be gained. As physical educators we need to give serious consideration to this problem of sports overemphasis, for it reflects upon our physical education programs as well.

A third problem area is *whether competitive sports is overemphasized in the physical education program.* Although competitive sports may be overemphasized by less skillful teachers, a good teacher will prepare a well-balanced program that exposes the students to all areas of physical activity. As physical educators we need to be constantly evaluating our programs to insure that we are providing physical *education,* not simply promoting physical *competition.*

The fourth problem area lies at the heart of this chapter: *What is the relationship of physical education and sport?* This topic is worthy of volumes, for to many people sport and physical education are the same and inseparable, and many people consider sport to lie at the heart of the study of physical education. However, we will try to give a simple

---

[29] D. A. Sargent, "History of the Administration of Intercollegiate Athletics in the United States," in Lockhart and Spears, p. 272.

answer to the question. Although there are many problems to overcome, sport and physical education have gradually been blended together to form a single area of interest. As they have blended together, each has benefited: sport from the educational aims of physical education; physical education from the activity and application opportunities of sport. Both sport and physical education are stronger as a result of the relationship, but much work is needed to realize the full benefits of the combination and to make the relationship a harmonious one.

Who has won the battle between physical education and sports? The question is still open to debate. Physical educators and athletic coaches are slowly coming to realize that they are closer together than they had realized. Each area is affected by the public reputation of the other. In the eyes of the public, the two areas are one. Whether physical education and athletics wish to be a single area, they are being forced together by the public. The question of which area will carry the greatest influence, if either one, has not yet been settled.

## Suggested Readings

Adelman, Melvin. "The Role of the Sport Historian." *Quest,* 12 (May 1969), 61–65.

Bennett, Patricia. *The History and Objectives of the National Section for Girls' and Women's Sports.* Microfiched Ed.D. dissertation, Mills College, 1956.

Betts, John Rickards. *America's Sporting Heritage: 1850–1950.* Addison-Wesley, Reading, Mass., 1974.

Boyle, Robert H. *Sport: Mirror of American Life.* Little, Brown, Boston, 1963.

"Club Sports in Colleges and Universities." *JOPER,* 46 (October 1975), 19–22.

Cozens, Frederick W., and Florence Stumpf. *Sports in American Life.* University of Chicago Press, Chicago, 1953.

Educational Policies Commission, National Education Association. *School Athletics.* National Education Association, Washington, D.C., 1954.

Gerber, Ellen, et al. *The American Woman in Sport.* Addison-Wesley, Reading, Mass., 1974.

———. "The Controlled Development of Collegiate Sport for Women, 1923–1936." *Journal of Sport History,* 2 (Spring 1975), 1–28.

Hart, M. Marie, ed. *Sport in the Sociocultural Process,* 2d ed. Wm. C. Brown, Dubuque, Ia., 1976.

Hodgdon, Paula Drake. *An Investigation of the Development of Interscholastic and Intercollegiate Athletics for Girls and Women from*

*1917–1970.* Microfiched D.P.E. dissertation, Springfield College, 1973.

Hoover, Francis Lentz. *A History of the National Association of Intercollegiate Athletics.* Microcarded D.P.E. dissertation, Indiana University, 1958.

Hopson, Sandra G. *The Socialization Process of the Black Athlete.* Microfiched M.S. thesis, Kent State University, 1972.

Johnson, William. "The Olympic Games: The Taking Part." *Sports Illustrated,* 37 (July 10, 1972), 36–44.

———. "After the Golden Moment." *Sports Illustrated,* 37 (July 17, 1972), 28–34, 39–41.

———. "Defender of the Faith." *Sports Illustrated,* 37 (July 24, 1972), 32–43.

Kenyon, Gerald S., ed. *Aspects of Contemporary Sport Sociology.* Athletic Institute, Chicago, 1969.

Koehler, Gretchen M.E. *Agents Who Have Influenced Women to Participate in Intercollegiate Sport.* Microfiched M.S. thesis, Brigham Young University, 1973.

Leigh, Mary H. *The Evolution of Women's Participation in the Summer Olympic Games, 1900–1948.* Unpublished Ph.D. dissertation, Ohio State University, 1974.

Leonard, George. *The Ultimate Athlete.* Viking Press, New York, 1975.

Lewis, Guy M. "Adoption of the Sports Program, 1903–39: The Role of Accommodation in the Transformation of Physical Education." *Quest,* 12 (May 1969), 34–46.

———. "Enterprise on Campus: Developments in Intercollegiate Sport and Higher Education, 1875–1939." In *Proceedings of the Big Ten Symposium on the History of Physical Education and Sport.* Edited by Bruce L. Bennett. Athletic Institute, Chicago, 1972, pp. 53–66.

———. "Theodore Roosevelt's Role in the 1905 Football Controversy." *Research Quarterly,* 40 (December 1969), 717–724.

Lockhart, Aileene S., and Betty Spears, eds. *Chronicle of American Physical Education, 1855–1930.* Wm. C. Brown, Dubuque, Ia., 1972.

Loy, John W., Jr., and Gerald S. Kenyon, eds. *Sport, Culture, and Society.* Macmillan, New York, 1969.

Lucas, John A. *Baron Pierre de Coubertin and the Formative Years of the Modern International Olympic Movement.* Microfiched Ed.D. dissertation, University of Maryland, 1963.

———. "Seminar on the Modern Olympic Games." *JOPER,* 47 (March 1976), 22–24.

Mandell, Richard D. *The First Modern Olympics.* University of California Press, Berkeley, 1976.

Marshall, Stanley J. *The Organizational Relationship Between Physical Education and Intercollegiate Athletics in American Colleges and Universities.* Microcarded D.P.E. dissertation, Springfield College, 1969.

Meadors, William J. *The History of the National Federation of State High School Athletic Associations.* Microfiched Ph.D. dissertation, Springfield College, 1970.

Michener, James A. *Sports in America.* Random House, New York, 1976.

Miller, Donna Mae, and Kathryn R. E. Russell. *Sport: A Contemporary View.* Lea and Febiger, Philadelphia, 1971.

Milton, Brian Gerard. *Sport as a Functional Equivalent of Religion.* Microfiched M.S. thesis, University of Wisconsin, 1972.

Mould, Michael William. *A History of the National Junior College Athletic Association (1937 through March, 1969).* Microcarded D.P.E. dissertation, Springfield College, 1970.

Pease, Dean A., Lawrence F. Locke, and Martin Burlingame. "Athletic Exclusion: A Complex Phenomenon." *Quest,* 16 (June 1971), 42–47.

"Perspectives for Sport." *Quest,* 19 (January 1973). Entire issue.

Reising, R. W. " 'Where Have All Our Heroes Gone?' Some Insights into Sports Figures in Modern American Literature." *Quest,* 16 (June 1971), 1–12.

Robicheaux, Laura. "An Analysis of Attitudes Towards Women's Athletics in the U.S. in the Early Twentieth Century." *Canadian Journal of History of Sport and Physical Education,* 6 (May 1975), 12–22.

Sage, George H. "Occupational Socialization and Value Orientation of Athletic Coaches." *Research Quarterly,* 44 (October 1973), 269–277.

——, ed. *Sport and American Society: Selected Readings,* 2d ed. Addison-Wesley, Reading, Mass., 1974.

Savage, Howard J. *American College Athletics,* Bulletin 23. Carnegie Foundation for Advancement of Teaching, New York, 1929. (Microcarded.)

Scott, Harry A. *Competitive Sports in Schools and Colleges.* Harper Brothers, New York, 1951.

Scott, Jack. *The Athletic Revolution.* Free Press, New York, 1971.

Sefton, Alice Allene. *The Women's Division, National Amateur Athletic Federation.* Stanford University Press, Stanford, Calif., 1941.

Torkildsen, George E. *Sport and Culture.* Microcarded M.S. thesis, University of Wisconsin, 1967.

Tutko, Thomas, and William Bruns. *Winning Is Everything and Other American Myths.* Macmillan, New York, 1976.

VanderZwaag, Harold J. "Sport: Existential or Essential." *Quest,* 12 (May 1969), 47–56.

———. *Toward a Philosophy of Sport.* Addison-Wesley, Reading, Mass., 1972.

"World of Sport." *Quest,* 22 (June 1974). Entire issue.

Zeigler, Earle F. *Problems in the History and Philosophy of Physical Education and Sport.* Prentice-Hall, Englewood Cliffs, N.J., 1968.

Zingale, Donald P. *A History of the Involvement of the American Presidency in School and College Physical Education and Sports During the Twentieth Century.* Microfiched Ph.D. dissertation, Ohio State University, 1973.

# 11 Problems and Ethics in Sport and Physical Education

We discussed ethics briefly in Chapter 6 and defined it as concerned with morals and conduct, with trying to decide upon proper rules of of conduct. We said it is a study of ideal conduct and the knowledge of good and evil, and that it seeks to determine what actions are right and wrong, what should and should not be done. The greatest problem that we face in discussing certain ethical problems is that no one perspective is absolute: Each person may have a different belief about what is right and wrong, and we have no objective standards by which we can judge some issues. For this reason, we need to understand that the ethical standards discussed in this chapter reflect the ethical views of the author.

## How Does Ethics Relate to Sport and Physical Education?

Ethics is vital to the successful functioning of any society—that is, people must have standards of value by which they live. The development of ethical standards has long been considered a vital part of the educational process. The Greeks spoke of the development of character as one of the most vital concerns, if not *the* most vital concern, of education. Many educational goals were optional, but character was a goal that could never be dropped.

If we agree that we need to develop character, or ethical standards, what does that need have to do with sport and physical education? We often refer to sport and physical education as a laboratory of human experience, for there, more than in any other organized area of the educational process, students are likely to show their inner selves. Sport and physical education challenge the student both physically and intellectually, and in the heat of intense effort, the person's true values will show through. One person will be more concerned with fair play, while another will be dedicated to winning in any possible way: This is the ultimate test of ethical standards, and no area of educational endeavor is so likely to put the student to the test.

Sport poses a dilemma in modern life, no less than in ancient times. H. A. Harris discussed the problem in the conclusion to his book on *Greek Athletes and Athletics:*

> Not only are games pleasant to play but many of them afford great enjoyment to spectators; all the problems of modern sport spring from this simple fact. In logical language the essence of sport is the enjoyment of the players; the pleasure of spectators is an accident . . . . So long as sport is true to itself, the only purpose of the organization of it is the enjoyment of the players; as soon as the interests of the spectators are allowed to become predominant, corruption has set in and the essence of the game has been lost. In other words, sport can be an entertainment for spectators, but what is primarily entertainment for spectators can never be sport in the true sense of the term.[1]

Originally sport was for the competitors, but in modern times the influence of television has increased many of the problems of the entertainment dilemma. When sport is still purely for the athlete, however, it is an excellent test of ethical behavior. Because sport and physical education can provide such a fertile ground for learning and testing ethical behavior, we face our next problem: Should physical educators teach ethics and values?

## Should Ethics and Values Be Taught in Sport and Physical Education?

If sport and physical education really *are* a "laboratory of human experience" as we claim, what better place could be found to try to teach ethics and values to the future leaders of the world? Delbert Oberteuffer has suggested that this issue is a major area of concern in contemporary physical education.[2] Whenever lists of objectives for physical education have been prepared, we see the area of developing social and moral competences included as a major concern. The supporters of sports programs have argued frequently that the contribution it makes to developing character is a major reason for having the programs.

We might be more accurate if we suggested that sport provides the opportunity to *display* character rather than develop it, but the ties between ethical character and sport and physical education are strong and of an ancient heritage. As physical educators and coaches we

---

[1] H. A. Harris, *Greek Athletes and Athletics,* Indiana University Press, Bloomington, 1966, p. 189.

[2] Delbert Oberteuffer, "On Learning Values Through Sport," *Quest,* 1 (December 1963), 23–29.

The 1976 Olympics, held in Montreal, were characterized not only by political problems, but also by the extreme security measures taken to protect the athletes. These precautions were taken to prevent the kind of terrorist activities that resulted in the death of Israeli athletes in the 1972 Olympics in Munich. (United Press International photo)

have an obligation to try to teach ethics and values, for in the ultimate judgment it may be the most important lesson we teach.

## How Do We Teach Ethics and Values?

As physical educators and coaches we teach ethics and values largely by example. Although we may talk about living by rules and treating others fairly, our students and athletes will be far more influenced by our practices than by what we say. People's true ethical beliefs are reflected in their daily actions. It does a teacher no good to tell a class to treat everyone fairly, if the teacher does not treat the students fairly. The old saying that "action speaks louder than words" is very true when we speak of ethical behavior. We are unlikely to teach *good* character if we exhibit *poor* character. Teachers and coaches must constantly be aware of the effect of their actions upon their students, for younger students will imitate their coaches and teachers in the belief that the actions are examples of accepted and proper conduct and ethics.

Today the concern over ethical behavior is rising as society becomes more aware of the need for ethical character in its members. In a special article on crime, *Time* magazine noted that behind the rapid rise in crime was a major element: "Morals: the ultimate problem." [3] The increasing consciousness of the need for the development of the older concept of ethical character is reflected by the reappearance of discussions in newer textbooks such as the one by Reuben B. Frost entitled "Human Values and Personal Ethics." [4] Our programs need to return to a stress on character, ethics, and sportsmanship.

---

[3] "The Crime Wave," *Time,* 105 (June 30, 1975), 17.

[4] Reuben B. Frost, *Physical Education: Foundations, Practices, Principles,* Addison-Wesley, Reading, Mass., 1975, pp. 382–403.

## The "Ethic" of Big-Time Sport, or Why Sport Has a Poor Reputation

Students and athletes learn many lessons from competitive sports, not all of them good lessons. Most people realize that competitive sports do not have a very good reputation today, particularly in the areas of ethics and values. When we think of sports today, we are often thinking of what has come to be called Big-time Sports—that is, top-level competition combined with big budgets. We may look at such competition in terms of professional athletics, or perhaps college or high school sports, but whatever the level of competition, many lessons are to be learned.

Sport has developed a poor reputation for many reasons. We will try to look at some of the philosophies and practices that have given sport this questionable reputation. One reason for many of these problems is that historically coaches and athletes at lower levels of competition try to imitate the practices they see in the big-time sports programs. Practices that might seem acceptable in professional athletics (which is essentially entertainment just as a circus is) are often inappropriate in amateur athletics. We see many of the ideas of professional athletics at the lowest levels of competition, unfortunately. That they reach these levels of sport and remain there must be the responsibility of the teacher-coach, for unless the teacher-coach opposes these practices, they will continue to spread. The following ideas or thumbnail philosophies are examples of practices that should be discouraged if sports is to be educational and attempt to develop a consistent system of values.

***The Supreme Importance of Victory.*** Two aspects of the current overemphasis on victory might be called the "winning is the only thing" ethic and the "agony of defeat" syndrome. The *"winning is the only thing" ethic* comes from the popular coaches' saying that "Winning isn't everything, it's the only thing." This idea, which is often attributed, probably incorrectly, to professional football coach Vince Lombardi, has been used by coaches on all levels to justify questionable practices ranging from mistreatment of the players to outright violations of the rules and practices of sport. The basic idea expressed here is that the only point of athletics is victory, so everything that is done has only one goal: winning. At best, this is a gross abuse of the idea of sport as a contributor to the educational process. If this philosophy is the philosophy of the coach or teacher, the school should have no sports program, for this motto has not the slightest pretense of values or ethics.

The *"agony of defeat" syndrome* covers the total range of sports, which is apparently "the thrill of victory, the agony of defeat." One small question arises in response to this view: *Why* should we think that defeat should result in agony? We compete with the hope of winning, but if we have given our best and still lose, why should we feel agony? One dictionary definition of agony is "intense suffering." Should this realistically be our response every time we lose? Sport is called by many coaches a "training ground for life," but if agony is our response to every defeat in life, would we be considered well adjusted? Defeat may be a disappointment, but the idea that it should be agony is another abuse of the place of sport in education and in life.

When we coach and compete in sports, we want to win. Winning, or trying to win, is a natural desire of the human race. It is true that we can liken life to a competition, but if we make victory with no holds barred the goal, we have removed much of the potential quality of that life. If victory is our ultimate lesson in school athletics, we have no lesson worth teaching, for the desire to win is inherent. The value of sport in the school curriculum lies in the other values that we teach or promote as we teach and train and compete. Victory is neither the only goal nor the highest goal in educational sport and physical education.

**Poor Sportsmanship.**  Sportsmanship has been used for many years as an example of the best trait athletics can develop. Unfortunately, we have no evidence that competitive sports participation actually does develop sportsmanship, while we do, unfortunately, have some evidence that sports competition can inhibit or lessen sportsmanship. Poor sportsmanship may primarily be a result of the examples given by coaches and teachers to their teams and to other students as they pursue victory and fame.

The *"nice guys finish last" rule* stands as a good example of what is wrong with educational sport, for too many coaches and athletes have tried to live up to this rule. The idea is that decency is a sign of weakness, that a person who shows signs of character probably does not have the force of will to become a champion. The result is coaches who abuse their athletes and ethical standards to pursue victory, because they do not think they can win if they play by the rules. If "nice guys finish last," sport will finish in that position in the list of educational priorities.

We might call the other aspect of poor sportsmanship the idea that *"the Lord* (or coach) *loves a poor loser."* We are increasingly treated to the spectacle of athletes who throw temper tantrums whenever they lose. This action is then cited by the coach or sports announcer as a sign of competitiveness or spirit, but if we want to be more honest, we can simply say it is a sign of childish immaturity, for most people are expected to have outgrown such behavior by the time they enter elementary school. Most coaches and athletes do not like to be referred to as cases of "retarded emotional development," but

the poor loser is just that. A person who cannot lose with dignity is not psychologically prepared to benefit from a competitive experience. Whether or not we can teach sportsmanship in the schools, we should at the least demand that it be exhibited by any person who wishes to compete.

**The Lack of Joy of Sport.** We traditionally think of sports activities as activities that people enjoy, or things that are fun to do. One aspect of contemporary sport seems to be the idea that sport should not be fun, because winning or losing is too serious to permit sport to be enjoyed. One example of this idea is similar to the last point made under poor sportsmanship, which is involved. *"Show me a good loser, and I'll show you a loser,"* as some coaches put it, is another example of the immature approach to sport. When we express the idea that only winning has a value, we are ignoring an important point: Everyone loses at some time. What is more, philosophies of this sort are self-defeating, for they turn everyone into losers. If everyone who participates in athletics will end up being called a loser, who will want to participate? Sport simply becomes futile under these conditions.

Another view of the no-joy-in-sport philosophy is expressed by the coach who says, *"We're here to win, not to have a good time."* If this is the coach's philosophy, the team has already lost, for the education this program will produce is entirely negative. We have all seen examples of the coach who believed that smiling was a sign of a poor competitive attitude. Whose attitude is really the poor one in a case of this sort? If there is no fun in sport, what will our competitive athletes be like in the future. Will they continue the idea that success equals misery?

**The Place of Education in Sport (Dead Last).** Actually we might more accurately refer to this as the place of the educator in sport, for we are concerned with the dedication of the coach to teaching. Most coaches in our schools will state that sport is an important part of the educational process. The question is whether their practices uphold their claim of believing the statement. We might call an example the *Dedicated Teacher syndrome,* or the coach whose education-minded approach is best reflected in his defensive statement that "I get paid to win, not to teach." The most obvious fact in the statement is that this coach is not a teacher, does not consider himself a teacher, and the statement makes the observer suspect that the coach has never been remotely interested in being a teacher. The statement itself is, in some cases, undoubtedly true, but is not a very supportable defense for doing a poor job, or no job, of teaching. A coach with this philosophy teaches his athletes far more than he realizes, primarily things schools would prefer not to have taught.

**Sports as Money.** We might view money as the greatest force affecting athletics today, for it lies at the heart of so many abuses of the educational goals of sport. The problem is a form of the Midas touch: We hope that everything we touch will pay off in dollars and cents. We see it reflected in the coach whose primary concern is salary and fringe benefits. We see it increasingly in the high school athlete whose primary concern about a college is "what will you give me?" Many of today's high school athletes are as interested in the ethics of scholarships and fringe benefits as a professional athlete is: not at all. We all too often see the picture of a functionally illiterate all-star high school athlete from a poor family who, after barely escaping high school, suddenly acquires a car, an improved wardrobe, perhaps a well-paid summer job, and the status of "amateur" college athlete. Too many coaches and athletes today believe that the cardinal rule of athletics is "money talks." What lessons are they teaching?

**The Nutcracker Reflex.** A favorite saying of coaches is that "when the going gets tough, the tough get going." The sentiment is worthy, for it teaches the rewards of sticking with a task until it is completed. Unfortunately, it also may be the catchword signaling the abuse and dehumanization of the coach's athletes. As teachers and coaches we should be sure that what the student-athlete is working for is worthy of the effort implied. Abuse simply for the sake of proving toughness or desire is never justified in an educational context.

**Coaching and the Idiot Syndrome, or Why the Coach Gets No Respect.** Perhaps the greatest failing of physical educators has been the growth of the idea of the anti-intellectualism of athletics and coaches. Sport is not thought of in an educational or intellectual atmosphere in most cases, primarily because of the actions of coaches. In our society the coach has come to be viewed as dedicated but not intellectual at all. Coaches are widely viewed as relatively ignorant people who have little interest in educational matters and less understanding of education. Unfortunately, because coaches and teachers of physical education often remain aloof from the rest of the school staff, many teachers hold this low opinion of their coaching colleagues. While much of the responsibility for this view lies with the poor job of public relations performed by physical educators, actual abuses are also at the heart of the matter.

Coaches who try to have an athlete's grade changed for the sake of the student's eligibility are showing fellow teachers that they have no concern for education or the primary task of the institution. Teachers who automatically give athletes good grades perform the same negative task in the eyes of the other teachers. College coaches who sign their all-star recruits as physical education majors regardless of the students' qualifications or interests show their own lack of respect for physical education's integrity as a field of study.

The use of a physical education major as a haven for the academically inept athlete has for decades been a popular concept among educators and citizens outside the field of physical education. One reason for this poor reputation as a subject area is the number of major students who obviously are not in college for an education, but who have come to be college athletes for as long as they can stay eligible. Physical education has suffered from the perpetuation of this sort of ignorance on the part of its coaches for far too long.

A psychological study of successful coaches has revealed that one of their characteristics is conservatism, or a resistance to change that is greater than the average person's resistance to change.[5] Coaches tend to be less flexible in their practices, which is more than likely to bring them into conflict with other teachers who do not share their views, but such inflexibility does not have to be a negative trait. If teachers and coaches will continue to work with their colleagues in other areas and let them see that their interests go beyond the gymnasium and playing fields and that they do want to maintain our academic integrity, they can gradually overcome the negative image the physical education teacher-coaches sometimes have.

These brief examples are not all the abuses that have contributed to giving athletics and physical education a poor reputation. We have taken decades to work ourselves into our current position, and changing that position will be neither easy nor quick. Now that we have con-

---

[5] Bruce Ogilvie and Thomas A. Tutko, *Problem Athletes and How to Handle Them,* Pelham Books, London, 1966, pp. 23–24.

sidered some of the things that have hurt the reputation, we need to look at the positive side of the task: our challenge. If we agree that we as physical educators should try to teach ethics and values, what ethical and value problems should we be facing as a part of the task?

## What Are the Ethical Problems We Face?

***Values Taught to Athletes and Students.*** One of our first ethical problems is a dual one: What values *do* we teach to our athletes and students, and what values *should* we teach to them? To answer the first part of this question, we must return to our earlier discussion of the way we teach with our actions. Regardless of what we say, the people we influence are watching what we actually do, to see whether our practices live up to our theories.

The 1960s was a time of much complaining about teachers and coaches being hypocrites, people who pretend to believe in one thing, or teach it, while they are doing something else that contradicts what they teach. If teachers do not live up to the theories they teach, the teachers will have a negative influence on the students. We must live what we teach.

Our next problem is really a question: What values should we teach our students and athletes? We could suggest many different values or aspects of ethical character that should be taught as a part of the educational process, for the list can be as long and detailed as each of us wants it to be. Instead, we will discuss five basic areas of ethics or values: justice and equality, self-respect, respect for others, respect for rules and authority, and a sense of perspective or relative values. This list is not intended to cover everything in the domain of values and ethical practices. It is simply a sampling of the areas the teacher-coach should keep in mind.

***Justice and Equality.*** Probably the greatest wish of any student or athlete is a simple one: fair and equal treatment. Students want a genuine opportunity to learn—to be exposed to what the teacher is teaching—as well as a fair opportunity afterwards to show what they have learned. Too often the average or poorly skilled student in physical education is neglected in favor of the gifted student. Educators should assist all students, regardless of their relative ability. Physical educators most often fail the students of poor ability in physical activities because they tend to neglect them. This practice is not justice to the student; it is unfair treatment of the student by the teacher.

Educators can fail to treat students equally because the students are different in any of several ways. We commonly think of the students who have not been given equal opportunity because they are of a different race than their teachers or other students. Teachers are equally unfair if they neglect a student whom they consider to be in a different social or economic group than the other students. A teacher can also fail students by neglecting them because they are not of the same sex as the teacher or other class members. This problem often occurs in athletic programs in schools that have tried to either prevent or ignore women's athletics. Finally, teachers fail to treat students fairly if they give them less attention because their level of physical ability—whether higher or lower—is different than the rest of the group.

The problem is complicated in athletics, for coaches have a tendency to give more attention to the more gifted athletes. This tendency is natural because the ultimate success of the team will likely ride more heavily on the shoulders of the more able athletes than on those of the other team members. However, a difference in physical talents should not affect the way the athletes are treated by the coach; all should be treated equally, regardless of ability. The coach should work with all the athletes as much as possible. Athletes will remember how the coach treated them long after they have forgotten everything else the coach taught.

**Respect and Consideration for Oneself.**  A coach who downgrades the athletes on a team, or a teacher who does the same thing to the members of a class, will make any success very difficult for students to achieve. A student or athlete needs a positive self-image and self-respect to be a success. The teacher-coach who treats all students equally will have made a major step in this direction, for no student will feel that he or she is unimportant or undeserving in the eyes of the teacher.

The teacher-coach should try to stress several concepts that relate to building students' self-respect. First, all that anyone can ask of people is that they do their best. If the teacher or coach demands that the students give their best, they will very likely give it. However, the teacher-coach should not abuse a class or team that gave its best and was still unsuccessful. If a runner competes and runs faster than ever before, does anyone have a right to complain if he or she still lost the race? Teachers cannot expect more than a student has to give, though they can raise the goals of the students to a higher level.

A second concept related to self-respect is simply the Golden Rule: Treat others as you wish to be treated. This rule holds true for teachers, coaches, students, and athletes. Self-respect is a delicate area, and students often feel insecure in the educational or athletic environment. The teacher can do much to remove the insecurity and help the student to develop a sense of self-respect that will lead to greater self-confidence and self-reliance.

**Respect and Consideration for Others.** Students and athletes need to learn to respect other people, whether they are their classroom or competitive counterparts, teachers, coaches, or any other person. The student needs to learn the value of treating other people with respect. The athlete who treats an opponent with respect is far more likely to receive the same treatment in return. In a competition in which the athletes treat each other with respect, the competition will be much more enjoyable for everyone involved. We have grown too accustomed to the idea that opponents are supposed to be abused; coaches are failing in their ethical duties if they teach this sort of conduct. They should, instead, encourage the students to extend respect to everyone, including parents and teachers.

When we speak of students and athletes learning respect, we need to remember that many athletes and students learn about respect from what they see their coaches do. A coach who screams at officials every time the team receives an adverse call is destroying any real opportunity to teach respect. Athletic competition may *seem* like war at times, but it is *not* war, and an opponent or official who makes a judgment against the team does not become a target for abuse in a sports program that is concerned with any aspect of ethical character. Coaches must *show* respect in order to *teach* it.

An aspect of learning to respect others relates to how the coach treats the athletes, or how a teacher treats the students. A teacher and coach must always be concerned with the students' and athletes' rights and feelings. A student should not become a target of ridicule because of an error, nor should the athlete who has an undesirable characteristic be subject to the coach's abuse. When students or athletes are abused by their teachers or coaches, the climate of respect disintegrates; a position of authority never includes the right to ridicule or abuse another person.

**Respect for Rules and Authority.** Students and athletes need to learn to respect rules and authority, for without them a society will not function. The first requirement in teaching this respect is that the rules need to be worthy of respect. The teacher who makes ridiculous rules simply to have rules to enforce has only complicated matters. The teacher-coach should set no ridiculous requirements—only those that genuinely contribute to the task at hand.

One aspect of respect for rules is how we teach the rules. Rules

This exaggerated drawing of an early Princeton–Yale football scrimmage indicates how college athletics programs may have earned the bad reputation they had before 1900. (Courtesy The Bettmann Archive)

are designed as a guideline of conduct in sport; they tell what can and cannot be done.  The teacher or coach can abuse the rules without explicitly violating them by pushing them to the allowable limits.  We sometimes hear the distinction made between the "letter of the law" and the "spirit of the law."  The "letter of the law" refers to what the law says shall be done, but underlying the law is the "spirit of the law," which is the intent of the law.  What is the *purpose* of a rule?  If a rule is designed to make basketball a no-contact game, what are coaches teaching if they hunt technicalities that may be used to help the team get away with contact?  If we teach the rules and then teach how they can be broken without detection, what are we teaching?  The object of all rules and laws is justice—to allow each person a fair opportunity.

We have to realize that living in a democracy requires respect for other people and respect for the rules.  If we do not respect other people, we will not be able to get along with them.  The result is conflict—and end to peace.  If we do not respect the rules of society, the result is anarchy, or disorder. A life of freedom and democracy is based on respect for our fellow citizens and our laws.

**A Sense of Perspective or Relative Values.** An important aspect of values is the relative values we place on things, or the viewpoints or perspectives we hold. In our discussion we will look at several questions related to the value of sport, but we will not seek ultimate or final answers for they should not be answered and passed over quickly. They require much thought and study.

A first question, perhaps the most important one, is *"how important is sport?"* Where do we place sport in the educational spectrum and in our lives? What part does sport play in life? For each of us, the answer or answers to the question of the importance of sport will give some indication of the part sport plays in our educational philosophies. Some of our answers may indicate that sport is more important than it really should be, but as educators, we need to place sport in a proper perspective.

A second question is *"what is the proper relationship between sport and physical education?"* We have already briefly discussed this difficult question in Chapter 10. We must determine the educational relationship between physical education and sport to be assured that sport receives the proper emphasis in an educational program, but without being overemphasized.

A third question is *"how necessary is victory?"* Do we believe in the idea of victory at any price? The value we place on athletic victory, which can be a choice between means and end in education, does much to show our ethical standards in sport. We must decide whether victory is more important to us than the educational values of competitive sports.

A fourth question concerns *academic integrity.* As educators we must decide what we stand for. Are we semi-educators, who will bend the academic rules to help ourselves gain a valuable athlete? Do we want our school to bend the rules to allow us to enroll a student who is unqualified to enroll or unprepared for the academic work expected of the typical student? Are we really educators if we encourage the academically inept to come to school because they are good athletes? We might consider the comments of Jacques Barzun in this area: "The analogy to athletics must be pressed until all recognize that in the exercise of Intellect those who lack the muscles, coordination, and will power can claim no place at the training table, let alone on the playing field." [6]

---

[6] Jacques Barzun, *The House of Intellect,* Harper & Row, New York, 1959, p. 95.

## Toward an Ethical Future

For almost an entire chapter we have been discussing various aspects of ethics and ethical problems and their relation to sport and physical education. We believe that ethical character and the learning of values are important aspects of education, but we are not sure how important they are, where they fit in, or exactly what we can do about them. Delbert Oberteuffer commented on our need to learn more in this area by saying

> ... what we needed in physical education was full blown research and clinical experience in the relation of movement to the teaching of ethics and morality, to the improvement of psychological states, and the cultivation of social gain between people and groups .... What kind of man-power does our society need for its preservation? This is the compelling question from the standpoint of national need and people in physical education had better have an answer or they will be lost in the oceans of sweat recommended by the muscle-building anti-intellectual.[7]

The future leaders of the nation in physical education and sport will determine the ethical practices and subsequent reputation of sport and physical education in the future. Whether physical educators are looked upon, as they have sometimes been in the past, as a group of not-too-bright, not-too-ethical sports people is up to future teachers and coaches. We need to see a marked improvement, and let us hope that the next generation of teachers will be more committed to the ideals of education and therefore more concerned with their own and their students' and athletes' ethical practices.

As educators and coaches, we should stand for something positive. We should have positive standards that show our respect for ourselves and others, our interest in fairness and justice, and our commitment to a strong sense of ethics. When we teach and coach, we can do no better than to convince those we teach that the often-quoted lines by the sportswriter Grantland Rice are the best judge of our ethical behavior:

> For when the One Great Scorer comes
> To write against your name,
> He marks—not that you won or lost—
> But how you played the game.

## Suggested Readings

AAHPER. *Values in Sports: Report of a National Conference.* AAHPER, Washington, D.C., 1963.

---

[7] Oberteuffer, pp. 23–29.

*The Academy Papers,* No. 9 (1975). Includes a section of discussions of various aspects of ethics in physical education.

Allard, Ronald Jean. *Sport: Tyranny of the Mind.* Microfiched M.S. thesis, University of Massachusetts, 1970.

Aly, Martha Alice. *Ethical Concepts for Recreation Professionals.* Microcarded M.S. thesis, University of Illinois, 1959.

Beisser, Arnold. *The Madness in Sport.* Appleton-Century-Crofts, New York, 1967.

Bennett, Bruce L. "Requiem for Sport." *1974 North American Society for Sport History Proceedings,* pp. 3–4.

Berryman, Jack W. "From the Cradle to the Playing Field: America's Emphasis on Highly Organized Competitive Sports for Preadolescent Boys." *1974 North American Society for Sport History Proceedings,* pp. 31–32.

Bucher, Charles A. *Athletics in Schools and Colleges.* Center for Applied Research in Education, New York, 1965.

Campbell, David N. "On Being Number One: Competition in Education." *Phi Delta Kappan,* 56 (October 1974), 16–20, 23.

Cobb, Robert A., and Paul M. Lepley, eds. *Contemporary Philosophies of Physical Education and Athletics.* Charles E. Merrill, Columbus, Ohio, 1973.

Crase, Darrell, et al. "Athletics in Trouble." *JOHPER,* 43 (April 1972), 39–51.

*Development of Human Values Through Sports.* AAHPER, Washington, D.C., 1974.

Edwards, Harry. *The Revolt of the Black Athlete.* Free Press, New York, 1969.

Fait, Hollis F., and John E. Billing. "Reassessment of the Value of Competition." In *Issues in Physical Education and Sports.* Edited by George H. McGlynn. National Press Books, Palo Alto, Calif., 1974.

Flath, Arnold, ed. *Athletics in America.* Oregon State University Press, Corvallis, 1972.

Ford, Gerald R., with John Underwood. "In Defense of the Competitive Urge." *Sports Illustrated,* 41 (July 8, 1974), 16–20, 23.

Fuoss, Donald E. *An Analysis of the Incidents in the Olympic Games from 1924 to 1948, with Reference to the Contribution of the Games to International Good Will and Understanding.* Microcarded Ed.D. dissertation, Columbia University, 1951.

Gardner, Paul. *Nice Guys Finish Last: Sport and American Life.* Alan Lane–Penguin, London, 1975.

Gerber, Ellen W., ed. *Sport and the Body: A Philosophical Symposium.* Lea and Febiger, Philadelphia, 1972.

Gilbert, Bill. "Drugs in Sport" (a three-part series). *Sports Illustrated,* June 23, June 30, and July 7, 1969.

Hart, M. Marie, ed. *Sport in the Sociocultural Process,* 2d ed. Wm. C. Brown, Dubuque, Ia., 1976.

Kelly, Barbara J. "Getting It All Together: The Integrated Learning Semester." *JOHPER,* 45 (October 1974), 32–35.

Kroll, Arthur M. *Issues in American Education.* Oxford University Press, New York, 1970.

Leonard, George B. *The Ultimate Athlete.* Viking Press, New York, 1975.

Lipsyte, Robert. *SportsWorld: An American Dreamland.* Quadrangle, New York, 1975.

Lockhart, Aileene S., and Howard S. Slusher, eds. *Contemporary Readings in Physical Education,* 3d ed. Wm. C. Brown, Dubuque, Ia., 1975.

McGlynn, George H., ed. *Issues in Physical Education and Sports.* National Press Books, Palo Alto, Calif., 1974.

Melnick, Merrill J. "A Critical Look at Sociology of Sport." *Quest,* 24 (Summer 1975), 34–47.

Michener, James A. *Sports in America.* Random House, New York, 1976.

Miller, Donna Mae, and Kathryn R. E. Russell. *Sport: A Contemporary View.* Lea and Febiger, Philadelphia, 1971.

Mravetz, Robert Joseph. *The Influence a Famous Athlete Has on the Development of the Ideal Self in Eighth Grade Boys and Girls.* Microfiched Ph.D. dissertation, Ohio State University, 1970.

Murray, J. Alex, ed. *Sport or Athletics: A North American Dilemma.* Seminar on Canadian-American Relations, University of Windsor, Ontario, Canada, 1974.

Noll, Roger G., ed. *Government and the Sports Business.* Brookings Institution, Washington, D.C., 1974.

Novak, Michael. *The Joy of Sports.* Basic Books, New York, 1976.

Oberteuffer, Delbert. "On Learning Values Through Sport." *Quest,* 1 (December 1963), 23–29.

Ogilvie, Bruce C., and Thomas A. Tutko. "Sport: If You Want to Build Character, Try Something Else." *Psychology Today,* 5 (October 1971), 60–63.

Olsen, Jack. *The Black Athlete: A Shameful Story.* Time-Life Books, New York, 1968.

Orlick, Terry, and Cal Botterill. *Every Kid Can Win.* Nelson-Hall, Chicago, 1975.

Osman, Jack Douglas. *The Feasibility of Using Selected Value Clarifying Strategies in a Health Education Course for Future Teachers.* Microfiched Ph.D. dissertation, Ohio State University, 1971.

Osterhoudt, Robert G. "The Kantian Ethic as a Principle of Moral Conduct in Sport." *Quest,* 19 (January 1973), 118–123.

Pearson, Kathleen M. "Deception, Sportsmanship, and Ethics." *Quest,* 19 (January 1973), 115–117.

Peters, R. S. *Ethics and Education,* abridged. Scott, Foresman and Company, Glenview, Ill., 1967.

Pustilnick, Jack, and Dale Riepe, eds. *The Structure of Philosophy.* Littlefield, Adams and Company, Totowa, N.J., 1966.

Ray, Harold L. "Let's Have a Friendly Game of War!" *Quest,* 14 (June 1970), 28–41.

Sadler, William A., Jr. "Competition Out of Bounds: Sport in American Life." *Quest,* 19 (January 1973), 124–132.

Sage, George H., ed. *Sport and American Society: Selected Readings,* 2d ed. Addison-Wesley, Reading, Mass., 1974, Chapter 7.

Sheehan, Thomas J., and William L. Alsop. "Educational Sport." *JOHPER,* 43 (May 1972), 41–45.

Siedentop, Daryl. *Physical Education: Introductory Analysis,* 2d ed. Wm. C. Brown, Dubuque, Ia., 1976.

Smith, Leverett T., Jr. *The American Dream and the National Game.* Bowling Green University Popular Press, Bowling Green, Ohio, 1975.

Snyder, Eldon E., and Elmer Spreitzer. "Basic Assumptions in the World of Sports." *Quest,* 24 (Summer 1975), 3–9.

"Sport and Value-Oriented Concerns." In *Sport and the Body: A Philosophical Symposium.* Edited by Ellen W. Gerber. Lea and Febiger, Philadelphia, 1972.

Telender, Rick. "Beyond the 35-Yard Line." *American Libraries* (January 1974), 20–24.

Tutko, Thomas, and William Bruns. *Winning Is Everything and Other American Myths.* Macmillan, New York, 1976.

VanderZwaag, Harold J. *Toward a Philosophy of Sport.* Addison-Wesley, Reading, Mass., 1972.

Weiss, Paul. *Sport: A Philosophic Inquiry.* Southern Illinois University Press, Carbondale, 1969.

Werner, Alfred C., and Edward Gottheil. "Personality Development and Participation in College Athletics." *Research Quarterly,* 37 (March 1966), 126–131.

Zeigler, Earle F. *Philosophical Foundations for Physical, Health, and Recreation Education.* Prentice-Hall, Englewood Cliffs, N.J., 1964.

———. *Problems in the History and Philosophy of Physical Education and Sport.* Prentice-Hall, Englewood Cliffs, N.J., 1968.

———, Maxwell L. Howell, and Marianna Trekell, eds. *Research in the History, Philosophy, and International Aspects of Physical Education and Sport: Bibliographies and Techniques.* Stipes Publishing Company, Champaign, Ill., 1971.

# V Modern American Physical Education

# 12 The Formal Profession of Physical Education

When we study physical education we eventually must face what many physical educators consider a question of major importance: Is physical education a profession or a discipline? Is it either one? After discussing this issue, we will study the different professional organizations in which physical educators are involved and the major publications that are used by physical educators. We will conclude the chapter by discussing how the physical education student works to develop professionally.

## The Field of Physical Education: Discipline or Profession?

In recent years many physical educators have been debating the exact status of the field of physical education, whether it is a profession, a discipline, or either one. Where does physical education fit into the academic scheme of things? This study need not divide the field, for physical education has many dimensions; one of these is a body of knowledge, which is required by a discipline, while other dimensions are the traits of a profession and professional concern. To determine the status of physical education, we need to understand exactly what a profession and a discipline are, then see whether physical education shows signs of the characteristics of either one. A field does not have to be *only* a discipline *or* a profession, however.

*Physical Education as a Profession.* For many years physical educators have referred to themselves as members of a profession, in this case the teaching profession. Although we often argue that we are members of a profession, the characteristics we use to show such a status are sometimes limited to our advantage. First we will look at the commonly accepted set of criteria for professional status suggested by

Abraham Flexner.[1] Flexner suggested six criteria or characteristics that determine whether a field is really a profession:

**1**    intellectual activity (a "body of knowledge")
**2**    a practical use
**3**    research resulting in new knowledge and ideas
**4**    self-organization
**5**    the capacity for communication (internal and external)
**6**    a dedication to helping others (altruism).

The first characteristic is that the activities are basically *intellectual.* While physical skills may be involved in performing the work, it must have an intellectual base, or "body of knowledge." The intellectual nature of the field must be one of the most important aspects of the work, rather than the physical or other skills used to apply the knowledge. This is perhaps where physical education is on the weakest ground when we say it is a profession, for some physical educators exhibit an anti-intellectual bent. This attitude may provide heated arguments with many non–physical educators.

The second characteristic is that the work is *practical.* The work has a genuine use, for while it must be based on knowledge, that knowledge has no value unless it is used. Most physical educators will argue that physical education has an intellectual base, and every physical educator will argue that the work is practical. The knowledge is applied to the practical use of developing and improving people's health, skills, and fitness.

The third characteristic of a profession is constant *research resulting in new knowledge and ideas,* which are then tested and applied in the professional work. This characteristic does apply to physical education, though many educators are dissatisfied with the small amount of research as well as the tendency to experiment only in the most narrowly practical areas. Some critics have also suggested that physical educators and coaches are the most resistant of all groups to change, even though research has shown that changes would be more useful.

The fourth characteristic of a profession is *formal self-organization.* Examples of such organization in physical education are the numerous professional groups—such as the American Alliance for Health, Physical Education, and Recreation (AAHPER)—many of which will be discussed later in this chapter. This characteristic is closely related to the fifth characteristic, which is the *capacity for communication.* A pro-

---

[1] Abraham Flexner, cited in Walter P. Kroll, *Perspectives in Physical Education,* Academic Press, New York, 1971, pp. 119–122.

fession sets up formal means of communication among its members not only to enable them to work together to solve common problems, but also to spread information. AAHPER assists physical educators in meeting these communication requirements not only by holding regular meetings at the state, district, and national levels, but also by sponsoring many publications.

The sixth characteristic of a profession is *altruism*—that is, the people who work in the profession are dedicated to helping others. The profession is characterized by concern for people's welfare, and it exists, at least in part, to help improve or protect others' lives. Few people would argue that this characteristic applies to teaching.

Most physical educators consider their field a profession. It does meet all Flexner's criteria to some degree (though there might be some arguments over the importance of some of the criteria). Charles A. Bucher, however, has given convincing arguments that physical education is not a fully matured profession; he suggests that it is an *emerging profession.*[2]

Do people see physical educators as rendering a "unique and essential social service," one that could not be rendered by a non-professional? Many people believe physical educators are doing a job that most well-coordinated people could do. Are physical educators selective about the people admitted to the field? Research has indicated consistently that the students majoring in the teacher preparation programs in our colleges are the least intelligent and gifted of our nation's college students—the least academically trained students—and that certification requirements sometimes vary so widely as to be almost meaningless. Are "rigorous training programs" provided for future members? There are many questions in this area also. Finally, is physical education "self-regulatory"? Are unethical or ill-prepared members dealt with within the field? This has not often been the case. Bucher suggests, rightly, that physical education still has not earned the full status of a profession, that it is still an emerging profession. Although some educators have argued that it has spent a long time emerging, its basic shortcomings are undeniable. While physical education's *goals* equal the characteristics of a profession, its *status* has not yet risen to meet those goals.

**Physical Education as a Discipline.** The difference between a discipline and a profession can be confusing, for a field can be a discipline while its members are the members of a profession. In essence, a discipline is an area of knowledge and theory that can exist purely for

[2] Charles A. Bucher, *Foundations of Physical Education,* 6th ed., C. V. Mosby, St. Louis, 1972, pp. 9–18.

itself; a profession must have a practical application. We have shown that physical education can have some practical use—such as developing people's health and fitness—and thus can be considered a profession. What, then, is necessary for physical education to be considered a discipline? Franklin M. Henry defines an academic discipline as

> . . . an organized body of knowledge collectively embraced in a formal course of learning. The acquisition of such knowledge is assumed to be an adequate and worthy objective as such, without any demonstration or requirement of practical application. The content is theoretical and scholarly as distinguished from technical and professional.[3]

Henry's definition, which is a synthesis of a number of definitions of the discipline, makes it clear that for physical education to be considered a discipline it must have what is often called a "body of knowledge"—that is, some scholarly knowledge with an important focus of attention. Is this the case with physical education? Henry and others believe that it is.

We might view a discipline as an area of basic science, concerned with the discovery of new knowledge, but not really obligated to find any use for that knowledge or apply it in any way. The primary object of the discipline is to *gain* the knowledge, while in the profession it is to *apply* the knowledge in a way that serves others.

Gerald S. Kenyon suggests that three criteria are necessary for a field to be a discipline: a focus of attention, a unique body of knowledge, and a particular mode of inquiry.[4] Other sources have suggested that the *focus of attention* of physical education as a discipline is the *human movement phenomena,*[5] or as Kenyon put it, a study of "man in motion." While there is some argument over whether physical education also possesses a *unique body of knowledge,* most physical educators do feel that such a body of knowledge does exist and that it is developing rapidly.

Kenyon suggests that physical education's problem in developing or claiming a discipline lies in the characteristic of having a *particular mode of inquiry* or research method used throughout the discipline, for

---

[3] Franklin M. Henry, "The Discipline of Physical Education," *Journal of Health, Physical Education, and Recreation,* 37 (September 1964), 32.

[4] Gerald S. Kenyon, "On the Conceptualization of Sub-Disciplines within an Academic Discipline Dealing with Human Movement," reprinted in *Contemporary Readings in Physical Education,* 3d ed., ed. Aileene S. Lockhart and Howard S. Slusher, Wm. C. Brown, Dubuque, Ia., 1975, 343–347.

[5] Celeste Ulrich and John M. Nixon, *Tones of Theory,* AAHPER, Washington, D.C., 1972, pp. 11–13.

several different research methods are used. Kenyon suggests that the field of study is still too broad and that the question of research method still must be settled. Many physical educators see a discipline of physical education emerging, not necessarily *from* the profession, but rather *parallel to* the profession—that is, a division of the field into the educators (profession) and the scholars (discipline). While neither the discipline nor the profession is fully developed, both are making rapid progress in physical education today. We need to remember that one need not exclude the other, however.

## Professional Organizations in Physical Education and Sport

Physical educators are involved in a multitude of professional organizations, the largest of which is the American Alliance for Health, Physical Education, and Recreation (AAHPER). AAHPER is a national organization dedicated to improving programs in all areas of physical education. With about 50,000 members nationally, AAHPER represents the major voice of physical educators in the United States today. Seven associations are included in the formal organization of AAHPER; these represent the largest interest groups within the membership:

1　American Association for Leisure and Recreation (AALR) is concerned with promoting leisure services and recreation education at the school, community, and national levels.
2　American School and Community Safety Association (ASCSA) is interested in all aspects of safety and safety education in the home, school, and community.
3　Association for the Advancement of Health Education (AAHE) is concerned with programs of health education in the schools, communities, and colleges, as well as with health-oriented legislation.
4　Association for Research, Administration and Professional Councils (ARAPC) might be viewed as a "catch-all" association of a number of smaller, more specialized interest groups, including administrators of different types of programs and persons interested in a number of areas of research in the field of physical education.
5　National Association for Girls and Women in Sport (NAGWS) is concerned with women's athletics at all levels, and its work includes producing rule books and sports guides in many areas. The women's intercollegiate sports organization, the AIAW, which is described later in the chapter, is part of this association.
6　National Association for Sport and Physical Education (NASPE), the largest of the associations, is concerned with people whose primary working interest lies in the areas of physical education and sport, which are promoted at all levels.

**7**    National Dance Association (NDA) is concerned with the development of dance both in and outside the educational systems of the nation.

AAHPER works in many ways to advance the profession. It holds annual national conventions—usually in the spring—which are rotated among the six regional districts of AAHPER. Each of the six districts also holds an annual convention, as does each state organization. These conventions provide an invaluable means of contact among physical educators of many different interests from across the country.

AAHPER also produces many publications. In addition to regular magazines in the largest areas of interest, it produces many materials designed to assist the teacher, clarify the work of physical educators, and promote the areas within physical education.

All members of AAHPER receive the newspaper *UPDATE* monthly during the school year (nine months). It is designed to give current schedules of meetings, tentative programs of conventions, and provide a few articles of general interest to the whole profession.

The *Journal of Physical Education and Recreation* (JOPER), which is the most widely read physical education magazine, also appears monthly during the nine months of the school year. Until 1975 it was the Journal of *Health,* Physical Education, and Recreation (JOHPER). While *JOPER* has slightly less current news than *UPDATE,* it contains many timely articles on both teaching practices and theory, columns devoted to the many special interest groups within physical education, and information on the new publications and products available to physical educators.

*Health Education* (formerly *School Health Review*) is the health educator's magazine, which appears six times yearly. It is concerned with all aspects of health education programs and practices.

*Research Quarterly* is a journal devoted entirely to reports of completed research in the fields of physical education. Appearing four times annually, it is designed to stimulate and communicate research among physical educators. It has research articles in all areas of physical education, though it tends to lean heavily toward physiological and motor skill learning research.

Each member of AAHPER receives at least two of the above four publications. The publications serve to improve communication within the profession and also help to improve teaching practices within the field.

The American Academy of Physical Education ("the Academy") was started by a small group of prominent physical educators in 1926 to advance knowledge and raise standards in physical education and to honor physical educators who show superior accomplishments. Its members, now numbering over one hundred, are elected by the other members. It is best known for its work in promoting excellence and initiating the discussion of new ideas in physical education. It also publishes *The Academy Papers* annually, which contains papers presented by its members on matters of importance or topical interest to physical educators. It is the highest honorary group in health, physical education, and recreation.

The National College Physical Education Association for Men (NCPEAM) was founded in 1897 under another name for men who worked in the areas of health and physical education at the college level. It seeks to promote the field at the college level and holds an annual national convention around New Year's Day. It publishes a number of articles and abstracts from its annual convention as the *Proceedings* of the group. It also publishes, in conjunction with the NAPECW, the quarterly monograph *Quest,* which is oriented toward the philosophical areas of the field.

The National Association of Physical Education for College Women (NAPECW) was formed in 1924, though its origins can be traced to 1909. It is concerned with studying and promoting all aspects of physical education programs for women, and its members are women who teach on the college level. It is the copublisher of *Quest,* along with the NCPEAM, and it holds a summer workshop on alternate years.

The American School Health Association (ASHA) was formed in 1926 by a group of physicians who were concerned about health services and instruction in the schools. Its members are people in the school health work areas, such as school nurses. It publishes the *Journal of School Health,* which appears ten times yearly.

The National Recreation and Park Association (NRPA) grew from the Playground Association of America, which was started in 1906. The association is concerned with all areas of recreation, parks, and park services.

The National Intramural Association was founded in 1950. It is interested in promoting and expanding intramural activities and promoting professional contacts among intramural directors. With close ties to both AAHPER and the NRPA, it publishes the *Proceedings of the Annual Intramural Conference.*

Some professional groups are beginning to pursue scholarly studies in areas of sport, such as the North American Society for the Psychology of Sports and Physical Activity (NASPSPA), which was begun in 1965. Its members are psychologists, psychiatrists, and physical educators who are interested in research in the psychological areas relating to sport and other physical activities. It publishes the *Sport Psychology Bulletin* four times each year.

The Philosophic Society for the Study of Sport (PSSS) was founded in 1972 in conjunction with a regional meeting of the American Philosophical Association. It is essentially interested in scholarly study of the philosophical aspects of sport and publishes the *Journal of the Philosophy of Sport.*

The North American Society for Sport History (NASSH) was founded in 1973. Its members are interested in historical studies of aspects of sport, which is interpreted broadly to include physical education. It publishes an annual *Proceedings* of its convention and also publishes the *Journal of Sport History,* a scholarly journal of articles in aspects of sport history, twice annually. Its members include the Canadian physical educators who publish the *Canadian Journal of History of Sport and Physical Education* twice each year.

The American College of Sports Medicine (ACSM), founded in 1954, is interested in promoting knowledge and research in areas concerning sporting activities and the accompanying injuries and disabilities, including their prevention, care, and treatment. It shares in the publication of the *Journal of Sports Medicine and Physical Fitness,* and it publishes the quarterly *ACSM Newsletter* and *Science and Medicine in Sports.*

The American Corrective Therapy Association (ACTA) was started in 1946. It is concerned with research and practice in areas relating to the physical and mental rehabilitation and therapy of persons with various types of disabilities. It publishes the *Journal of American Corrective Therapy* twice monthly.

The Physical Education Society of the Young Men's Christian Association of North America was begun in 1903. Its objects are to promote the goals of the YMCA and to promote physical education activities as well. It publishes the *Journal of Physical Education* every two months.

The Phi Epsilon Kappa Fraternity was started on a small scale in 1912. It is interested in promoting research and an international exchange of information in the areas of health education, physical education, recreation education, and safety education. It publishes the magazine *The Physical Educator,* which appears quarterly.

Delta Psi Kappa is an organization begun in 1916 for women professional students in health, physical education, and recreation. It works to raise professional standards and encourage women to conduct distinguished research. It publishes *The Foil* twice each year.

The National Education Association (NEA), founded in 1857, is the nation's largest professional organization of teachers, with over one million members. Its primary concern is promoting education in the United States, at the same time working for the best interests of the teachers. AAHPER is affiliated with the NEA. Its most widely circulated publication is *Today's Education.*

Physical educators work not only in
school systems, but also at recreational
centers such as YMCAs and YWCAs.
(Courtesy Cary Wolinsky, Stock, Boston)

There are many professional fraternities for all educators, just as
there are for physical educators exclusively. A prominent example is
the Phi Delta Kappa educational fraternity for men, which works to
advance educational standards and research and includes among its
publications the monthly *Phi Delta Kappan.*

The United States Olympic Committee (USOC) was discussed in
its relationship with the International Olympic Committee (IOC) in Chapter 5. It works to promote the Olympic games in the United States,
raises the funds to send the U.S. Olympic teams to the games, and conducts the Olympic trials, in which the team members are chosen.

The Amateur Athletic Union (AAU) was founded in 1888 to protect
amateur sports from the growing threat of professionalism. It is run by
volunteers across the United States and conducts contests in many
different sports at local through national levels. Its counterpart and frequent antagonist is the largest collegiate sports body, the NCAA.

The National Collegiate Athletic Association (NCAA) grew from a
body formed in 1906. It seeks to uphold the member institutions' control of their collegiate sports programs for men. It publishes rule books,
establishes policies, and organizes national collegiate championships
in many sports. Membership in one of the three divisions or classes of
the NCAA depends primarily on the amount of emphasis (mostly financial) the member institution places on its intercollegiate sports program.

The NCAA has had jurisdictional arguments with the AAU throughout its existence.

The Association for Intercollegiate Athletics for Women (AIAW) was begun in 1971 by AAHPER's Division of Girls' and Women's Sports (DGWS, now NAGWS) to provide a national body to control women's intercollegiate athletics. Its goal is to promote women's athletics while trying to avoid the problems that have continued in programs of men's athletics.

The National Association of Intercollegiate Athletics (NAIA) was started in 1940. Although it has a number of large schools among its members, it is still considered the body representing "small college sports." Its member schools generally (though not always) put a lower priority and financial investment into sports than do the schools in the NCAA, though some colleges hold dual membership in the NCAA and the NAIA.

The National Junior College Athletic Association (NJCAA) was started in 1938 to sponsor intercollegiate sports competition in the junior colleges. It conducts a number of national championships and invitational events in many sports each year.

The National Federation of State High School Associations (NFSHSA), which has changed its title since it was founded in 1923, was originally concerned with promoting high school sports and protecting school teams from some of the early excesses of competition. It has dropped *Athletic* from its name because many state versions of the National Federation included activities such as band and speech contests that did not fit into the definition of the old national title. The National Federation sets suggested eligibility standards, issues national sports rule books and officials' guides, and suggests standards for intersectional high school competitions. It has begun issuing rule books for women's high school sports as the women's programs have begun to expand rapidly in the 1970s.

Many other national, regional, and local associations of teachers and coaches throughout the country are also of interest to physical educators, and just as there are many professional journals of education and physical education, there are also coaching journals and publications. Some of the publications are devoted to single sports, while others include all sports. Two of the most widely used coaching magazines are *Athletic Journal,* which has an emphasis slightly closer to the college level than *Scholastic Coach,* which is directed more toward the high school level. Because both periodicals cover all major sports and contain articles that relate to coaching problems and practices, they are very useful to coaches and physical education teachers. As a beginning teacher, you should try to become familiar with the publications available in the fields of education and physical education, and if you plan to coach, you should become well acquainted with the more specialized publications available in your coaching area or sport.

## Becoming an Involved Professional: Development and Responsibilities

Becoming an involved committed member of a profession is an ongoing process. As a student preparing for a career in the fields of physical education, you are working to meet the minimal standards for admission to the profession. After graduation when you join the profession, you need to work to upgrade yourself as a professional. Beverly Seidel and Matthew Resick have written about the various aspects of becoming a professional, and we will study briefly the categories or areas of professional commitment or involvement at both the student and practicing professional levels.[6]

*School Selection.* The future physical educator is first concerned with picking a college or university for undergraduate or graduate preparation. In many cases students give too little thought to the institution and what it has to offer. An undergraduate institution should have a strong major program in your area of interest, whether it be in physical education, health education, recreation, safety education, or dance, for you are not likely to specialize beyond this point at the undergraduate level. In fact, you can receive a good undergraduate program in the many combined health and physical education major programs found primarily in the smaller schools, though you should make sure that a broad, well-balanced preparation is available at the school.

You should study the requirements of the school for admission to the major program: What type of nonmajor courses are required by the department or the school? Who teaches the undergraduate students: the professors, or teaching assistants? What kind of reputation does the school have in the state and the region? Are its graduates respected? Are its graduates successful? AAHPER regularly revises a directory of all schools in the United States with major programs, which may help in choosing an undergraduate school.

These concerns change in emphasis when you prepare to go into graduate school. Matters such as the regional and national reputation of the school and department should be considered. What do the faculty of other schools think of the school and its graduates? Where

---

[6] Beverly L. Seidel and Matthew C. Resick, *Physical Education: An Overview,* Addison-Wesley, Reading, Mass., 1972, pp. 186–192.

do its graduates find employment? What are the admission and retention standards of the school? Are its professors respected specialists with advanced training in their area of specialization? Where were the professors trained? Finally, you should remember that many benefits are gained by studying at several schools, rather than earning all of the degrees at a single institution. More reputable graduate institutions are refusing to allow their students to earn all their degrees through the doctorate at the same institution because of the risk of inbreeding and developing a narrow, provincial viewpoint.

*Library Development and Use.* This category might be called "developing the tools of the trade," for at the undergraduate level it is concerned with building a strong personal library of professional publications and at the same time with learning to use the public or school library and its resources. Library skills are critical to success in the professional work; you must be at home in the library, and your personal library should be broad. As you begin to work in specialized areas, however, your more narrow outlook of interests may be detected as your personal library grows.

A common complaint is that too many physical educators seem to be nonreaders and that their reading habits reflect a seeming lack of general education and only a very narrow professional education. As professionals, we should read widely, including current newspapers and general periodicals as well as the professional publications, for they help us to establish common lines of communications with non–physical educators.

*Professional Preparation.* A good program of professional preparation is also essential. The physical educator needs a strong, broad undergraduate education, but the process of education does not end with the bachelor's degree. Not only do most states require further academic work before any type of permanent certification is awarded, but more specialized work, such as is available in graduate programs, will assist you in developing expertise in some area or areas. The process of professional preparation can consume many years, but it can be a challenging, stimulating experience rather than a discouraging one.

*Professional Membership.* Membership in professional organizations is one sign of true professional commitment. As an undergraduate, you will find such organizations as student major clubs and such professional fraternities as Phi Epsilon Kappa on campus. You will also find that reduced membership fees are available in most state organizations and AAHPER. These student memberships include most professional privileges, as well as receipt of the professional publications.

When you graduate and become a member of the profession, you should also become a member of organizations such as AAHPER and the state-level version of AAHPER. Many other professional organizations, such as those we mentioned earlier in this chapter, can benefit an active professional member. As a physical educator with a genuine commitment to the profession, you will want to be involved in some of these professional groups in some active way; they are all dedicated to advancing the profession in some area of interest and work.

***Professional Meetings.*** Professional membership shows some interest in the condition of the profession, but a real commitment involves attendance at professional meetings. Many types of professional meetings take place regularly around the world—more than any physical educator could hope to attend and still do any other work. The professional meetings are the most exciting means of communication among members of professional groups, for here the physical educator can meet many people from different backgrounds and share common problems and discoveries. In many respects the greatest impetus to change may be said to result from the stimulus and challenge of professional meetings.

At the undergraduate level, you will find such activities as state student major conventions that are completely planned and run by students. Attendance at these will help you to experience a feeling of involvement and to gain experiences and contacts that are similar to those gained at professional meetings. You may also wish to attend the specialized clinics, which are held for such areas of interest as sports coaching or officiating particular sports, or the physical fitness and sport clinics of the President's Council on Physical Fitness and Sports. These meetings are useful because they can help broaden your outlook and your experiences as a student physical education major.

As a practicing physical educator, you may still wish to attend the clinics but you will perhaps become more aware of the regular professional conventions. Physical educators most commonly attend such meetings as the annual AAHPER national conventions held at each of the state, district, and national levels. As an involved physical educator, you should try to attend one or more of these conventions annually, if possible, for the experience is invaluable. Most other professional groups have an annual convention, and the members are depended upon to plan the meetings and the programs.

Mere attendance at the professional meetings is not enough, however: For a profession to grow and improve, the members must be directly involved in its activities. Many professionals have become involved in high-level organization work simply because no one else was willing to help. The opportunities for direct involvement at all levels of professional activities are very great, and as undergraduate and graduate students, you should try to get involved. Most larger conventions have special sections and meetings for the students, so you should not feel that your involvement will not be wanted before graduation. There is room for any person willing to help.

**Research and Writing.** All too few physical educators are involved directly in research and writing activities. A profession and discipline need continual research to grow. Only through research can we extend the boundaries of our knowledge and improve our practices. While the areas in which research can be useful are almost unlimited, physical educators as a group have been occasionally ridiculed for both the lack of much research and the low quality of some research projects. The only real solution for such a shortcoming is to make the members of the field realize that *every* member is capable of conducting research at some level. In many cases the reason why members have not conducted research is because they were not encouraged and because they doubted their ability to do so successfully. While the lack of time is often used as an argument for why research has not been conducted, the real reasons are more likely to be a lack of self-confidence and encouragement. Physical educators should feel obligated to conduct research on some small scale regularly, whether or not it is "major" or "significant" research.

The same reasons are also cited for the failure of physical educators to write about their activities or the state of the profession. How many times have people read professional articles and reacted with "I could have written that"? So why was it not done? We need to write to share our ideas, our concerns, our theories. Articles can show others how we solved problems they are now facing.

A profession and a discipline run and grow on the professional meeting and the written word. Write about your ideas, and encourage others to write theirs. Do not be afraid to write because you fear ridicule or lack confidence in your opinions. As physical educators we must be willing to accept valid criticism if we are to grow as professionals; we must also encourage writing and research on a massive scale. The idea behind encouraging writing and research on a grand scale is not to inundate the field with poor-quality work: Rather, the more work that is done, the greater the odds that we will produce more and better scholars and writers to help us improve the field.

While the national meetings may be flooded with people willing to write and speak, this is often not the case at the district level, and only rarely is it the case at the state level. Get involved, and see where it leads you. The field of physical education will be the better for it.

Whereas some physical educators teach a broad range of general skills, others are specialists in a particular skill area and give private as well as group lessons. (Courtesy Cary Wolinsky, Stock, Boston)

**Teaching.**  When most people think of physical education they think of teaching, for we think of most physical educators as being teachers, whether or not this is the case.  The physical educator should be dedicated to quality teaching, just as to quality research and writing, for our greatest contact with the public is as teachers.  The future of physical education rests largely on the opinions of the future citizens whom we teach in the schools.  Coaching is another form of teaching, when it is done well.  We should attempt quality coaching, but it should never interfere with the quality of our teaching, for our teaching programs are also the base unit of our public relations programs.

**Commitment.**  If any word is to be chosen to describe the most desirable characteristic in the professional physical educator, or in any member of any profession, it is *commitment.*  True professionals must be committed to their fields.  Only by being committed, totally involved physical educators can we hope to achieve the genuine state of member of our profession or discipline.  Furthermore, our commitment will be most valuable if it is a *commitment to excellence.*

## The Next Step: Work in the Field of Physical Education

We have now discussed the profession and discipline of physical education to understand how to prepare for and become involved in the field.  We now need to look at the employment opportunities in the areas of physical education, for your training would seem pointless if you were unable to use it. We will study all the employment opportunities, for physical education is a broad field indeed, and even if you do not plan to teach, many nonteaching opportunities are available.

## Suggested Readings

Abernathy, Ruth, and Maryann Waltz. "Toward a Discipline: First Steps First." *Quest,* 2 (April 1964), 1–7.

Brackenbury, Robert L. "Physical Education, An Intellectual Emphasis?" *Quest,* 1 (December 1963), 3–6.

Falls, Harold B., and Wayne C. McKinney. "A Philosophy of Research Preparation for the Physical Educator." *Quest,* 14 (June 1970), 44–49.

Fraleigh, Warren P. "A Prologue to the Study of Theory Building in Physical Education." *Quest,* 12 (May 1969), 26–33.

Gardner, John W. *Excellence: Can We Be Equal and Excellent Too?* Harper & Row, New York, 1961.

"Graduate Study in Physical Education." *Quest,* 25 (Winter 1976). Entire issue.

Griffin, Patricia S. "What's a Nice Girl Like You Doing in a Profession Like This?" *Quest,* 19 (January 1973), 96–101.

McIntyre, Martin. "A Model for the 70's." *JOHPER,* 44 (November-December 1973), 28–30.

Morford, W. R. "Toward a Profession, Not a Craft." *Quest,* 18 (June 1972), 88–93.

"The Nature of a Discipline." *Quest,* 9 (December 1967). Entire issue.

"The Scholarly Enterprise." *Quest,* 20 (June 1973). Entire issue.

Teeple, Janet. "Graduate Study in Physical Education—What Should It Be?" *Quest,* 12 (May 1969), 66–70.

# *13* Career Opportunities in Physical Education

Today's student in physical education is increasingly concerned with the future job opportunities in the fields of physical education. The decade of the 1970s continued an economic decline that affected the hiring and retention practices of the schools and resulted in an unstable employment situation in the very stable area of teaching. Although there are many nonteaching options in physical education, we traditionally think of teaching when we ask of the employment situation in physical education.

## What Is the Job Situation in Education?

The job situation in education is increasingly tight, especially so in physical education. We usually think of physical education as a teaching field, and a popular one at that. As a college major, it is popular with athletes, many of whom are interested primarily in coaching in the schools. Although there was a shortage of teachers in the early 1960s, by the mid-1970s the education situation had reversed itself: The number of students in the public schools (through the high school level) was decreasing, while the number of teachers had increased far beyond the needs of the schools. A considerable oversupply of teachers had appeared in most subject and grade areas, and the number of teachers being produced each year exceeds the number of teaching vacancies by a respectable margin.

During the 1950s and 1960s the school population made rapid, vast increases. As the children born during the series of "baby booms" that began during World War II and continued during the Korean War reached school age, the schools had to be enlarged rapidly; American education seemed to turn into an exercise in building construction. This expansion was also felt in the colleges and universities during the mid- to late 1960s, for a larger proportion of the high school graduates were continuing their education past the high school level.

Two other developments of the 1960s furthered the growth of the student population above the high school level: the rise of the community college and technical school across the United States, and the trend of many schools toward an "open admissions" policy. Although a few states, most notably California, had strong systems of community colleges before 1960, the period of the sixties saw almost every state begin to push the founding and development of local two-year community colleges—which were oriented toward the work of the first two years of liberal arts and sciences college study—and technical schools —which were oriented toward one- and two-year degree programs in many different trades. As a result, the post–high school population in education multiplied at a startling rate.

During the 1970s evidence of a surprising reversal of the school population trend appeared. Adults were becoming more concerned with birth control; younger women were preferring to have fewer children; and the size of the typical family began to drop. Although the "zero population growth" goal of many birth control advocates was hardly being realized, the number of students in the schools hit a high-water mark, then began a gradual decline. This decline is expected to continue for at least another decade.

The effect of the declining birth rate on the school population and teacher needs was compounded by another trend: the consolidation of schools, particularly at the middle, or junior high, school and high school levels. Smaller schools were combining into larger schools for several reasons; two of the major reasons were to permit the schools to offer a broader educational program while eliminating the unnecessary duplication of teachers within the school district and to allow the cities to try to end the age-old problem of racially segregated schools.

All these changes were compounded during the mid-1970s by another unexpected problem: a long-lasting period of recession that affected the ability of the people to support the system of education as it had been in the past.

What is the result of these several trends? We are faced with an unexpected decline in the number of teachers needed—just as the earlier products of the "baby boom" began entering the market as newly qualified teachers. And because of the financial problems of the schools, many teachers have found themselves out of work. In a period of a few years, a time of the schools' working to attract teachers has changed to a time of the teachers' having to work to attract the schools.

What does the oversupply of teachers mean, in practical terms? At the elementary through high school levels, two possibilities are obvious, but they may never materialize because of the financial crisis.

First, the schools have an unprecedented opportunity to hire only the most qualified applicants as teachers and also to remove teachers who are poorly qualified or incompetent. Unfortunately, teachers are usually retained on the basis of seniority, and the quality of their work does not often figure in determining who will be released from employment. To a considerable extent, the first possible result has failed to happen.

The second possible effect of the oversupply of teachers would result from the schools' using them to make radical cuts in the size of the classes taught by the teachers. A commonly held, though not well proven, view of educators is that more and better learning is possible in a smaller class than in a larger one. Unfortunately, this possibility also has failed to come true. In fact, the financial crunch has in many cases resulted in the release of so many teachers that the typical class size has increased despite the teacher surplus.

The situation is somewhat different at the college level. The increased number of two-year community colleges and technical schools, combined with the growing trend to continue school after high school, will result in continued increases in the college population. Although there is currently a teacher surplus at the college level, the opportunities for college teachers will probably improve again in a few years.

So what is the demand for physical education teachers? The demand for male teachers is small. In fact, there are far more qualified male teachers of physical education than there are jobs. Although there are more qualified females than jobs, the demand for women physical educators is strong, and if anything, it is increasing. The controversial Title IX federal funding programs that were aimed at eliminating sexual discrimination in the schools resulted in a huge growth of women's sports in the schools and colleges, and the demand for women coaches is almost impossible to meet. While the job situation in physical education is much better for women than for men, there are numerous exceptions for people with specialities, as we will discuss later in the chapter.

## Teaching as a Career: Pro and Con

Most people who consider physical education as a major field are thinking in terms of teaching and coaching, yet they often have given little thought to the good and bad points of teaching as a career. Before we can discuss the opportunities in the teaching areas of physical education we need to understand these positive and negative factors that affect one's enjoyment of teaching.

***Positive Aspects of Teaching.*** Teaching is generally considered to have many benefits as an occupation. The teacher has traditionally held a position of respect in the community. The reason for this respect can be traced to another aspect of the teacher's work, for the teacher makes a definite contribution to society. Teaching is vital to the survival of the community, and a good teacher is a positive influence on many young people.

Teaching is considered an occupation with good job security, though the recent financial crisis has affected this security to some degree. Generally speaking, teachers are well paid for their services. Although salaries might be higher, which can be said of almost any occupation, the last two decades have seen tremendous changes in the level of teachers' salaries. Also, teachers generally receive automatic pay raises each year, which is true of very few other occupations. Teachers also enjoy the benefit of long vacation periods; they work an average of nine to ten months of the year. While the extra time may be devoted to an additional job, it is available for travel, study, and many other opportunities. The long vacation periods have made teaching attractive to persons who wish to have more free time to pursue their other interests.

Perhaps the greatest positive aspect of teaching as a career, however, is the personal satisfaction it provides. A person who really wants to teach will find many aspects of the work satisfying, for teaching carries a degree of personal involvement in the success of others that is found in few other occupations. Many teachers continue to teach for this reason alone.

**Negative Aspects of Teaching.** Too few prospective teachers stop to look at the negative aspects of teaching as a career, for teaching can have as many bad points as it has good ones. Perhaps the best known negative aspect of teaching as a career is that teaching is an overcrowded field, though this is not a negative aspect of teaching as a practice. The competition for teaching jobs is very difficult, and it becomes more difficult each year. More candidates are appearing annually, and they are better qualified candidates for the available jobs, in terms of educational training, degrees, and teaching experience.

While teaching has traditionally been a respected occupation in the abstract sense, teachers as a body are increasingly viewed by many people with a lack of respect. The schools and teachers have begun to suffer from a lack of public support from a public that is increasingly dissatisfied with the schools and their work. This problem carries over into the area of the teacher's salary. While salaries are not low, and while they have risen rapidly, salaries are low compared to the education and expense required to qualify for them. While schools much prefer to hire teachers with master's degrees, the salary increase gained by earning this degree will be only a small fraction of the cost of the degree, and if the degree is earned in a full-time study program, the loss of a full year's teaching salary must be added to the cost of the degree. The educational requirements for the jobs are not consistent with the salaries offered when the requirements are met.

Finally, today's teachers are finding that they have increasingly heavy workloads, which makes doing a good job more difficult. Although a large surplus of qualified teachers is available, fewer teachers are being employed because of the schools' financial problems. The result is larger student loads per teacher, combined with less time for recovering from and preparing for teaching the classes. The large quantities of paperwork that are a traditional part of the educational bureaucracy make the workload heavier, for too few school systems provide enough clerical workers or teaching aides to keep the teachers from being bogged down in nonteaching duties.

**To Teach or Not to Teach.** As you can see, teaching has both its good side and its bad side. As a prospective teacher, you must look at both sides carefully, for you must decide which aspects of teaching carry the most weight for you. For many teachers the overall satisfaction of a career devoted to helping other people outweighs all of the negative considerations, while for other persons the workload or pay situation is enough to drive them away from teaching. You must decide which of these positive and negative aspects is most important to you as you consider teaching as a career.

## Basic Qualities of the Successful Teacher

What makes a successful teacher? We have talked about the good and bad points of a teaching career—and later we will discuss how the physical educator is trained for a career—but what are the basic, general qualities needed if a person hopes to become a successful teacher? While each person can produce a list of suggested necessary qualities, we will look at a brief list of important qualities for the successful teacher.

**Teaching Personality and Interests.** Successful teaching requires a good combination of personal qualities and interests. A good personality is necessary; the teacher should enjoy people, work well with them, and have a good sense of humor. The teacher must be interested in the educational process and in the students. An interest in the needs and interests of the students is an important part of successful teaching. Even if a prospective teacher possesses the other qualities already mentioned, a poor personality can severely hamper the chances of teaching success. A teacher must *want* to teach and must *enjoy* teaching.

**Strong Educational Background.** In addition to having intellectual ability, the successful teacher needs a good, broad educational background, which means more than having a good preparation in the major field. Teaching calls for a broadly based high school and college program of study in the liberal arts and sciences. The teacher needs to have some exposure to and understanding of the breadth of human experience and knowledge. The teacher's educational background and intellect are closely allied to the next quality.

**Communication Skills.** Teachers need to be skilled in both verbal and written communication. They must be able to express themselves clearly, to be able to explain their thoughts and ideas to other people. Teaching also involves many written reports; in fact, much of what teachers learn comes from information written by other teachers. Without communication skills, successful teaching is almost impossible. Unfortunately, communication is one of the areas where prospective teachers today are the weakest.

**Health and Physical Skills.** The successful teacher needs to be healthy, simply because the unhealthy person is physically less able to do a thorough job of teaching, particularly in an area involving physical skills as physical education does. In physical education in particular, the teacher must have good motor ability, a good combination of coordination, flexibility, strength, and speed. The teacher needs to be skilled in performing the activities that are going to be taught, for not only will the teacher have to demonstrate the skills in many cases, but the ability to perform the skills gives the teacher a far better understanding of the components of the skills and the problems that may be encountered by the student in learning the skills.

**Intellectual Ability.** If one single quality of the teacher is to be considered the most important, perhaps intellectual ability would be that quality. While a person does not have to be a genius to teach successfully, a person of poor or even average intellectual ability is at a distinct disadvantage. Good teachers must be able to understand what they are teaching at higher levels than they present the material to the students. Also, the teacher should be able to serve as an example to the students, which is difficult if the students consider the teacher an intellectual inferior. All education has an intellectual base, and a prospective teacher needs the intellectual ability and intelligence to work at a reasonable level of accomplishment. The teacher needs to be intelligent and have a strong interest in learning.  A person with little respect for learning can hardly be expected to be a very dedicated teacher.

## Types of Teaching Jobs

When most people think of employment opportunities in physical education, they think in terms of teaching opportunities.  The field of physical education is so closely tied to teaching and coaching that we rarely stop to realize the many nonteaching opportunities.  Before we look at the nonteaching possibilities, however, we should look at some of the many types of teaching jobs in the different areas of physical education, for it is a broader field than many teachers realize.

*Physical Education.*  While we have consistently referred to physical education in the broad sense—that is, by including all the areas of the field, such as health and recreation—we will now refer to jobs in physical education under the narrow definition.  Most physical educators who teach do so in the area that most people refer to as physical education.  Although we usually think physical education teachers work with basic activity classes at the high school level, the field has many levels of teaching opportunities.

The lowest level of employment, in terms of age, is working with preschool and elementary school children.  This age group is sometimes broken into two groups, with the younger group referred to as "K–3," or kindergarten through grade 3.  Teaching at this level is increasingly being done by specialists rather than traditional classroom teachers.  They most often work with activities in the movement education and perceptual motor activities area, rather than teach games and sports skills, for children at this age benefit more from activities aimed at developing the most basic of movement skills.

The upper elementary grades are sometimes combined with the grades of the middle or junior high school to cover a range of grades from 4 through 9.  For this age group, the teacher moves more into games and sports skills, though they are not of a strenuous nature, for the bodies of students in this age range are developing rapidly.  The teachers of this age group will find that the wide range in body sizes, strength, endurance, and skills of their students requires careful adjustments in the physical education program.  Many teachers who wish to teach at the high school level begin their teaching careers at the middle school level, in grades 7 through 9.

The next level is the high school level—sometimes referred to as "senior high school"—which includes grades 10 through 12.  At this level the teachers ideally teach more advanced skills, more strenuous activities, and some lifetime sports, and they may work with coeducational activities. In most cases the teachers at this level (and many teachers at the middle school level) are also involved in coaching some sports activities. At this level the prospective teacher is highly likely to encounter job openings in private schools or academies, in addition to the public schools. These private schools may have been started for a number of reasons—some of them academic, some religious, some essentially political.

Beyond the high school level there are two basic types of educational institutions. One type is aimed at terminal degree programs of a practical nature. These are most often technical schools or community colleges whose programs usually last one or two years. Whether physical education is offered in schools of this nature depends on the educational philosophy and goals of the state, county, or community sponsoring the school.

The other type of institution is the traditional college, such as the junior college (with two-year programs, usually liberal arts oriented) and the senior college or university (with four-year programs and, in many cases, graduate programs). The goals of these institutions may seem less practical, for they are less often aimed at learning to perform a single, money-earning skill. Most of these institutions have physical education programs, and many of the colleges and universities also have programs for physical education majors.

The teacher is more likely to be a specialist at the college level. Some college teachers primarily teach activity classes, and they may do most of their teaching in the narrow range of four to six specific activities rather than teach a little bit from every type of physical activity. Some college teachers work primarily in the teacher preparation program, either in the coaching theory area, the professional skills areas, the scientific foundations areas, or the other theory areas, such as administration and measurement and evaluation. Some college teachers work primarily in intramural activities or in research areas, while others work primarily as administrators of programs in physical education. As the academic level at which the teacher works gets higher, the variety of teaching jobs increases considerably.

Many job possibilities in the teaching areas have been discussed by Bryant J. Cratty and James E. Bryant.[1] We have indicated the basic type of job performed by the physical education teacher through the college level, but there are other teaching possibilities in addition to those in the regular public and private schools. A teacher may work for

---

[1] Bryant J. Cratty, *Career Potentials in Physical Activity,* Prentice-Hall, Englewood Cliffs, N.J., 1971; and James E. Bryant, "Some Possibilities for Employment in Physical Education's Allied Fields," *Physical Educator,* 31 (December 1974), 193–195.

the government and teach in schools on armed forces bases, both in the United States and in foreign nations. These teachers enjoy many of the benefits of governmental service employment. A teacher may teach for the United States government or for a foreign government under government-sponsored programs, such as the Peace Corps.

*Health Education.* Health education has become a field that is often separated from physical education. Health educators are concerned with improving the health knowledge and practices of all people, though we commonly think of this work being done with school-age people. More schools below the college level are now hiring specialists in health education rather than having the health education classes taught by the physical education teacher, who often has very little training in health education. Many of the jobs in the field of health education and school health services are nonteaching jobs, which we will discuss later in the chapter.

*Recreation.* Recreation specialists are another group of workers who are growing rapidly, particularly at the community level. The number of recreation teachers is not great, though it is increasing. Recreation is taught primarily at the college and university level to persons majoring in the field of physical education or to people planning to specialize in recreation and recreational services. As many nations become more affluent and leisure time increases, the recreation specialist will gain increasing importance both inside and outside the educational system.

*Coaching.* The coaching of athletic teams has traditionally been an important part of the teaching duties of physical educators in the schools of the United States. Many persons will argue over whether coaching is, in fact, a form of teaching, but when it is done well and with a regard to more than the immediate aim of victory, coaching can be a very important type of teaching. Its effects seem to stay with students longer than other types of teaching.

Coaches are hired as teacher-coaches at the junior high or middle school level, high school level, and the college and university level. While state regulations usually require a middle or high school coach to be a teacher, this is not true at the college level. The larger the college is, the less likely the coach is to be a teacher as well. Coaching is perhaps the most popular aspect of physical education activities. It is largely responsible for creating much of the interest of future physical educators in the field. The interest and importance of coaching can be exaggerated, but we should not overreact by trying to cast out coaches as unworthy physical educators, for they have much to contribute to the field.

**Safety Education.** Safety education is a broad area that includes all areas of safety practices, including driver education. Many states have begun to require all younger drivers to complete an approved course of driver education before they can receive a license to drive. Many insurance companies offer lower rates to young people who have completed driver education courses. Safety in the use of bicycles and recreational vehicles has been a more recent addition to many programs of safety education. The field is concerned with the development of consciousness of safety procedures and an awareness of the dangers that exist in many activities.

**Dance.** The teaching of dance is also growing in interest in physical education. Many of the students who major or minor in dance activities become teachers either in the schools or by offering private lessons to students. While the larger number of teachers of dance are women, the number of men in dance is increasing. At the college level students have become interested in learning folk dances of many nations as a recreational activity, and at earlier ages, more students are specializing in activity areas, including dance, which is especially popular for young women. It offers many benefits in the development of coordination and grace.

**The Need for Specialists Is Increasing.** More specialists are needed in the schools in a number of areas. While physical education teachers and coaches are in oversupply as a group, many areas of teaching and coaching still are far from crowded. *Special education* is one area of need for teachers who can work with the "exceptional child." Teaching special education classes, or using "adapted activities," refers to teaching any person who is unable to benefit from the ordinary program of physical education activities. It can include working with gifted children, whose needs for more intellectual content or approaches to physical activities are rarely met. It can include working with children who have mental disabilities, such as the retarded, and with children who have any type of physical disability, ranging from temporary injury to blindness, deafness, and diseases such as muscular dystrophy and polio. The need for people who are skilled in the special education area is great.

Specialists are needed in areas such as aquatics and gymnastics, for some *specialized coaching areas* are still far from crowded. The oversupply of coaches is primarily in the so-called major sports, such as football and basketball. At this time the number of different sports

Because dance and movement skills are growing in popularity so rapidly, more specialists need to be trained in those areas. (Courtesy Anna Kaufman Moon, Stock, Boston)

offered in the schools is being expanded rapidly, but the expansion is handicapped by a lack of trained coaches. Because some sports that were primarily regional are beginning to spread across the nation, specialists are now needed in many parts of the country where they are rare.

Specialists are also needed in areas of *lifetime sports and coeducational activities,* which are also expanding rapidly. Many schools have changed the orientation of their program from fitness activities to lifetime sports, which requires some changes in the training of the teachers. At the same time governmental regulations and popular demand are calling for a greater emphasis on programs of coeducational activities rather than those in which all classes are grouped by sex. This change in the composition of the classes can affect the teaching content and methods, which requires new training and teachers with different areas of specialization.

The *women coaches* are perhaps the fastest growing group of specialists in the field today. The late 1960s and early 1970s have seen a massive increase in the number of women's athletics teams at the high school and college level. The need for trained women to coach these teams has far outstripped the supply, almost regardless of the

Another opportunity for physical educators is outdoors work with programs such as Outward Bound, which builds participants' self-confidence and self-image by showing them how they can fend for themselves in nature. (Courtesy Cary Wolinsky, Stock, Boston)

sport. This need, combined with the usual lack of a large surplus of women physical educators, has combined to open a very large job market for women physical educators who are specialists in one or more sports.

*Elementary school specialists* are another growing group. They are currently in short supply, though many schools have begun to work to fill that void. More elementary schools are hiring specialists to teach physical education in the elementary school or to act as advisors/supervisors of the classroom teachers who may do the actual teaching in the lower grades. The demand at this level is increasing, and teachers of both sexes are needed. The traditional elementary specialist has been female, which has created a greater market for male specialists.

*Challenge-oriented specialists* are in increasing demand. Examples of people in this area of work are the teachers or instructors in programs such as the Outward Bound program. These activities, which are designed to provide a tough challenge to the participants, began outside the school, but the programs are gradually being added to college and high school physical education programs. They provide an extended test of the individual that is difficult to reproduce in the usual school situation.

*New areas of scholarship* are also appearing at the college level, though they may not be teacher-oriented activities. Increasing numbers of physical educators are beginning to specialize in research areas such as we have described in our discussion of disciplines. Areas of research related to the fields of physical education that have been opened in the last one or two decades include motor learning research, the sport psychology or sociology fields, the history and philosophy areas of physical education and sport studies, along with new dimensions of physiological research oriented toward sport. New opportunities are developing in these areas as they are opened by growing numbers of physical educators interested in concentrating in the scholarly studies areas of the field.

This survey is just a sampling of some of the types of teaching jobs that are available in physical education and its allied fields. While the field has an overall surplus of teachers, many areas within the field do not have enough teachers to supply their needs. As a prospective teacher, you can improve your employment potential by developing a specialty in some area in which the need for teachers is great. The teaching possibilities in physical education are by no means limited, unless your interests are limited to the most common, traditional teaching areas.

## Types of Nonteaching Jobs

Not every student of physical education is interested in teaching as a career. While the basic orientation of the field is toward teaching, many other areas of work are available to the trained physical educator. While these are essentially areas of physical education, some of the areas may require specialized degrees in other areas, such as recreation or physical therapy. In some areas a business minor or even a major may be very helpful, especially in administrative positions that involve long-term planning or handling large sums of money.

*Administration.* Administrative work may be the end result of teaching in physical education, for the teacher may become the administrator of a large program or department of physical education. Administrators are needed in teaching areas, but they are also needed in areas not connected with teaching, such as sports programs. Sports administration can include work as an athletic director or as a business manager for school or professional sports teams. An administrator needs some academic training in administrative needs and procedures, in addition to practical experience, for a successful teacher coach will not necessarily be a successful administrator.

*Health Education and Services.* While we think of the health education area as a teaching area, it is closely allied to many activities that do not involve teaching. This area of work includes school nurses and doctors, health specialists in the schools who either provide services or supervise health programs, and workers in the many areas of public health services. Health educators may work for local, state, or national governments to provide services, give information, and develop health or health education programs to be used in the schools or communities. Many positions are available for administrators of areas of health education work and services.

**Therapy and Special Training.** While we usually think of therapy as physical therapy, which involves work with people with some temporary or permanent physical disability, the areas of therapy are much broader in nature. There are four basic types of therapy: physical therapy, corrective therapy, occupational therapy, and dance therapy. We will briefly discuss each area as a possible occupation.

*Physical therapy* is primarily physical activity planned by a physician to help people make a physical recovery from severe disease or disability. It is planned to correct problems that are primarily physical in nature, so it might be considered a more narrow area of corrective therapy. Although a physical education degree is helpful, the specialist needs specialized training before qualifying as a physical therapist.

Broader in scope than physical therapy, *corrective therapy* is concerned with the mental aspects of rehabilitation as well as the physical aspects. It is a team approach to rehabilitating people with physical and mental illness. Rather than treat only the physical symptoms, it aims at the mental and social problems that are a result of the disability. This area of specialization has developed largely since World War II.

*Occupational therapy* involves working with people who are emotionally disturbed or suffer from perceptual motor problems. Physical education activities are used as one of several approaches to the problems of the patients. As with other types of therapy, the occupational therapist needs special training beyond a bachelor's degree.

*Dance therapy* is a relatively new area of therapy. The dance therapist works with people of all ages in programs that use the expressive movement aspect of dance as a means of guidance and to improve communication among people with problems. The dance therapist needs training in dance, movement activities, and psychology to develop the broad background needed to work in this area.

**Recreational Services.** The recreation area is growing rapidly for many smaller communities are developing programs of community recreation and recreational facilities, just as the larger cities did years ago. People are needed to develop and administer recreational pro-

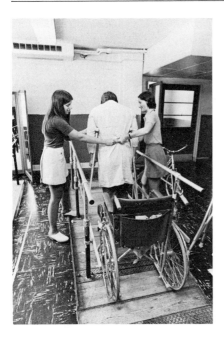

Physical educators need not be teachers of dance or movement or athletics; they can use their knowledge of movement and physiology in careers such as physical therapy, which is an area in need of more and more specialists. (Photo by Dan Bernstein for Tufts–New England Medical Center)

grams on a number of levels. Although community recreation is the area we think of most commonly, the government uses specialists connected with the national parks system, many business and industrial concerns hire people to run company programs of intramurals and competitive sports, and many larger churches are hiring trained specialists to run church recreation programs.

As nations become more affluent, citizens gain much more free time. One of the major problems of the future may be the question of how we will use our leisure time. The area of leisure services has become a major national business, with many millions of dollars spent annually on recreation and recreational supplies in the United States alone. Businesses are sponsoring recreational activities not only because they are enjoyed by the employees—which keeps them happier, the companies believe, with their employers—but because the employees tend to stay in a better state of health. Churches are adding recreation programs to provide more acceptable activities for the members within the church. The activities also help the churches in holding the interest of the young people. Church recreation is a rapidly developing area in the recreational services field.

***Full-time Coaching and Athletics.*** Many coaches at the college level devote their full time to coaching duties, while some coaches also run coaching clinics, schools, and camps, especially during the summer months. This type of activity has become very popular in the United States during the last decade or so, and as the professional sports teams increase in number, more professional coaching positions are becoming available.

Many high school and college athletes hope to make a career of professional athletics. The one thing to keep in mind in this area is that the competition is *extremely* keen. The odds against a high school athlete playing and doing well in college, then continuing on into professional sports successfully are in the million-to-one range. The most unfortunate aspect of the interest in playing professional sports and coaching at a high level is that too many athletes neglect to prepare themselves to do anything else if they fail to meet their goal. A student interested in professional sports should be educated for a second career as a basic precaution.

**Sports and Health as Business.** Many "health clubs" have been opened to develop and maintain the health of anyone who will pay the bill regularly, while many existing sports clubs are devoted to particular sports, such as golfing, swimming, tennis, skiing, ice skating, and bowling. Most of the sports clubs hire specialists as "club pros" who will teach or coach the members in the activities of the sport. Although the primary prerequisite of a job of this nature is a highly developed level of skill in the chosen sport, a physical education background can be very helpful in the teaching aspects of the duties. The "health clubs" can use people with training in physical education, though the dominant hiring interests of some of them seem to relate to an attractive appearance and the ability to sell memberships, rather than any evident ability to improve the health of the paying customer.

Some of the private sports concerns that run their own schools in a sport require trained teachers, while some organizations have set up resorts dedicated to a single sporting activity, which also requires highly skilled teachers. Some more general organizations, such as country clubs, also hire sports coaches to train private sports teams composed of the children of the club members.

**Sports Medicine and Athletic Training.** A great need in sports is for more specialists in sports medicine (doctors) and specialists in athletic training (paraprofessionals in athletic medicine).

The title "athletic trainer" can be confusing, for in amateur athletics the trainer does not really train the athletes or plan their program of training. The trainer is concerned with the care and prevention of athletic injuries. Prevention may include activities such as providing liquids for athletes to drink during workouts in hot weather or taping ankles or other body parts for safety or support before practice sessions or contests. Treatment includes activities such as first aid and emergency treatment of injuries and may include planning the program of rehabilitation for an athlete after an injury. The trainer may be considered an intermediate step between the coach and the physician who specializes in sports medicine. Well-trained, ethics-conscious athletic trainers are necessary to prevent the abuse of training and drug-handling practices that can occur in the treatment of athletic injuries. Ethically, the trainer cannot dispense drugs or give shots unless supervised by a physician, but in practice in athletics this may not be the case. This is an area of major concern in modern athletics, for too few people are accustomed to dealing with athletic injuries.

Although specialized training is necessary, the need for specialists in the area of athletic injuries and their treatment is growing rapidly. Many states are moving to put trainers in the high schools, which would create a huge demand for certified trainers, both male and female. Not all colleges have athletic trainers at this time, but a move toward requiring trainers as a safety factor in athletics could make this area one with excellent job opportunities in the future. The National Athletic Trainers Association has information on training programs and colleges with certified training programs. The number of doctors who are trained in handling sports injuries is also limited in most communities, though the addition of certified trainers in the community could improve this situation because there would be fewer injuries.

**Sports Supplies and Equipment.** As participation in sports and recreational activities increases, sales and business opportunities in sporting goods increase rapidly. Private companies need persons with an understanding of physical activities—both competitive and recreational sports. People are needed who are familiar with the equipment needs and changing demands. Many companies are specializing in the design and construction of athletic facilities, indoor and outdoor, and they need people with a knowledge of the requirements of sporting events.

**Publishers.** Publishers of books on sports and textbooks in the area of physical education and its allied fields need people who are knowledgeable about physical education in several areas. Editorial workers are needed who are familiar with the needs and demand for publications in areas related to physical education and sport, which requires a knowledge of both physical education and writing and editorial skills. Other people are needed in the sales areas, including direct sales, which often involves traveling across the country to sell the books. These jobs require a knowledge of physical education and the comparative values of the available books, combined with sales ability and an understanding of the available markets for publications in the area of physical education and sports.

## The Employment Future of the Physical Educator

As we have noted, the need for general teachers of physical education is low, for teachers are in an oversupply. However, there will always be more demand for the better-than-average graduate—the A or B student—than for the C student, who exists in a considerable oversupply. Prospective teachers who have the greatest chance of finding a job are those with good grades and at least one well-developed area of specialization, such as we have discussed in this chapter.

Too few students realize the many job opportunities that exist outside the teaching field for the student interested in physical education and sports. The greatest demands are connected with the many recreational activities and services, which in turn create a greater market for sporting equipment and supplies. The student of physical education can, by studying the job market carefully and at an *early stage* in the training process, find many good potential forms of employment. However, the student who maintains only ordinary grades and does not develop any area of specialization will have a difficult time locating a job after graduating from college.

## Suggested Readings

Bryant, James E. "Some Possibilities for Employment in Physical Education's Allied Fields." *Physical Educator,* 31 (December 1974), 193–195.

Calandra, Gerald A., and Jack Baker. "Job Hunting for Fun and Profit." *JOPER,* 46 (November–December 1975), 19–22.

Cratty, Bryant J. *Career Potentials in Physical Activity.* Prentice-Hall, Englewood Cliffs, N.J., 1971.

Fardy, Paul S., and Herman K. Hellerstein. "An Emerging Role for the Physical Educator." *Quest,* 24 (Summer 1975), 80–84.

Finn, Peter. "Career Education and Physical Education." *JOPER,* 47 (January 1976), 29–31.

Freed, Mike, ed. "The Leisure Industries: Investigations of Commercial Recreation and Tourism." *JOPER,* 46 (November–December 1975), 33–48.

Johnson, Granville B., Warren R. Johnson, and James M. Humphrey. *Your Career in Physical Education.* Harper & Row, New York, 1957.

Palmer, Chester L. *Physical Education as a Career: A Guide for Vocational Guidance Counselors and Prospective Physical Educators.* Microcarded Ed.D. dissertation, Teachers College, Columbia University, 1951.

Pape, Laurence A., and Louis E. Means. *A Professional Career in Physical Education.* Prentice-Hall, Englewood Cliffs, N.J., 1963.

Smith, Hope M., and Marguerite A. Clifton. *Physical Education: Exploring Your Future.* Prentice-Hall, Englewood Cliffs, N.J., 1962.

Stinnett, Timothy M. *The Profession of Teaching.* Center for Applied Research in Education, Washington, D.C., 1962.

"Grass-Roots Phys. Ed.": What the Physical Educator Does

In the last chapter we discussed some of the many employment opportunities—both teaching and nonteaching—that are open to physical educators. This chapter is devoted to the task of the physical educator, what the physical educator actually *does*. For this reason we will discuss the physical educator's most common role: a teacher and coach. Most of our ideas about physical education as a field of study and as a career come from this role, but many beginning physical education majors have only a very limited idea of what the actual daily work of a physical educator is. This chapter is an attempt to explain the types of duties that school physical educators commonly perform in their day-to-day work.

## Program Development

Although this category of work falls under a broad designation, we need to understand what we are talking about when we refer to the task of planning the physical education program. Many people have the mistaken idea that physical education programs follow one of two patterns in their developmental stages: either (1) the teachers do whatever they feel like doing on a given day (the "roll-out-the-ball" school of physical education), or (2) they list six or eight sports in the order of their seasons and then have the students play them during the school year (the "advanced roll-out-the-ball" program). Planning a good curriculum for physical education at any level involves considerable work and follows a fairly consistent pattern of stages of development (see the chart).

For a program of physical education to be of value in a school, it must be a well-planned program that meets the needs and interests of the students and also meets the general objectives of physical education. The first step in planning a curriculum involves studying both

The curriculum-planning process
simplified.

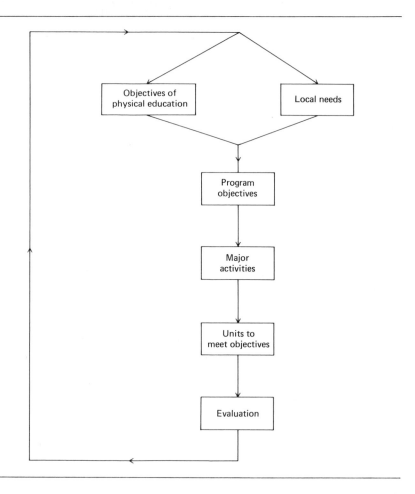

these areas. The teacher must consider the *objectives of physical edu-cation,* or what the program tries to do and how it should fit into the total educational program of the school, then the objectives should be compared to the *local needs,* or the areas of physical education in which the students are weak or are interested in improving themselves. These two areas are combined, ideally, to yield the *program objectives,* or the aims or specific goals for which the local program of physical education will be designed.

The objectives of the local program should be consistent with the traditional objectives of physical education—that is, the program should be a broad, well-rounded one.  Once the objectives of the program have been determined, the teacher can begin to develop the basic program. This consists of choosing a set of *major learning activities* that will enable the students to meet the program objectives.  To choose the major activities means only to select the basic activities or sports that will compose the heart of the curriculum.  The next step in the process, after the major activities have been chosen, is to develop program *units to meet the program objectives.*  As an example, if one of the major activity areas is dance, the teacher must next decide on the content of the unit on dance, what its objectives will be, what teaching methods and procedures will be followed, and how the unit will be evaluated.  This process is followed for each major activity, until the year's activities are planned. As the planning details are completed, the teacher can show how each part of the year's program will work to meet the various objectives of the total physical education program.

A well-planned program is necessary if the teacher hopes to fulfill or meet the objectives that have been set for the program, for the next step is the *evaluation of the program.*  The teacher should plan at least a brief evaluation after each major unit and then an in-depth evaluation at the end of the course.  The students should be involved in this in-depth evaluation.  Each evaluation will try to determine the answer to several important questions:

1    Were the objectives *worth* meeting?  Were they valid, worthwhile objectives for the unit or program?  Should any of the objectives be dropped as unnecessary?  Should any new objectives be added to the list?

2    Were the objectives met?  Did the program meet its goals?  Were plans to fulfill the program carried out?  If the objectives were not met, why?  Was the program poorly planned or taught?  Did the students fail to make the necessary effort?  Were the objectives worthy of their effort?

3    Should the objectives or the units of instruction be changed, either in part or in whole?  If the units or course need revision, what changes would contribute more to the student's total education?

As the program is evaluated, the curriculum-planning process returns to the first step to consider the basic objectives of physical education and the needs and desires of the local people.  Evaluation is a never-ending process.  A program should be continuously changing, even if it is only in a small way, for even if the basic objectives of physical education do not change, the constantly changing needs of the people in the local communities require constant, though gradual, revision of the local physical education program.  Program development is perhaps the most critical task of the physical educator. Not only does it determine exactly what the physical educator will be trying to do; it also determines what goals and outcomes will be sought in the future.

## Types of Physical Education Duties

Let us now discuss the activities and tasks you will do as a teacher of physical education by listing the categories of your future work, rather than by trying to follow a "typical" physical education teacher through a "typical" schoolday, for there are many differences in duty, routine, and customs from one school to another. We will discuss the type of work you will do as divided into five different categories: planning duties, teaching duties, evaluative duties, administrative duties, and various unclassified duties.

***Planning and Consultation Duties.*** We have already discussed in some detail the best example of the sort of planning physical educators have to do. The physical education program is continuously being evaluated and regularly replanned. Much of the teacher's efforts go into planning the daily schedule of activities. As a physical education teacher, you must not only plan the activities of the regular classes in some detail to be able to calculate the time needed for each portion of the lesson and to determine what facilities and equipment will be required, but you must also consider several concurrent problems. What changes will be necessary in case of inclement weather? What will be necessary if some of the students in a class are highly skilled and others in the same class have very poor skills? How will the teaching plan be affected? Are there any classes of adapted activities? If so, their program must be planned very carefully. If possible, their program of activities should be as close to the regular program as possible. If there is no adapted class, are there any students in the regular classes who need adapted activities? What will you do with them during the class periods?

If you are a coach as well as a teacher, you will have to plan the team practice sessions and take into account the same problems or questions of objectives, available facilities, weather conditions, and characteristics of the participants. Many of your duties as a coach will more accurately be in the categories of teaching and administrative duties, however.

The physical educator often has to plan athletic events or other special activities, ranging from the small and simple to the large and complex. If the event is held outside the school, you will be concerned with matters such as travel arrangements, meals, housing, and moving equipment and supplies. If the event is at the home school, you will be concerned with matters such as clearing the plans with the school's administration and perhaps the local school board, checking the condition and needs in facilities and equipment, making arrangements to accommodate the visitors, and arranging for tickets and other financial matters. You should plan for all possible things that might happen, and you should assign people to handle them. In this particular area the teacher's duties edge into administrative work, for planning is an obligation of administration. However, the actual planning is not necessarily the duty of the administrator; it is the administrator's duty to see that planning occurs.

You may also be responsible at times for assisting with the planning of facilities, whether in school buildings or parts of buildings (such as the gymnasium) or in the facility needs of the school or the community. The physical educator is expected to be the resident expert in matters of recreational and physical activity needs, including construction needs, at all levels. If a new facility that has any bearing on physical education or athletics is in the planning stages, you should be an active participant in the planning.

You may also be asked to consult or help with the planning of community recreation programs, for this is yet another aspect of the physical education program as it affects the community. Community recreation programs are becoming increasingly popular, and the physical educator needs to be able to help the community in planning both the program and the facility needs for good community programs. As a physical education teacher, you may discover yourself helping in the planning of many physical activity programs or facilities that seem to have little direct connection with the school program of physical education.

**Teaching Duties.** Although the teaching duties may not seem to be a large portion of the total duties of the physical education teacher at times, teaching is the essence of physical education to most physical educators. As a physical educator, you will find many different types of work or duties in the daily teaching activities. The teacher must firmly control the teaching methods used in the class. The teacher must be seen by the students as a leader. To many students the physical education teacher is an example of conduct or a way of life. While the teacher is not expected to be perfect, he or she is expected to be fair —to be just in the treatment of the students, and logical in all dealings with them. While the teacher should not be lax or loose in class discipline, there is no place for the bully or autocrat who wants to own and manipulate the class. Students should be shown as much fairness and respect as the teacher hopes to receive from them.

The physical education teacher is heavily involved in skills work and instruction. You will frequently have to demonstrate the skills to the class, which is why you should have a broad selection of basic physical skills. A class is going to have little respect for a teacher who expects the typical student to be able to do what the teacher cannot do. As a teacher, you will also have to use teaching skills to help the students to learn the required physical activities. The teacher cannot simply give a skill assignment, show how it is performed, then leave the students to perform it for themselves. You will have to be able to show the students *how* to learn it, rather than simply *what* they have to learn.

You will spend much class time observing and analyzing students' performance of skills. You will need to be able to watch a skill performed, analyze it to determine what its problems are, then suggest possible ways of correcting the unwanted actions, or possible approaches to correcting the problem. To be able to teach physical activities, you will have to be able to evaluate the skill with which they are performed and know how to react to a given problem.

You will also be involved in safety practices and accident prevention, for there is a great potential for physical accidents in physical education activities. You must teach the students how to perform activities safely and make them conscious of good safety habits. Accident prevention is an important aspect of planning in the school physical education program.

The physical education teacher is also frequently involved in counseling the students. In some cases this is career counseling, with students who are interested in pursuing physical education as a career, but more frequently the counseling involves other matters. The most common type of counseling involves students with problems, for students often want to talk to an adult other than the parent or the school guidance counselor. Many students will feel closer to you as their physical education teacher or coach than to other teachers in the school; thus when problems appear, your students may talk first with you. When this happens, you need to try to give the student the attention that the problem deserves. In many cases the student may need a friendly ear more than any particular advice. Providing that ear can be very beneficial to the student, and very much appreciated.

We will include the coaching duties within the realm of the teaching duties, though many physical educators would consider coaching a category of duty separate from the other categories. We are including it with teaching because it may be the most influential part of the educational process to many students. We should not isolate the coaches from teaching or from physical education; rather we should try to influence the coaches toward what physical educators consider the positive values of sports, for the coach is constantly teaching the athletes a system of values that can hardly be overlooked.

The rapid increase in the popularity of women's athletics has increased the need for female coaches. Although they are probably the fastest-growing group of specialists, they are still in great demand. (Courtesy Pam Schuyler, Stock, Boston)

Teaching lies at the heart of coaching, for no person can coach well without teaching. As a coach, you will be involved in the analysis of complex skills and strategies. You will have to work toward the correction or solution of problems and constantly work toward teaching new or better skills and methods. Coaching is a more highly concentrated version of teaching—with a more narrow goal as the object of the teaching—and it also involves some of the most permanent teaching in physical education.

**Evaluative Duties.** The physical education teacher also performs many evaluative duties—that is, evaluating or judging things and assessing their value or success. This is particularly true in the area of skills analysis, for in essence you will be evaluating the student's skills or performance, deciding how well the student performs, and perhaps assigning a grade to that performance.

We generally think of evaluation as taking place in three particular areas: students, self, and program. You should evaluate students constantly by using a regular series of tests of some nature (not necessarily objective tests). The evaluative process is designed to assess the progress of the individual student toward the goals that you set for the program at the start of the year. You should determine whether the student is meeting the program objectives at a reasonable rate and decide whether any changes need to be made in the program. You may discover that a teaching method is not succeeding, or that a unit does not seem to be helping the students achieve a desired objective. In this case, the task is to discover shortcomings (or notable progress) in the student.

We also must include evaluation of the physical education teacher, for while evaluating ourselves compared to an ideal is not popular or necessarily much fun, it is necessary if we are to insure that we are continuing to do a good job. The teacher should be making a major contribution to the success of the physical education program, so the teacher is one place to look if the students are not meeting the objectives of the program.

You must evaluate the quality of your own performance: Has the job been done well? Are the students responsive? Are there any particular problems evident? How can the quality of your teaching be improved? You can get some idea, if a biased one, of how your teaching job is going by having the students make anonymous evaluations. While this practice has its handicaps, it can give you some good answers as to where problems may exist.

The third area of evaluation is the evaluation of the program itself. Has the program been successful? Did the students meet their objectives? If they did not meet their objectives, what was the reason? You must evaluate your program for its strong and weak points, for what it includes and what it fails to include. Your program should be evaluated constantly, but it should undergo an in-depth analysis at the close of each school year, with input at least from yourself and from the students who were in the program. This step is critical in revising the program to make it better.

Your evaluative duties will include testing the students in many different areas. While you may commonly think of testing only their physical fitness and motor skills in the program, you may also conduct testing and evaluation of the students in areas such as nutrition, social areas (how well they get along with other people), and other areas of concern to the total development of the student, physical, mental, social, and psychological. This broad program of evaluation can help show you which way to go in more successfully fulfilling the needs of the students.

**Administrative Duties.** A physical educator performs many administrative duties, more perhaps than most people realize. As a teacher, you will be running the program of physical education, usually with little or no direction from higher up the administrative ladder. In addition, you may be required to organize and administer an intramural program in the school; these duties involve finding convenient times when the students can participate, then encouraging the forming of teams, arranging facility schedules, officiating services, and gathering equipment and supplies.

Because of the extensive facilities often needed for physical education, and the extent and bulk of equipment and supplies required, physical educators generally perform more administrative duties than teachers in most other areas of the school program. The physical education teacher is usually responsible for the gymnasium and equipment, and you may be responsible for seeing that it is supervised and maintained. You may also encounter this type of duty if you perform coaching duties, for there are administrative duties connected with organizing the training and competitions, and the purchase and maintenance of equipment.

The physical education teacher may also have to develop budgets in areas such as the physical education program, the intramural program, and athletics. You will be responsible for keeping the expenses of the program in line with the approved budget, which requires care in the purchase, use, and care of equipment and supplies. Developing a budget is a difficult but necessary task, if you as a teacher or coach hope to get the best use from the available money.

Much paperwork is also involved in teaching physical education. While written tests generate paperwork that threatens to drown teachers in other areas, the paperwork of the physical educator tends more heavily to inventories of equipment, purchase and budgeting matters, and reports. Every teacher is required to keep records of matters such as attendance and illness, grades, accident reports, and numerous other matters that vary from state to state. As a teacher, you must be well-organized in thought and able to write a coherent, easy-to-understand report whenever necessary.

You may be responsible to other people who are higher in the administrative ladder, and there may also be people below you in the administrative order. You may become a department chairman responsible for several other teachers, a coach responsible for several assistant coaches, or an athletic director responsible for all of the coaches. You will be working constantly with other people in various administrative functions, which requires the ability to take and to give directions well.

If you are to be successful in the administrative duties of the teacher, you will find that one particular ability is as necessary as the ability to organize: the ability to delegate. Delegating authority means to give the responsibility for a task to another person who then has the obligation to get the work done as well as the power necessary to carry out the obligation. Many administrators are limited in their skills because they are either unable or unwilling to delegate. You must learn the limits of a person's ability to perform activities and then develop the ability to delegate tasks that might push the person beyond that point. Because the successful physical education teacher and coach frequently ends up in administration, as we will see in the next chapter, it is important for you to develop your administrative abilities as much as possible.

**Unclassified Duties.** The category of "unclassified duties" might also be called "miscellaneous duties," for it involves any duties that do not fit into the previously discussed categories. We will mention only three such areas in this discussion, though others can be found.

A common example of the other duties you might have to perform is *teaching subjects that are not physical education activities.* Physical education teachers often teach such subjects as health education and driver and safety education, where they are not taught by specialists, but they also frequently teach unrelated subjects. Although almost every field is represented, the most common other teaching areas of physical education teachers are in the sciences, especially biology, and in the social studies area. And although many schools continue to hire people to teach double subjects such as these, the teaching of physical education would be much stronger if this practice were ended.

You may also be involved in *working with athletic training and injuries,* or with the connected programs of athletic rehabilitation. In many schools the coach is also the trainer, team doctor, and chief ankle-wrapper. For this reason, a good course in athletic training and injuries is vital to a well-balanced physical education major. The athletic injury can happen as easily in the physical education class as on the athletic playing field, and you need to be ready and able to treat almost any injury that might occur, or at least know what to do until the doctor comes. Medical emergencies are a part of physical education, for vigorous activity always produces some risk.

As another unclassified—and often unwritten—duty, you may *become involved in community affairs.* Often teachers are expected to be active in civic concerns, to work with community-betterment groups. The teacher is considered a vital member of the community, and many members of the community expect the teacher to show a maximum of involvement in things that are important to the community. Many teachers work in areas such as charity drives, community improvement projects, scouting, and church activities.

## Characteristics of the Teaching Job

To conclude a discussion of the many activities and duties of the physical education teacher, we need to discuss an aspect of teaching that is of concern to new teachers but is not always discussed ahead of time: What the beginning teacher can expect to find in the first teaching job. Charles A. Bucher has suggested that the typical teaching job, when it is first encountered by a new teacher, has four characteristics.[1]

1   *Long workday and workweek:* Magazine articles and politicians will make much of the short workday or week of the teacher, but it simply is not true. While the school day is not very long, it is an intense experience for the teacher, which can be draining emotionally, if not physically. As a teacher of physical education, you often will have to act as a coach after school and then go home to grade papers and prepare for the next day's classes. As a coach, you may be at school from 7:30 or 8:00 A.M. until after 6:00 P.M. and still have several hours of work at home to be fully prepared for the next day of school.

2   *Strenuous daily schedule:* As the working hours indicate, the day is rarely short. You may teach six classes, take a quick lunch break, and do several hours of coaching work, all with no genuinely restful break. Research has shown that even a five-minute break each hour can improve a person's performance, but most teachers have no such break in practice, for changing classes hardly constitutes a restful break from the routine.

3   *Heavy clerical work:* Although some school systems are beginning to hire paraprofessionals to do some of the teacher's paperwork, you should expect to do a large amount of paperwork, much of which may seem pointless. Details of class attendance, injuries, absences, and grades are examples of the statistical and written reports that are regularly required. At times you may feel more like a hired secretary than a teacher; the feeling is not rare.

4   *Inadequate materials and facilities:* While many teacher preparation programs may have the latest in teaching equipment, or limitless physical facilities, this may not be the case in the school where you begin teaching. (The situation may also be reversed; the college you attend may have little equipment and the school where you first teach may have many things you have never used.) This problem should be considered a challenge to your skill and ingenuity. Obviously, the scope of your program and its potential success will be largely determined by the available materials and facilities, so you must be prepared to work with (and without) almost every type of equipment and facility. Many community

---

[1] Charles A. Bucher, *Foundations of Physical Education,* 7th ed., C. V. Mosby, St. Louis, 1975, p. 523.

resources can be used if you carefully study the many resources that exist.

## What the Physical Educator Does: A Comment

We might summarize this chapter by asking, "What does the physical educator do?" "Everything."

This answer is not too inaccurate, for a physical education teacher is often expected to be a jack of all trades and physical education may require a greater variety of talents than any other teaching area. Perhaps that is one reason why so many people want to become physical educators, and why so many physical educators continue to find teaching a wonderful challenge.

## Suggested Readings

Friedman, Toby. "Fitness for the Space Age." *Quest,* 3 (December 1964), 31–36.

"The Physical Educator as Professor." *Quest,* 7 (December 1966). Entire issue.

# 15 Preparing Tomorrow's Physical Educator

The college training of the physical educator has traditionally been referred to as "professional preparation," according to the belief that
teaching is indeed a profession. Such a formal training regimen is a
relatively recent development in educational history, particularly in the
broad areas that constitute physical education, for organized collegiate
programs designed to train physical educators, particularly for teaching,
are little more than a century old.

Although the physical educator may perform many different functions with little involvement in the educational systems, the traditional
patterns of preparation have been teacher-oriented. Although more
programs are beginning to permit specialization that does not involve
this teacher-training approach, the primary orientation of the field is
toward teaching of some nature. The term physical *education* shows
why this is true.

Our current patterns of professional preparation are largely a result
of the development of the major in the normal schools, which were
simply teachers' colleges. The teacher-emphasis of those schools has
had a major impact on how physical educators are trained. Physical
educators have made attempts to ally themselves more closely with the
sciences, but the traditional patterns are not easily changed.

## What Are the Components of Professional Preparation?

Traditionally there have been four areas of professional preparation for
future physical educators. The first of these areas is the *academic
courses* required by the institution the student attends. This portion of
the collegiate program is frequently referred to as "general education,"
for it is designed to provide every college and university student with
academic training of a broad nature. It provides some concept of the

The future physical educator needs a
thorough background in the sciences,
particularly those dealing with physiology
and biology, to understand the workings
of the human body. (Courtesy Frank
Siteman, Stock, Boston)

breadth of human knowledge.  This part of the preparation is commonly
done during the first two years of college.

The second area of professional preparation is in the *foundation
sciences,* or those areas of science that must be a part of the physical
educator's base knowledge if a good grasp of the major field is to be
expected.  The basic emphasis has been toward the biological sciences,
especially anatomy and physiology, but increasing emphasis is being
directed toward an understanding of chemistry, which underlies biology
(particularly in the area of exercise physiology), and toward more exposure to physics, which is necessary in studying aspects of movement,
such as the mechanics of human movement and the outside forces that
affect it.

The third area of professional preparation is often referred to as
the *professional education.*  It comprises the major courses in education
itself, which are entirely oriented toward teaching.  It includes the
student-teaching experience, which is generally considered the most
valuable portion of the area.  Student teaching is an area of some controversy in the educational program, but it is also required for teacher
certification if you wish to teach below the college level, and in some
cases at the junior college level.

The fourth area of professional preparation is the area of physical
education, the *major program.*  In many colleges it is a combined major
in health education and physical education, though it might be a major

concentration in a single area of the broad field of physical education, such as physical education itself, health education, recreation, dance, safety education, or any of the newer areas of specialization that are appearing as schools consolidate and more specialists are sought.

## What Are Some of the Issues of Teacher Education?

One of the oldest issues in the education of teachers is the question of *time:* How long should the training program last, if it is to be effective? The generally accepted minimum is four years, though most educators insist that five years is a more reasonable period: four years to become well-trained in the field of specialization, followed by a year devoted to the professional training in education. In many cases, however, the fifth year blends into work toward the master's degree.

Another issue causing considerable controversy is the amount of work devoted to the *subject matter versus professional education training.* The root of the issue is that more preparation is needed in the subject matter—so you will know *what* to teach—while other arguments are that the professional education training is more important, for it does not matter if you have mastered the field, if you do not know *how* to teach it. This controversy may be the reason for the push toward the fifth year of preparation, for it permits more work in both areas.

A third persistent problem is the *approach to the subject matter.* Should it be taught with the emphasis on the subject matter itself, or should it be taught with the emphasis on how the students will teach it after they have graduated? In other words, should the teaching methods instruction be integrated into the subject matter instruction, or should it remain segregated and taught in "methods" courses outside the subject courses?

A fourth problem is the question of whether there should be *more philosophical or more scientific emphasis.* The question arose early in the twentieth century as educators sought to develop a "science" of teaching. They never really succeeded, and the issue has not yet been settled.

A fifth issue relates to *laboratory experiences,* or the time spent observing teaching activities and practicing teaching as students. The many questions in this area range from involving the students in small teaching-observation experiences regularly from the first year of college, to the more traditional approach of concentrating the experiences during one or more terms of the last year of college, to the idea of requiring a full year or more of successful teaching before actual certification.

A final persistent issue is the *general education* of the student. How much time should be spent in areas outside the major field and the other areas of study directly related to the teaching field? How broad should the general education be? Professional educators have frequently argued against additional work in general education, because they believe it further limits the amount of work that can be devoted to the areas in which the student hopes to teach. This issue involves us most with people outside the field, for at the heart of the issue is the far-from-simple question that lies at the heart of all education: What is education? What is its ultimate goal? What education is most worth having? The question has not been resolved for centuries, nor is it likely to be settled in the near future, but physical educators should not be too dogmatic or closed-minded to the views of the liberal arts supporters. By ignoring their areas of study we may be isolating ourselves from the other areas of the educational experience more than we realize.

As we look at the broad area of physical education, the dichotomy between the arts and the sciences is still visible. Physical education is still torn over which way to go. As a result we are neither art nor science, though the tendency is toward the sciences. In health education two directions may also be seen. The traditional approach has been to combine health with physical education, with between one-fourth and one-third of the time spent in health. Increasingly, specialization in health education begins at the undergraduate level rather than in the graduate schools as in the past. Recreation education is also developing rapidly as an undergraduate area of specialization. It may be the most rapidly developing specialization, particularly in a time of radically increasing quantities of leisure time for people in many areas of the world.

## Traditional Patterns of Professional Preparation

A study of the traditional patterns of professional preparation reveals a startling variety of conditions under which people are prepared as physical educators. While many educators believe this variety of programs hampers the development of a well-coordinated, thorough training program nationwide, many other educators consider it one of our greatest strengths, for no one is forced to prepare under a single, rigid national system. We need to discuss some of the many variables that exist among the programs of professional preparation.

***Certification Procedures.*** A teacher must be certified by the state before being allowed to teach in the public schools of that state. Each individual state sets its own requirements for teacher certification. There are two basic approaches to teacher certification in setting the state requirements. The first is the *hours-and-credits approach,* in which the prospective teacher must have a required number of courses or credit hours in various areas of the professional program. The second approach is the *approved-program approach,* in which the state studies the teacher preparation program of the school and then approves it. If the program of the school is approved, then any prospective teacher graduating from that program will be granted a teacher's certificate. The approved-program approach permits more flexibility in the development of school programs of professional preparation. It also permits the use of the competency-based approach to teacher education.

Competency-based teacher education (CBTE), also called performance-based teacher education (PBTE), is a trend of the late 1960s and the 1970s. It is based on the idea that successful teaching requires the teacher to possess skills or knowledge of certain types, or "competences," if the teacher is to be successful. When a prospective teacher has met all of the required competences, he or she is certified to teach. Because the program itself is more difficult to evaluate, the program itself is assessed, rather than the teacher-candidate graduating from the program. If the certifying body, such as a state department of education, considers the program requirements to meet the needs of their teachers, then the program is approved. After the program has been approved, any graduate of the program will be certified to teach, usually upon the recommendation of the school, rather than the evaluation of the state.

Although CBTE has been the subject of much professional discussion and writing, as of 1974 only eight states (see Table 15.1) had actually adopted CBTE programs of certification; twenty-two states were considering the idea or were moving in that direction; and twenty states were making no plans for such a change.[1] Of the eight states that had adopted CBTE by 1974, only one (Texas) was considered to have changed to a genuine, completely competency-based program. The other programs appeared to be more tentative or experimental. The concept and practice of CBTE, as well as its potential value, are still open to considerable controversy.

Just as the requirements for certification vary from state to state, so do the types of certificates that are awarded. The certificates fall into three basic types: temporary, conditional, and permanent certificates. A *temporary* certificate usually permits the teacher to teach for one year; it is used to permit the hiring of a teacher under unusual circumstances. Temporary certificates are not usually renewable.

---

[1] Melvin G. Villeme, "Competency-Based Certification: A New Reality?" *Educational Leadership,* 31 (January 1974), 348–349.

**Table 15.1**
The Status of Competency-Based
Teacher Education

Competency-Based Requirements in Use

| | |
|---|---|
| California | Texas |
| Minnesota | Vermont |
| North Carolina | Washington |
| Ohio | Wisconsin |

Competency-Based Certification Being Planned or Considered

| | |
|---|---|
| Alabama | Maryland |
| Alaska | Massachusetts |
| Arizona | Michigan |
| Connecticut | Montana |
| Florida | New Jersey |
| Georgia | New Mexico |
| Idaho | New York |
| Illinois | Oregon |
| Kansas | Pennsylvania |
| Kentucky | Utah |
| Maine | West Virginia |

No Present Study or Move Toward Competency-Based
Certification

| | |
|---|---|
| Arkansas | Nevada |
| Colorado | New Hampshire |
| Delaware | North Dakota |
| Hawaii | Oklahoma |
| Indiana | Rhode Island |
| Iowa | South Carolina |
| Louisiana | South Dakota |
| Mississippi | Tennessee |
| Missouri | Virginia |
| Nebraska | Wyoming |

A *conditional* certificate permits the teacher to be employed under certain restrictions. Most often the conditions involve the teacher's undergoing additional training of some nature within a set time. Under some conditions this type of certificate is renewable. Usually it will set a time limit on how long—three years, for example—the teacher is permitted to qualify for a higher certificate.

A *permanent* certificate might more accurately be called an "unconditional" certificate, for it may not be permanent. Most states have moved away from the idea of permanent certification and require instead that the teacher continue to work for professional improvement. A teacher may be required to take additional college or graduate work at certain intervals for such a certificate to be held. This certificate is a "full" certificate, however. The teacher is considered fully qualified to teach.

**AAHPER Recommendations: Hours and Credits.** In 1962 a professional preparation conference was sponsored by AAHPER and held in Washington, D.C., to suggest patterns the nation's colleges and universities should follow in developing good programs to prepare teachers in the fields that constitute physical education. The report of the conference has perhaps been the most influential book on what should be included in a professional preparation program involving hours and credits. Although another professional preparation conference has been held since 1962, it was directed toward the competency approach, which does not lend itself as readily to assessment as the hours-and-credits programs. To gain a fuller understanding of the breadth needed in a good program of teacher preparation, we will look at the recommendations of the 1962 conference.

These recommendations are referred to as hours-and-credits not because certain numbers of hours are suggested, but because certain courses or content areas are suggested. As we mentioned earlier, the first area of preparation is the general education. The recommendations suggested courses in English composition, literature, history, philosophy, sociology, psychology, the arts (art, music, drama), and mathematics as areas of study that should be included in the program. For the most part the general education portion of preparation is the bulk of the first two years of college training.

The second area of preparation for a physical educator is in the foundational sciences. This area includes some portions of the general education area of preparation, plus some areas that may be included in the courses required as part of the major concentration. At the lower levels of the foundational sciences, students should have some course work in the introductory or general courses in chemistry, physics, and biology. At the more advanced level should be courses in human anatomy and physiology. At the top undergraduate level should be courses in kinesiology or biomechanics and the physiology of exercise, which are most often taught by the physical education department. The anatomy and physiology courses may be taught by either the physical education or biology departments.

The third area of professional preparation includes the professional education courses designed to prepare the student for teaching in general, regardless of the subject the student intends to teach. This portion of the study may be done in a "block" design—that is, all in one semester (or one or two quarters)—and will include all the required education courses and the student-teaching experience. The courses suggested include the social and philosophical foundations of education, human growth and development, educational psychology (which may be offered by the department of psychology or of education), educational curriculum and instruction, and the directed (supervised) student-teaching experience.

The fourth area of education is in the major field, such as physical education. We might look at the major preparation as including four areas of experience. The first area is *personal skills,* or the physical skills you must have to be able to demonstrate the skills you will teach. These skills should cover a broad range that includes aquatics, dance, elementary-level activities, team sports, and individual and dual sports, plus the combative sport of wrestling for male students. While you need not necessarily be an expert performer in the skills, you need to be able to perform reasonably well any skills you teach to the students, both for reasons of demonstrating the skills and for understanding the problems of their execution, plus the aspect of student respect (or disrespect) that may result if the students are required to do what you cannot. This concept does not necessarily extend to the level of the advanced performer or athlete.

The second area is that of the *teaching and coaching skills.* Not only should you be able to perform, but you must also be able to *teach* the skills. It is very possible that a person will be able to perform at a high level, yet be unable to teach the skills being performed. This is the weakness in hiring a good athlete with no preparation for teaching. The skills of performance and teaching do not always go hand in hand.

The third area might be called the *general theory* area. This area involves instruction in the meaning and purposes of physical education, developing and maintaining programs, and developing a broad understanding of the other fields related to physical education, if you are specializing in physical education. Your course work in the history, philosophy, and principles of the field will act as an introduction to the field, and you should take other courses in the areas of administration

The future teacher and coach needs to
develop personal performance skills to
enhance demonstrations and to understand the learning process better.
(Courtesy Peter Vandermark, Stock,
Boston)

and supervision of the physical education program, curriculum and instruction, and the measurement and evaluation area, sometimes called
tests and measurement. If you are majoring in physical education in the
narrow sense, additional work in the broader areas is necessary to a
well-balanced competence in understanding the whole field and realizing the importance of all of its components. Work should include health
education and safety education, recreation, and adapted programs of
physical education. These examples cover a broad field, but they do
not go into much depth. More work in other areas, particularly in health
education, is necessary to a good program.

The fourth area included in the major field might be called the
*practicum,* for it consists of practical experience in the teaching of
physical education—apart from the work involved in the professional
education courses. It can include observing other people teaching,
small teaching or assistant-teacher experiences in nearby schools and
in your own classes, and working with young people in almost any situation, whether by assignment for credit or simply on your own. The
trend is toward having more such practical experiences earlier in students' college years. The reasons for such a trend are simple and
understandable. College is expensive and time-consuming. Some persons can do well in the skill and theory areas of the field, yet they either
dislike the actual teaching or discover they have no aptitude for it. It
is to the student's advantage to discover any such problems at the

earliest possible stage, so the student can either arrange a nonteaching major or find another major field that will not cause the same problems. If you will not enjoy teaching or be able to do it well, the best time to discover that fact is *now,* rather than shortly before graduation when too much time and money have been invested to permit a practical change of emphasis or major.

The newer nonteaching major programs that are developing are oriented toward the student who wishes to prepare for a career of scholarship and research as we discussed with the discipline of physical education. As the field of physical education expands we will probably see increasing numbers of students who do not go through the teacher-preparation program because they are not preparing for a teaching emphasis, but *do* plan on a career of academic work in the field. This discussion is not meant to give the impression that a physical educator will be either a teacher *or* a scholar. The two areas may have different emphases, but they overlap considerably. No physical educator would be likely to exclude *either* one; the difference lies in the comparative emphasis and where it is put.

Most collegiate programs for physical education majors will include most, if not all, of these elements in their program of professional preparation, particularly if the school is still working under the hours-and-credits system, as most schools are. However, if you examine the major programs at many different schools, you will discover that a wide variety of course combinations and program emphases can be found throughout the nation. If you dislike the emphasis or arrangement of one school's major program, there is almost certainly some other school that will have a major program to meet your needs and preferences.

**AAHPER Recommendations: Competency-Based Teacher Education.** Competency-based teacher education (CBTE), sometimes called performance-based teacher education (PBTE), is based on the idea that successful teaching requires the individual to be competent in certain areas, and that these areas of competence can be tested objectively and can be taught to prospective teachers. While research has not yet proved this idea to be true, since the late 1960s a number of states and schools have become heavily committed to this approach to teacher preparation.

The 1973 Conference on Professional Preparation utilized this approach in its suggestions for updating or developing programs of professional preparation. The publication that resulted *(Professional Preparation in Dance, Physical Education, Recreation Education, Safety Education, and School Health Education)* cannot be cited to any single individual or group, for each division of the broader area of physical education had its own task force to work at developing guidelines.

In some respects the document is very forward-looking, for it moves from an hours-and-credits approach to a conceptual approach. It suggests major areas of concern, primary concepts in those areas, and competences to be developed relating to those concepts. In other respects it is more narrow, for it shows no concern for the other three-quarters of the college educational experience. The hopeful suggestion that the institution should have good requirements is a lack of stated concern that physical educators cannot afford to show.

Rather than discuss the competences or even concepts suggested, for the number is considerable, we can give a general idea of the components for the major field preparation by citing the major areas for which concepts and competencies were suggested. The first major area is *meaning and significance,* which places movement concerns within the context of history and modern society. This area is divided into subareas that cover the sociocultural, philosophical, and historical facets of meaning and significance.

Another area is human *growth and development,* which may be taught outside the department of physical education. Another area taught largely outside the department is the *introduction to sciences,* which includes subareas of the physical and biological sciences and the behavioral sciences (psychology and sociology).

Other areas suggested are the *research foundations,* to provide a basis for conducting research; the area of the *development of personal performance competences,* or developing personal and teaching skills; and the area of *modes facilitating learning,* which is concerned with the development of situations that will encourage learning and help it to come about more easily.

Some self-explanatory areas of preparation are those of *administration, curriculum planning and organization,* and *intramurals,* which is a rising concern of the well-balanced physical education program. These areas are concerned primarily with the development and operation of successful programs in the schools.

While the competency-based approach has grown rapidly in popularity, there is no evidence that it is any more successful in the production of successful teachers than the traditional methods, nor is there any evidence that it is less successful. The primary question with this approach is whether its heavily evaluation-oriented system will cause it to be such an administrative burden that the system will choke on its own paperwork. Even if the competency-based system fails to work, it has characteristics of the long-term trend in teacher education toward even greater flexibility in developing training programs and planning personal programs of education for teaching.

**Variations in Patterns of Professional Preparation.** It was mentioned earlier that there are many variations to the patterns of teacher education in the nation's schools. We need to consider briefly some of the major variations. The first variation is the addition of *extra science courses* to the required program. This idea is in keeping with the idea that physical education is a science, or allied to the sciences. The courses are also added in an attempt to raise the quality of the academic program. Whether this additional emphasis is really justified is difficult to say, for the answer is more philosophical than concrete. If the student plans to go on to graduate study and perhaps research in the areas of the scientific bases of physical education, a stronger scientific background would be a necessity.

A second variation is the *addition of major courses,* either to give a broader coverage of the major field or to provide some specialization in an area within the field. This might be viewed as similar to the older concept of the "minor" field, or an area in which the student has taken several courses or done concentrated work, but not enough work to qualify the area as a major field. Examples of this type of concentration are the development of minors in areas such as coaching, athletic training, elementary school physical education, therapeutics, health education, recreation, aquatics, safety education, or other areas that are not offered as full major fields in many schools. Such work can help in developing a better-qualified teacher, and the additional qualifications can improve the student's chances of finding employment after graduation.

A third variation is preparation for a *second teaching area.* This has been a physical education tradition for decades, for physical educators have often been asked to teach in areas other than those in which they are best prepared. Because of the peculiarities of hiring practices, a second teaching area can help very much in finding a teaching job. On the other hand, the practice of teaching two subject areas is one of the major reasons for the lack of respect many people feel for physical education. Many physical educators have taught in areas in which they were poorly qualified or unqualified, and the result has been a poor performance and a blot on the reputation of our field. Physical education comprises so many areas that the student's full time is needed to develop the single major. Any time spent in developing a second major most often results in a weaker physical educator who, rather than being strong in one field, is fair-to-poor in two fields.

A fourth variation in the professional preparation program is the *fifth-year program.* This variation was strongly recommended by the 1962 Conference on Professional Preparation as a standard practice, though this is not the case in most schools. The first four years are devoted to training in the supportive areas and the major field, and then the fifth year is devoted to developing the teaching competences, plus additional strengthening work in the major field. Although the arguments for the fifth year of professional preparation are strong, many social and economic arguments counterbalance them. Delaying the start of the professional career another year means that the teacher cannot be self-supporting until after the age of about twenty-three. The additional year of schooling is very expensive, almost prohibitive in many cases. In addition, students cannot take their places as responsible members of society until the age of 23, which creates many problems for them and for the society. In many cases the fifth year of the professional program is devoted to the earning of a master's degree. If a master's degree results from the fifth year, more people consider the year worth the additional time, effort, and money.

***Graduate Education in Physical Education.*** A large proportion of physical educators continue their training beyond the undergraduate level and work toward one or more graduate degrees. Graduate study is at an advanced level; it aims at preparing the physical educator in some specialized area of the field or is designed to prepare the student to carry out some higher task. Physical educators with graduate degrees may be preparing to be teachers, but with a more thorough program of professional preparation. They may be training to teach at the junior college or college level, preparing to do research or administrative work in some area, or preparing for one of the specialized areas, such as health education or recreation education, after concentrating in physical education at the undergraduate level.

The most common degree at the graduate level is the master's degree, which represents roughly one year of work beyond the level of the bachelor's degree. A typical master's degree program may require from 30 to 36 semester hours of graduate work (45 to 54 quarter hours), depending on the different degrees and school requirements. Examples of the different types of master's degrees are the M.S. (master of science) degree, which usually involves a concentration in an area of physical education and may require some work in the scientific foundations of physical education. In many cases the M.S. degree work will include the preparation of a master's thesis, or an advanced, original research project that the student will plan, carry out, and then present in writing. Many degree programs at the master's level provide an option for the student to earn the master's degree without writing a thesis: Further course work is usually substituted for the thesis requirement.

Another option of the graduate degrees is the language requirement. The ability to read a foreign language is commonly required for higher degrees in the arts and sciences, but it is not usually required at the master's degree level in physical education. The ability to read one or two foreign languages reasonably well is a common requirement for the Ph.D. degree, regardless of the major field, but a language usually is not required for an Ed.D. degree. In recent years many schools have begun permitting students to substitute well-developed research skills for the language requirement. An example might be the substitution of a number of courses or an amount of other work involving the use of computers in research, or highly developed skills in the use and application of statistical tools, since the object of the requirement is to insure that the holder of the degree possesses the skills needed to conduct research without relying upon the talent or assistance of other people.

Another program at the master's degree level is the M.Ed. (Master of Education), which may be a concentration in either physical education or education alone. It is usually a degree oriented toward teaching. Another degree aimed toward teaching, but with a more academic orientation than the M.Ed. degree is the M.A.T. (Master of Arts in Teaching). The M.A.T. degree is usually a program designed for people who have a solid academic preparation in their field of study but do not have the education courses required for certification. It prepares them for teaching and at the same time adds more work in the major field. Frequently a teaching internship is included as a part of the degree program. Finally, the M.A. degree (Master of Arts) is occasionally seen in physical education, but it is generally a liberal arts degree with a language requirement rather than a science- or education-oriented degree.

A master's degree program is very helpful in adding depth to the student's professional preparation. It can serve as the often-recommended fifth year of teacher preparation. It can improve the student's qualifications in physical education, and it is also helpful in showing the student whether further graduate work might be fruitful. Generally speaking, if no problems are encountered while involved in the program, the student would expect to spend one calendar year in earning the degree.

The doctoral degree is the highest academic degree, though there are several types of doctorates. The Ph.D. (doctor of philosophy) is the traditional arts and sciences degree. It usually requires languages or other research competences, and it is oriented toward research. Although a person earning a Ph.D. in physical education will often become a teacher, the degree is more oriented to the academic or discipline side of the field.

The other most common doctoral degree is the Ed.D. (doctor of education), which is aimed toward the teaching side of the field, rather than the research side. No languages and little or no research preparation is usually required, for the degree holder is expected to be more concerned with the teaching itself and less likely to be engaged in research. While the degree may be an Ed.D. with a major in physical education, the actual field often is simply education, with physical education, health education, or the preferred physical education area being a smaller portion of the actual course work.

Other degrees similar to the Ed.D. degree are sometimes encountered in the field of physical education. Examples are the D.P.E. and P.E.D. degrees (doctor of physical education). Their training emphasis may be toward either the research side or the teaching side of the field, depending on the program of the individual school. There is considerable overlapping of the research-teaching emphasis among doctoral degrees in physical education.

The doctorate is necessary if the physical educator plans to teach at a very high level, such as teaching the general theory levels at the college or university level, whether teaching undergraduate or graduate courses. While an instructor without a doctoral degree may be very qualified through experience, most colleges prefer their faculty members to be either holders of a doctoral degree or actively working toward the degree.

The doctorate represents about three to four years of full-time study past the bachelor's degree, though the actual time involved is usually longer. This time includes the year of course work involved in the master's degree program, another year or two of course work devoted to the doctoral concentration and its supporting areas, and a final year involved in preparing for the comprehensive doctoral examinations and preparing the dissertation, a research project that is more extensive and original than the master's thesis (with the Ed.D. degree the dissertation may not be required to be an original research topic at some institutions). Other outside factors, including remedial work to correct any deficiencies in the undergraduate program of preparation, will increase the amount of time required to earn a doctoral degree. Some schools will require several years of teaching experience before permitting a candidate to undertake a doctoral program, and most schools set a seven-year limit on completing the degree requirements.

The number of schools that offered bachelor's, master's, or doctoral degrees in physical education, health education, and recreation education in the United States during the 1974–1975 school year are shown in Table 15.2. About 700 schools offer a degree of some type in some area of physical education in the United States, with over 250 schools offering master's degrees, and over 60 schools offering doctoral degrees.

## Trends in Professional Preparation

The professional preparation programs through which physical educators travel are gradually changing. Although the process is usually slow, it is also relatively constant. Because the needs of people change,

**Table 15.2**
Schools Offering Degrees in Health,
Physical Education, and Recreation

|  | Bachelor's Degree | Master's Degree | Doctor's Degree |
|---|---|---|---|
| Physical Education* | 674 | 262 | 62 |
| Health Education | 200 | 115 | 36 |
| Recreation Education | 157 | 65 | 23 |
| Total Schools Offering Degree Programs | 690 | 264 | 65 |

* Includes combined degrees in health and physical education.

the skills that physical educators need also change. These changing skills needs are reflected in changing patterns of professional preparation as the schools try to find better ways to prepare their students to meet these needs. Several of the more noticeable trends in professional preparation programs should be understood clearly.

**Increased Specialization.** Perhaps the most noticeable trend in professional training is the increase in specialization; many more people are concentrating in smaller areas of the physical education fields. Many students are developing concentrations at either the undergraduate or graduate level in areas such as health education, recreation education, safety education, dance, athletic training, coaching areas, and the area of adapted and therapeutic work, as examples. In the past the physical educator majored only in a broad degree that could be called health and physical education. The combined degree is gradually dropping from use as the generalist is replaced by the specialist. One reason for this is the increase in the size of schools, as districts and schools consolidate, while another reason is the large increase in the number of teachers available. The gradual result of this increase in specialization is an expansion of the programs available to students in the many fields of physical education, which is a great improvement in the schools' services.

**Certification of Coaches and Trainers.** A number of states have begun to certify their coaches and trainers. By requiring some background training in these areas, such as the equivalent of a "minor" program in college, they can provide a safer, more knowledgeable level of coaching in the schools. The concern over the safety of school athletes has increased rapidly in recent years, for as sports competition has expanded, so has the number of injuries. Too many schools have no trainers to work with problems of athletic injuries. Some states are working to establish groups of high school trainers who have been certified by the state so that high school athletes will receive better, more knowledgeable care as quickly as possible if they are injured.

**Elementary School Specialists.** As the trend toward specialization continues, one of the rapidly-growing specialties is the teacher of elementary school physical education. The elementary ages might be considered the most important ages for the application of good physical education programs, yet in many states the elementary school children are taught their physical education by the classroom teachers. The result has frequently been a poor program of physical education at a critical age for the development of coordination skills. Specialists are being trained who will either teach physical education at that level or act as consultants and supervisors of the physical education program at several elementary schools.

**Adapted and Therapeutic Specialists.** The areas of adapted physical education and therapeutic or physical rehabilitation are also rapidly developing. This area is concerned with persons who cannot take part in the normal physical education programs. In the adapted area the reasons for needing a special program can range from temporary injury, to below-average physical skills and abilities, to working with the mentally retarded. An example of one of the programs that has developed from this type of work is the Special Olympics for the mentally retarded, which is growing rapidly across the nation. In the area of physical therapy or physical rehabilitation, the object is to work with people who are trying to make a comeback from a very serious injury, disease, or handicap. Examples of work in this area include working with persons who have lost limbs and are learning to use artificial arms and legs, or with persons suffering from the effects of diseases such as polio or muscular dystrophy, to improve their ability to walk or perform other common physical skills.

**Paraprofessional Training.** The training of paraprofessionals or teachers' aides is still a small area of physical education training, but it is expected to grow rapidly in the future. The paraprofessional is a person who has had technical training—such as a one- or two-year program in a junior or community college—and who assists the teacher by fulfilling many of the duties that require less training. Examples of some of the duties that paraprofessionals can perform are taking roll, issuing and receiving equipment, preparing facilities, and giving and grading tests. Essentially the paraprofessional is used to lighten the work load of the teacher by doing many of the time-consuming non-teaching duties that cut into the teacher's actual teaching time.

**Competency-Based Teacher Education (CBTE).** We have mentioned competency-based teacher education earlier as the idea that there are certain competences that a teacher must possess to be successful. CBTE permits the student to save time in college by passing competency tests to demonstrate abilities or skills that are already developed, thus saving the time that would be required in course work in those areas. The four- or five-year program may also be shortened by other approaches; for example, by giving college credit for practical outside work experiences and allowing credit (usually nongraded) for tests of knowledge in required course areas, such as the CLEP (College-Level Equivalency Program) testing and credits, which are allowed by many schools in the nation. These changes permit far greater flexibility in developing the individual student's program according to the individual wishes and needs; they reward earlier competence, but do not necessarily handicap those who are not ready for work on a higher level.

**After Graduation.** The preparation of a physical educator does not end after graduation from college. Most teachers are faced with preservice and in-service training, or programs designed to keep them in touch with the latest developments in educational theory and practices. Many states require further college work at regular intervals, regardless of how long the teacher has been teaching. This trend is in keeping with the idea that the process of education never ends. Many other people pursue scholarly studies with no intention of teaching or coaching.

**Whole-School Involvement in Teacher Education.** This trend, involving using all the departments of the college in planning the teacher-training process, is a reaction to the problem of isolation of specialists in education and physical education. There is a tendency to try to do everything, including the academic preparation, wholly through the department of education, which can give teachers a rather limited idea of the views and knowledge of the areas which they may be teaching in later years. The idea of involving all the departments on the campus in planning the teacher-preparation programs and their content is a move to insure that the concern for methodology will not overlook or replace an equal concern that the teachers actually *know* something to teach.

***Open Admissions Versus Higher Teacher Standards.*** This problem may have no solution. At the same time that educators are trying to raise the quality of teaching by setting higher grade or knowledge requirements for prospective teachers, many schools have become "open admissions" colleges, which means that they have few or no admissions standards: Any student may be admitted, regardless of ability or seeming lack of ability. There are many reasons for the rise in the number of open admissions schools, but a major reason is to try to balance the earlier problems of discrimination in admissions. In an open admissions school every person has a chance to demonstrate the ability to do college work. This does not make higher standards impossible, or even necessarily more difficult to develop. The school can require that the bulk of the general education and foundational sciences work, along with some introductory areas of physical education theory courses, be completed with set grade restrictions before the student is admitted to the professional preparation program. Although this work should be the equivalent of two years of college work, the student is not limited to two years to meet the requirements. Time can be permitted for academic deficiencies to be made up in addition to taking the required programs.

## Toward the Future in Curricular Planning

Physical education, like all areas of education and life, is changing, and so must our patterns of teacher education change. One of our greatest problems, however, and the one that most hurts the reputation of educators, is our tendency to snatch an idea from the air and put it into effect in our programs with no greater justification than how nicely the theory rolls off the tongue at professional conferences. One reason for the disrespect with which educators are treated today is that while claiming to know how to teach better than any "noneducators," we have shown no objective proof to establish that we know what we are talking about.

A prime example of this blindness toward proof is the massive move of the educational community toward competency-based teacher education. No one can deny the logic of the theory that there are objective, provable competences necessary to successful teaching. So why not base our programs on developing these competences, then require the competences for state certification, rather than a mass of courses, hours, credits, and grades? Many states have rushed to do just that. One tiny problem remains: No scientist or educator has ever proved the existence of even a single competency area to successful teaching. We have *no proven* competencies.

Before we make changes in our patterns of professional preparation, we should show (1) the value of the changes and (2) that the changes *work*. If we cannot establish these two points, not only will we receive no respect from the academic and nonacademic communities, we will *deserve* no respect. We should establish these values and outcomes *before* making the changes, rather than after the fact, for changing before proving is ideology, rather than education. This does not mean we should not experiment, but we should not push for *large-scale* changes based on unproven ideas, as in the CBTE movement. It is difficult to plan education for the future, because we often have little idea of what the future holds either in educational practices and conditions or in job opportunities and needs. If we did have the answers to everything, most of the challenge of teaching would be gone.

One solid need of physical educators is for more work in the liberal arts and interdisciplinary studies areas. There are several reasons for suggesting this shift in direction. One is supplied by James B. Conant, who is considered by many persons to be an opponent of physical education. Whether he is an opponent or not, he expresses some compelling arguments for such a broadening of the educational background of physical educators:

> Because the physical education teacher is likely to be a coach and because of the high visibility of the coaching staff, the road to administrative positions is open and attractive . . . . The future is likely to be like the past in this respect. Unless there is a change in the direction of this trend, I conclude that *the physical education teacher should have an even wider general academic education than any other teacher* . . . . More likely than not, the man preparing to be a physical education teacher is, perhaps unconsciously, preparing to be an educational administrator. He needs to start early on a course of wide reading in the humanities and the social sciences [italics added].[2]

Large numbers of coaches eventually become administrators in the public schools, and Conant's suggestions are meant to direct their training toward the broader liberal arts studies that will make them more aware of the ideas and viewpoints of the other disciplinary areas of the educational spectrum. Although he touches on the edges of the reason for these wide studies, he misses one basic reason for them that should occur to most physical educators: lack of communication.

---

[2] James B. Conant, *The Education of American Teachers,* McGraw-Hill, New York, 1963, pp. 185–186.

A great communications gap exists between physical educators and other educators, academic and otherwise, simply because we cannot speak their language. We sometimes seem out of touch with the liberal arts and with their required development of communications skills so that even if physical education has become more academically respectable, we seem to be unable to prove it or communicate it to the academic community outside our own field. There is little value in our telling ourselves that our field is a respectable area of the educational process; we must sell it convincingly to those who have no ties to the field. We must broaden our horizons so we will be able to open new lines of communication to the many academic fields with which we have no present communication. Only when they begin to understand us— and we begin to understand them—will physical education begin to attain the respect that we as physical educators believe it deserves.

## Suggested Readings

Bain, Linda L. "The Hidden Curriculum in Physical Education." *Quest,* 24 (Summer 1975), 92–101.

"Competency-Based Teacher Education." *Briefings,* 2 (NAPECW and NCPEAM, 1975).

Conant, James B. *The Education of American Teachers.* McGraw-Hill, New York, 1963.

Dunn, Patricia Carolyn. *An Exploration of the Status and Future Directions of Graduate Programs in Health Education in the United States.* Microfiched Ph.D. dissertation, Ohio State University, 1972.

"Educational Change in the Teaching of Physical Education." *Quest,* 15 (January 1971). Entire issue.

Goodman, Paul. *Compulsory Mis-education.* Horizon Free Press, New York, 1962.

Grace, Robert E. *Competency-Based Professional Education in Physical Education.* Unpublished Ed.D. dissertation, State University of New York at Buffalo, 1974.

*Graduate Education in Health Education, Physical Education, Recreation Education, Safety Education, and Dance.* AAHPER, Washington, D.C., 1974.

"Graduate Study in Physical Education." *Quest,* 25 (Winter 1976). Entire issue.

Highet, Gilbert. *The Art of Teaching.* Vintage Books, New York, 1950.

Hill, Charles E., and Donald Hilsendager. "Research Competencies for the Undergraduate." *JOPER,* 46 (November–December 1975), 61.

Hoffman, Hubert A., Louis E. Bowers, and Stephen E. Klesius. "Selective Admissions: A First Step in Professional Preparation." *JOPER,* 46 (October 1975), 29–30.

Joyce, Bruce, and Marsha Weil. *Perspectives for Reform in Teacher Education.* Prentice-Hall, Englewood Cliffs, N.J., 1972.

Koerner, James D. *The Miseducation of American Teachers.* Houghton Mifflin, Boston, 1963.

Kroll, Walter. *Perspectives in Physical Education.* Academic Press, New York, 1971.

Lindvall, C. M., ed. *Defining Educational Objectives.* University of Pittsburgh Press, Pittsburgh, 1964.

McCarty, Donald J., and Associates. *New Perspectives on Teacher Education.* Jossey-Bass, San Francisco, 1973.

McClellan, James E. *Toward an Effective Critique of American Education.* Lippincott, Philadelphia, 1968.

*Professional Preparation in Dance, Physical Education, Recreation Education, Safety Education, and School Health Education.* AAHPER, Washington, D.C., 1974.

*Professional Preparation in Health Education, Physical Education, Recreation Education.* AAHPER, Washington, D.C., 1962.

"Teaching Teachers." *Quest,* 18 (June 1972). Entire issue.

"What's New in Professional Preparation." *JOPER,* 46 (March 1975), 35–45.

# VI The Future of Physical Education

# Toward the Twenty-First Century: Trends and Problems

After studying where physical education has come from, what it is, and how we are prepared as physical educators, we still face a major concern: What does the future hold for physical education? What are the developing trends in our lives, and what effect will they have on our field ten, twenty, or thirty years from now? We need to consider not only trends and directions that seem to be apparent in education and society today but also some of the problems that we are facing in education and society as well.

## Toward the Future

People have always been fascinated by the future. As we study the history of literature we find many examples of people's predictions of the future. Writers have expressed their views of the future, sometimes as a warning, other times as a suggestion of their view of what the ideal society should be. The suggestion of an ideal lies behind Plato's *Republic* written in ancient Greece, and Thomas More's *Utopia* written in the sixteenth century. Examples of other views of the future and the problems it creates are Aldous Huxley's *Brave New World,* George Orwell's *1984,* and Alvin Toffler's *Future Shock.* While we want to know what the future holds, the thought of the changes it may bring leaves many of us apprehensive, for we know that changes will take place, but we do not know whether the results will be better or worse for the human race.

***The Problems of Predictions.*** While educational theorists are usually full of ideas about how to improve education and society, a "mood of caution" has overtaken many educators, according to the *U.S. News* *and World Report.*[1] During the last almost two decades educators have been given unprecedented opportunities to put their theories into action, but the results have rarely been impressive. Theorists are becoming more cautious in their easy predictions of successful, meaningful change, for too many of their earlier predictions failed to come true.

At one time the population was expected to rise indefinitely; the school population, and therefore the need for teachers, would also rise forever into the future. Many schools began expansion programs with this prediction in mind, just as masses of teachers began to be turned out. We have discovered, sometimes too late, that this prediction was incorrect. A change in family habits has taken place: a trend toward smaller families. The result has been a leveling-off of the school-age population, so that around 1982 the number of students at each grade level is expected to stabilize.[2] The college population is expected to continue to increase, though this is not related to a population increase, but rather to a change in societal views of the college experience. The U.S. population is expected to keep slowing its growth until it reaches approximately 250 to 300 million people, at which point it *may* stabilize, though this stabilization is difficult to predict. However, because many other parts of the world have done nothing to decrease the growth rate, the world population will continue to rise at a phenomenal rate.

**World Trends.**    Several world trends are easily visible. The most visible of these is the *population explosion* we have already discussed. The number of people in the world is increasing rapidly, with the greatest rates of increase most often found in the nations that are least able to support their present population. Such growth creates a great conflict both within and between nations, as the wants and needs of the people clash with the concrete problem of availability of resources.

Another problem is the growth of the industrialized world into a heavily *technological world.* The knowledge explosion has tended to move people toward more specialization as it becomes more impossible for a person to have a broad store of the world's knowledge. The world is increasingly computerized and miniaturized, so that many of the older distinctions between regions and people no longer hold true. Many of the old regional differences between areas of the United States are all but impossible to discover today, for the influences of national television, instant world news, and increasing wealth at most levels of

---

[1] "Crisis in the Schools," *U.S. News & World Report,* September 1, 1975, pp. 42–59.
[2] National Center for Educational Statistics, *The Condition of Education,* U.S. Government Printing Office, Washington, D.C., 1975, p. 132.

society have done more in a generation to make the United States a single people of a single nation than all of the changes of the past two centuries.

The technological world is a complex one; today more than ever the person who hopes to survive and be a successful, contributing member of society needs many skills. Our educational process must change to meet these technological needs so that schools can help prepare tomorrow's citizens to fulfill their roles in society. The "old-fashioned" education was designed to prepare a person for a civilization that was also "old fashioned." We must prepare people to live in the future, rather than the past or even the present.

The *knowledge explosion* has created educational conflicts: We cannot expect students to gain more than a portion of the world's knowledge, but we face the dilemma of deciding what portion of that knowledge will be most valuable. The period of the 1970s seems to have ushered in a new aspect of education in the United States that has not existed before: a massive disagreement over what the people want from education and the schools. The result of this discord is confusion; different schools are trying different approaches to education. The results tend to be confusing rather than enlightening. The question is asked and repeated, "What knowledge is most worth having?" Educators do not agree on the answer.

Another trend is the *emergence of the Third World,* which we discussed earlier in Chapter 5. These nations were previously the world's "have-not" nations, but they are now becoming factors in world politics because of the size of their populations or other factors, such as the petroleum reserves of the Arab nations. They are a factor in world politics because the effects of their population growth affects the future of the planet in terms of life-support resources, and the money that some of them have come to control is sufficient to exert a strong force upon the world economy. As these nations work toward political maturity, the other nations of the world must work to help them understand the long-term effects of their actions on the world, but the emphasis must be upon international understanding and tolerance.

Another trend might be termed the *growth of ethical dilemmas.* The problems causing the dilemmas are those—as we have mentioned in our discussion of ethics—involving questions for which there may be no clearly "right" or clearly "wrong" answers. An example of an ethical dilemma is how to deal with the effects of the world population boom, for the growth in the world population is a serious threat to the ability of the world to support its citizens. The natural need is for a world policy of birth control, but many newly emerging nations see such suggestions as a threat to their power; they believe that the suggestions are made as an effort to keep their nations small and weak. Such nations face the dilemma of having small populations they can feed, or large populations and a starvation problem.

The same ethical dilemma appears in the problems of environmental concerns, which we might refer to as "economy versus ecology." The ecology of a nation may be hurt by industrialization, yet the effect of strict ecology moves may be a weaker economy. The issue in some cases has been simplified to jobs or the ecology, and many people believe that any possible compromise will hurt both to some degree. In a problem of this sort, there may not be a "right" answer, but if this generation cannot solve the problem, the next generation will have much greater problems to solve.

Another ethical problem of sorts is the question of education of the masses. Each nation has its own ideas regarding who should be educated and to what extent they should be educated. The United States has traditionally attempted to educate a larger proportion of its people than any other nation on earth. Is this idea the best one in modern times? Should every person be educated? If so, what should be the process, what should be the content, and to what degree should they be educated? Again, there is no "correct" answer to problems of this nature. Each nation must make its own educational decisions for the future, but as the world changes, these decisions affect the other nations more than ever before.

When we look at these and all the other current trends, we realize we are facing different aspects of a single problem: The earth is continually changing. Nothing remains the same, including us. We must prepare ourselves for the future, and we must prepare physical education for the future. Our first big question is what the future holds for physical education.

## Trends and Directions in Education and Society

In considering the trends and directions of apparent changes today, we want to look at three areas of trends: those of society, the schools or education in general, and physical education in particular. Societal trends give us a broad picture of what the future may hold, while the school trends give us a bit more specific idea of the directions that physical education might take. A study of the trends and directions in physical education will give us our clearest idea of the implications of the future for physical educators.

*Societal Trends and Directions.* The population change is perhaps the most noticeable societal trend, and it has a great effect on the directions of most changes we anticipate. While only a few decades ago the

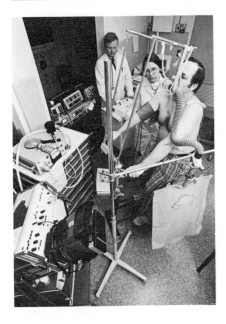

Along with the increasing concern about learning relaxation skills and tension relief has been the development of the study of exercise physiology, which investigates the limits of human performance and the relation between nutrition and exercise. This photo shows a bicycle stress test, such as might be used to test the heart's reaction to stress or the body's capacity for taking in and using oxygen. (Photo by Dan Bernstein for Tufts–New England Medical Center)

population of the United States was expected to continue to increase in a geometric progession, we have already begun to see the death of that trend. The birth rate in the United States has begun to decline, though in the foreseeable future it is not expected to reach the "zero growth" rate (where the birth rate is equal to the death rate), which many population control advocates are suggesting, and which will result in a stable population level.

The gradual stabilizing of the U.S. population will require much rethinking of national educational priorities: The unexpected decrease in students means less need for teachers. This reason for the oversupply of teachers is further complicated by the fact that the number of trained college graduates who expect to go into teaching will continue to grow for years. This oversupply of teachers can be both a curse and a boon, for while it means more unemployed teachers, it also means an increased chance to enlarge the number of highly qualified teachers and to remove the poorly qualified.

The growth in world wealth has resulted in an increased availability of leisure time for the general population, particularly in the United States. This trend creates a need for people who can teach and direct programs of recreational activities, plus creating a greater need for the teaching of recreational skills and attitudes toward exercise in the schools. Some growth will also be seen in programs relating to relaxation skills and tension relief, especially as society becomes more technological and complex.

An increased concern for the environment has also grown in recent years, as people have become more conscious of nature and civilization's impact on it. As people become more concerned about the environment, they also become more involved in the developing programs of outdoor education and recreation. Environmental concerns will tie in with the increase in leisure time to lead to an explosive growth in the recreational area of physical education.

**School Trends and Directions.** Many changes are appearing on the school scene today. The first really noticeable trend is the gradual decrease and stabilization of the student population, which we have already discussed. Although the student population will stabilize through the high school level, it will continue to increase at the college level for some time. In this case the growth results not from any population change, but from a change in the American attitudes toward post–high-school education, combined with the radical growth of two-year schools in the United States during the 1960s and early 1970s. More technical schools, community colleges, and junior colleges are providing a much greater variety of programs to high school graduates than ever before. Thus there has been a great trend toward continuing on to college after completing high school.

The concept of education is also changing, as is the question of the proper emphasis of the educational process. A battle has developed between the cognitive and affective domains of educational objectives. The "taxonomy of educational objectives," a method of classifying more exactly the many objectives of education into types and their meanings, was developed by Benjamin S. Bloom and others.[3] According to this method, the objectives of education fall into three broad categories, or "domains":

1   *Cognitive:* This area might be thought of as factual, for it includes the gaining of knowledge and its use by the person. It is the area of intellectual abilities and skills.
2   *Affective:* This area basically involves our attitudes and values, or how we feel about things; the quality of our character; and our appreciations and interests. While most education has traditionally been in the cognitive domain, the affective domain is increasingly being emphasized in the educational process. The greatest difficulty with teaching in the affective domain is determining what

---

[3] Benjamin S. Bloom, ed., *Taxonomy of Educational Objectives; Handbook I: Cognitive Domain,* David McKay Company, New York, 1956; and David R. Krathwohl, Benjamin S. Bloom, and Bertram B. Masia, *Taxonomy of Educational Objectives; Handbook II: Affective Domain,* David McKay Company, New York, 1964.

is to be taught and then devising an objective test to determine the degree of success or failure of the learning, for attitudes and appreciations are very difficult to test objectively. The idea of *precisely* putting a feeling into words or numbers is a contradiction in terms.

**3** *Psychomotor:* Bloom also referred to this area as the "manipulative or motor-skill area," [4] which gives a clear indication of the meaning of the term, for it is concerned with the development of the motor skills of the student.

While we are not concerned with studying the nature of the taxonomy and its educational application (for this area of study is in another part of the program of professional preparation), the conflict its appearance has generated will last for years to come, for it has brought forth once more an opposite aspect to be considered within current educational disagreement: the "back to basics" movement.

Today's student appears to have poorer language and math skills than the typical student of twenty or even fifty years ago. Among the often-given reasons for this decline in basic skills, or the three Rs, are the rise of permissive education, a move away from discipline and direction in the schools, and a move toward emphasizing the affective domain—attitudes and appreciations—rather than knowledge and concrete skills. One result of the dissatisfaction of many parents with today's public education is rising attendance at alternative institutions.

The number of "alternative schools," both public and private, has been increasing over the past several years. Though the schools known as alternative schools were originally started to provide a more humanistic or free-form educational environment, the term is now being used for almost any school that differs from the typical public school in method or emphasis. Some alternative schools are designed to provide students with more discipline and direction; others are planned to re-emphasize basic education; and still others (primarily private schools) wish to provide a more religious or patriotic environment.

The rise of interest in the affective domain results from the feeling that people need a greater concept of values, and that a vital part of the educational process is the development of attitudes and appreciations consistent with those of the society in general. One reason for disagreements with the idea of affective education is that its supporters often forget that it can be developed only on a cognitive base, for facts must come before theories and values, if the theories and values are to survive. Proponents of affective learning sometimes overreact by rejecting the cognitive domain, without realizing that the affective cannot

---

[4] Bloom, p. 7.

survive without the cognitive base. For an education to be well rounded, however, *both* areas need to be developed. There is no reason for a "battle" between the cognitive and affective domains.

One outcome of this conflict over what the schools should teach has been an increasing community involvement in the schools. More citizens are interested in what is happening in the schools and are working to make the school programs more responsive to community and citizen needs. There is a developing attitude that education is a lifetime experience, rather than something that happens within the walls of a schoolhouse within a certain age-span of each person. Education is seen less as a function of age and more as a continuing experience as the knowledge and interests of each person change throughout life.

This involvement and change in attitudes is reflected by an increasing move toward relevance in the education. People are beginning to demand that their education be functional, that it be relevant to their needs when they are outside the school. These concerns are part of the demand for accountability of the schools and of the teachers, who are expected to show that they are indeed accomplishing something in the schools, and to show that it is *worth* accomplishing. There is massive resistance to the old idea of the school as an "ivory tower" where reality and the outside world never enter. Today the outside world is moving into the school and the educational process.

A greater consciousness of a future of work is being developed in students as career training develops. It shows students the place of work in society, teaches them about work, and introduces them to many career options at an earlier age. It is intended to counteract the problem of students who graduate from school with absolutely no idea of what they want to do in the future, and in many cases with no idea that they *need* to do anything.

Another trend is toward humanizing the curriculum. One complaint about education has been that it dehumanizes students, or puts them into a lowly position of little respect or human value. The humanization of education and the curriculum is one aspect of the affective concerns: Increased emphasis is put on the idea of caring more for the students. The curriculum is also becoming more flexible, as an increasing variety of options are being designed to vary the curriculum to fit the needs of the individual student rather than bend the student to fit the curriculum. Use of block or modular scheduling, along with a growth in independent study and advanced placement testing, is also increasing.

The school curriculum has become broader, with more areas of study and interest permitted than in previous decades. The narrow bounds of traditional educational subjects and interests are gradually disappearing, as more interdisciplinary studies appear and cross the boundaries of subject matter. In physical education, the program is becoming much broader, with a move toward lifetime sports and less well-known sports and fitness activities in the place of the small number of traditional sports and the calisthenics-oriented fitness activities. More electives are being permitted in the schools, though the idea of a totally elective program has shown little sign of public acceptance, or of success if it were allowed.

Teaching methodology is undergoing many innovative changes. Specialists are being utilized more, as are such teaching techniques as team teaching (several teachers teach a single class) and differentiated staffing (staff members teach primarily in their areas of specialization rather than in all areas of their subject). A much greater use of teaching machines and audio-visual media is also evident. The laboratories that have been developed use taped sound cassettes or video cassettes, as well as records, slide shows, and motion picture shows as a part of the teaching process. More teachers are trying more experimental teaching and learning methods and tools than ever before. The growth of innovative teaching techniques has been rapid, and it is not likely to slow down very much.

**Physical Education Trends and Directions.** Physical education is beginning to emerge as a discipline, as we discussed earlier. The development of a discipline is helping to put the field of physical education on a more academic footing, while raising the standards of education required by the field.

The increased specialization of teachers will show up clearly in physical education, for it is a broad field with many potential areas of specialization. More people will develop teaching or research specialties, which will result in more qualified teachers, and which can permit the hiring of better qualified teachers. However, the tradition has been to retain older teachers on the basis of seniority, rather than teaching quality or qualifications, which can hamper the development of a better, more academically qualified body of physical educators and other teachers.

More specialized degrees may appear, and very likely some schools will begin to concentrate their undergraduate or graduate programs in one or two specialized areas of physical education, rather than try to prepare generalists alone in a world increasingly taken over by specialists. Not only will more specialized fields develop, but students majoring in physical education will probably be required to work more in skill-development activity areas in the future.

Among the growing specialties for workers are the areas of adapted and handicapped activities—that is, working with people physically or mentally unable to participate in the regular physical education program or with those who need some type of rehabilitation program. Government studies indicate that about 11 percent of school students in the United States have some type of handicap, such as

As mentioned in the text, one of the growing areas of specialty is rehabilitation. Rehabilitation programs are not limited to schools; exercise programs rehabilitate heart patients and teach them how to live their lives as normally as they can in spite of their handicaps. (Courtesy American Heart Association)

speech impairment, learning disability, mental retardation, emotional disturbance, or other problems that remove them from the regular school programs.[5] More services will be provided to students who are disadvantaged, whether for physical, mental, emotional, or primarily social or economic reasons, as in the case of members of minority groups.

A greater variety of activities and areas of interest will be developing in the next decade or two. Women's sports activities are undergoing a period of rapid growth (which may, however, level off within a decade), and more use of intramural activities is appearing in the high schools and colleges. This rise in nonvarsity club sports in the colleges might be considered a return of the athletic programs to the students for their enjoyment and a move away from athletic departments and coaches as a way of life and a business. A parallel trend toward physical education as a purely elective subject is also growing.

Finally, there is a growing interest in the social and aesthetic areas of physical education and sport, both as studies and as simple areas of personal interest. Physical educators are following their interests into areas of dance, the liberal arts, humanities studies, psychology, and sociology, as examples of broad aspects of study that are being used more and more by physical educators. There is a growing emphasis on the joy and beauty of movement.

## Problems and Challenges in Physical Education

Although there are many problems and challenges facing educators in general and physical educators in particular, we will look at only half

---

[5] National Center for Educational Statistics, p. 164.

a dozen problems and challenges, as examples of what the future holds for us. We could cite many more examples, but these few are enough to give a general idea of the scope and nature of the existing problems and challenges.

**The Place and Function of Physical Education in Education.** This issue is the source of a number of long-standing questions: What is the place of physical education in the educational process? What function does it fulfill? Can we justify it as a part of the curriculum? Can we justify requiring it of all students? These questions are being asked, loudly and often, across the country, and as physical educators we must have answers that will satisfy our critics. In a time of accountability we must show that physical education has a definite, positive value in the educational process, and we need to show why physical education is a vital part of the curriculum.

**Other Curriculum-Oriented Problems.** Many curricular problems exist in education and physical education. In addition to the need to make the curriculum more relevant, which we have already discussed, we need to establish educational priorities for our society if we are to settle some of these long-standing issues. We need to end the separation of reality and education, but we cannot go so far into the idea of "relevance" that we succumb entirely to the idea of having the student at any age plan the curriculum for us. As one educator said, "The trouble with gearing a curriculum to the interests of children is precisely that: they *are* children. But education is for life." [6]

We do not want to plan an inflexible curriculum, however. We must be open to change and innovation. Students need to have options that will permit them the optimum realization of their latent talents. For this reason the students need to be included in program planning and evaluation, for the programs are supposed to be designed to benefit the students, not the teachers.

We have also discussed the cognitive-affective struggle—the quarrel between three Rs–learning and values-learning or unstructured education—earlier in this chapter. Theodore W. Hipple makes an interesting observation in this area by remarking that "the chief weakness in contemporary education may not lie within the institution itself, but within the expectations held for it by the larger society." [7] We might say that people have used it as a means to an end (employment, societal

---

[6] Max Rafferty, *The Future of Education: 1975–2000,* ed. Theodore W. Hipple, Goodyear Publishing Company, Pacific Palisades, Calif., 1974, p. 167.

[7] Theodore W. Hipple, ed., *The Future of Education: 1975–2000,* Goodyear, Pacific Palisades, Calif., 1974, p. 135.

law and order, discipline), but have not considered it valuable simply for itself alone. Perhaps we use it simply to make up for our own personal mistakes, shortcomings, and failures.

We also face the challenge of developing more and better leaders, for physical education is not a field noted for its nationally recognized leaders or authorities. At the same time we need to develop greater creativity in our practitioners—that is, their ability or talent to think and act innovatively. Reuben Frost has suggested the term *copeability* as a great need, the development of the ability to cope with problems and to solve them.[8]

We particularly need to work to make athletics more genuinely educational. One of the greatest failures of physical educators is that we seem to lose sight of the purposes of physical education and education where school athletics is concerned. We have had no real action to correct the gross ills of sports since the 1929 Savage Report (and even that had little noticeable effect upon college practices). Many people outside the field are questioning the value of athletics in the schools, and if we do not move to show *and* practice those positive values, we may find sports starting to disappear from the trimmed budgets of the future.

**Oversupply of Teachers.**  We have also discussed this problem at some length. We need to raise the standards of admission to the field of physical education so that we will have less of a "glut" of potential physical education teachers joining an already overcrowded field. Raising admissions standards may be the best way to make a major improvement in the quality of physical education teachers and programs.

**The Gap Between Research and Practice.**  We need to work to close the gap between our current teaching methods and facts and what we have discovered about teaching and skill acquisition in research. We have allowed a gap to appear between the physical educators who are researchers and those who are practitioners. We need to work to see that we improve the practice of physical education as a result of the research we are doing in physical education.

**Financial Problems.**  In the early 1970s school budgets across the nation began facing severe budget problems. Part of this problem is the result of a temporarily down economy, but there is also a warning for

---

[8] Reuben B. Frost, *Physical Education: Foundations, Practices, Principles,* Addison-Wesley, Reading, Mass., 1975, p. 92.

the future: Money is going to be less available. If physical education expects to continue to receive a fair share, we must prove the value of our programs to the schools, or we may see our programs dropped or at least cut back severely in scope. The same difficult lesson is doubly true for athletics in the schools. We must *show* the value, or have our programs included among the "frill" programs that disappear when money is less available for the schools. We must be more conscious of budgets and more careful of our spending habits.

**Alienation of Students.** This type of student may actually be the greatest problem in education today: Can the "turned off" student—the student who is not interested in school, who does not care—be reached? The problems of drug and alcohol abuse that we see in students and the larger society are symptomatic of a sense of loss of personal worth, a feeling of making no contribution to anything. In part the feelings of alienation are probably a result of the overcrowded population conditions, but we must try to cope with the problem of alienated students, for the consequences of a large number of alienated people are grave. This worry is one of the major reasons for the interest in humanism in education.

**Again, Toward the Future.** Throughout this text we have looked at physical education as a broad field in the context of its historical past, its patterns of development, its function in today's society, and the most likely trends it will follow into the future. Hopefully you now have some idea of what physical education is all about. We have tried to show physical education as an important part of the total educational process, but without making exaggerated claims for it.

Physical education is a worthy field, for in its activities and experiences we can find elements of value to people of all ages and conditions. The greatest question that faces physical educators today is not anything we have looked at directly in this text, but it is one more question concerning the future of physical education: When you have become a physical educator, what will you do with it? What directions will physical education take under your guidance and leadership? That is the most important question about the future of physical education.

## Suggested Readings

Aerospace Education Foundation. *Technology and Innovation in Education.* Frederick A. Praeger, New York, 1968.

Berman, Louise. *New Priorities in the Curriculum.* Charles E. Merrill, Columbus, Ohio, 1968.

Bucher, Charles A. "Change and Challenge." *JOPER,* 46 (November-December 1975), 55–56.

Committee for Economic Development. *Innovation in Education: New Directions for the American School.* Committee for Economic Development, New York, 1968.

————. *The Schools and the Challenge of Innovation.* McGraw-Hill, New York, 1969.

Flournoy, Don M., and Associates. *The New Teacher.* Jossey-Bass, San Francisco, 1972.

Hipple, Theodore W., ed. *The Future of Education: 1975–2000.* Goodyear, Pacific Palisades, Calif., 1974.

Hirsch, Werner Z., et al. *Inventing Education for the Future.* Chandler, San Francisco, 1967.

Kroll, Arthur M., ed. *Issues in American Education.* Oxford University Press, New York, 1970.

Lawler, Marcella R. *Strategies for Planned Curricular Innovation.* Teachers College, Columbia University, New York, 1970.

Leonard, George B. *Education and Ecstasy.* Delacorte Press, New York, 1968.

Lieberman, Myron. *The Future of Public Education.* University of Chicago Press, Chicago, 1960.

Miller, Richard I. *Perspectives for Educational Change.* Appleton-Century-Crofts, New York, 1967.

Pease, Dean A., and Darrell Crase. "Commitment to Change." *JOHPER,* 44 (April 1973), 35–37.

"Quest for Tomorrow." *Quest,* 21 (January 1974). Entire issue.

Reimer, Everett. *School Is Dead: Alternatives in Education.* Doubleday, Garden City, N.Y., 1970.

Rich, John Martin. *Challenge and Response: Education in American Culture.* John Wiley and Sons, New York, 1974.

Von Haden, Herbert I., and Jean Marie King. *Innovations in Education: Their Pros and Cons.* Charles A. Jones, Worthington, Ohio, 1971.

# Resource Reading Materials

This list of books and magazines is a departure point for students and teachers interested in a deeper study of aspects of physical education and sport. It is by no means all-inclusive.

## Resource Books

Bennett, Bruce L., Maxwell L. Howell, and Uriel Simri. *Comparative Physical Education and Sport.* Lea and Febiger, Philadelphia, 1975.

Betts, John Rickards. *America's Sporting Heritage: 1850–1950.* Addison-Wesley, Reading, Mass., 1974.

Davis, Elwood Craig, ed. *Philosophies Fashion Physical Education.* Wm. C. Brown, Dubuque, Ia., 1963.

————, and Donna Mae Miller. *The Philosophic Process in Physical Education,* 2d ed. Lea and Febiger, Philadelphia, 1967.

Gerber, Ellen W. *Innovators and Institutions in Physical Education.* Lea and Febiger, Philadelphia, 1971.

*Graduate Education in Health Education, Physical Education, Recreation Education, Safety Education, and Dance.* AAHPER, Washington, D.C., 1967.

Hart, M. Marie, ed. *Sport in the Sociocultural Process,* 2d ed. Wm. C. Brown, Dubuque, Ia., 1976.

*HPER Omnibus.* AAHPER, Washington, D.C., 1976. Includes contributions from sixteen winners of the Gulick Award, AAHPER's highest honor.

Kroll, Walter. *Perspectives in Physical Education.* Academic Press, New York, 1971.

Leonard, George B. *The Ultimate Athlete.* Viking Press, New York, 1975.

Lipsyte, Robert. *SportsWorld: An American Dreamland.* Quadrangle, New York, 1975.

Lockhart, Aileene S., and Howard S. Slusher, eds. *Contemporary Readings in Physical Education,* 3d ed. Wm. C. Brown, Dubuque, Ia., 1975.

Lockhart, Aileene S., and Betty Spears, eds. *Chronicle of American Physical Education, 1855–1930.* Wm. C. Brown, Dubuque, Ia., 1972.

Loy, John W., Jr., and Gerald S. Kenyon, eds. *Sport, Culture, and Society.* Macmillan, London, 1969.

Lüschen, Günther, ed. *The Cross-Cultural Analysis of Sport and Games.* Stipes Publishing Company, Champaign, Ill., 1970.

Michener, James A. *Sports in America.* Random House, New York, 1976.

Miller, Donna Mae, and Kathryn R. E. Russell. *Sport: A Contemporary View.* Lea and Febiger, Philadelphia, 1971.

Murray, J. Alex, ed. *Sport or Athletics: A North American Dilemma.* Seminar on Canadian-American Relations, University of Windsor, Ontario, Canada, 1974.

Novak, Michael. *The Joy of Sports.* Basic Books, New York, 1976.

*Professional Preparation in Dance, Physical Education, Recreation Education, Safety Education, and School Health Education.* AAHPER, Washington, D.C., 1974.

Sage, George H., ed. *Sport and American Society: Selected Readings,* 2d ed. Addison-Wesley, Reading, Mass., 1974.

Siedentop, Daryl. *Physical Education: Introductory Analysis,* 2d ed. Wm. C. Brown, Dubuque, Ia., 1976.

Ulrich, Celeste. *To Seek and Find.* AAHPER, Washington, D.C., 1976.

Van Dalen, Deobold B., and Bruce L. Bennett. *A World History of Physical Education,* 2d ed. Prentice-Hall, Englewood Cliffs, N.J., 1971.

VanderZwaag, Harold J. *Toward a Philosophy of Sport.* Addison-Wesley, Reading, Mass., 1972.

Vendien, C. Lynn, and John E. Nixon. *The World Today in Health, Physical Education, and Recreation.* Prentice-Hall, Englewood Cliffs, N.J., 1968.

Webster, Randolph W. *Philosophy of Physical Education.* Wm. C. Brown, Dubuque, Ia., 1965.

Weiss, Paul. *Sport: A Philosophic Inquiry.* Southern Illinois University Press, Carbondale, 1969.

Weston, Arthur. *The Making of American Physical Education.* Appleton-Century-Crofts, New York, 1962.

Zeigler, Earle F. *Philosophical Foundations for Physical, Health, and Recreation Education.* Prentice-Hall, Englewood Cliffs, N.J., 1964.

————. *Problems in the History and Philosophy of Physical Education and Sport.* Prentice-Hall, Englewood Cliffs, N.J., 1968.

## Resource Periodicals

*Canadian Journal of History of Sport and Physical Education.* Published twice yearly. Subscriptions available from Alan Metcalfe, Faculty of Human Kinetics, University of Windsor, Windsor, Ontario N9B 3P4, Canada.

*Current Index to Journals in Education.* Published monthly in cooperation with ERIC (Educational Resources Information Center) to index the articles from over 700 journals related to areas of education. Available from Macmillan Information, a Division of Macmillan Publishing Company, Inc., 216R Brown Street, Riverside NJ 08075.

*Education Digest.* Published nine times yearly. 416 Longshore Drive, Ann Arbor MI 48107.

*Family Health.* Now includes former magazine *Today's Health.* Published monthly. 149 Fifth Ave., New York NY 10010.

*Health Education.* Published eight times yearly by the American Alliance for Health, Physical Education, and Recreation (AAHPER). Can be selected as a periodical by AAHPER members or ordered separately from membership. 1201 16th Street, N.W., Washington DC 20036.

*Journal of Leisure Research.* Published quarterly by the National Recreation and Park Association, 1601 North Kent Street, Arlington VA 22209.

*Journal of the Philosophy of Sport.* Available through Business Manager, Department of Physical Education, University of New Mexico, Albuquerque NM 87103.

*Journal of Physical Education.* Published six times annually by the National Physical Education Society of the YMCA, Lee Circle, 936 St. Charles Ave., New Orleans LA 70130.

*Journal of Physical Education and Recreation (JOPER).* Published nine times each year by AAHPER. Can be selected as a periodical by AAHPER members or ordered separately from membership. 1201 16th Street, N.W., Washington DC 20036.

*Journal of School Health.* Published ten times a year by the American School Health Association, Kent OH 44240.

*Journal of Sport History.* Published twice annually by the North American Society for Sport History. Available through Department of History, Radford College, Radford VA 24141.

*Journal of Teacher Education.* Published quarterly by the American Association of Colleges for Teacher Education, One Dupont Circle, Washington DC 20036.

*Parks and Recreation.* Published monthly by the National Recreation and Park Association, 1601 North Kent Street, Arlington VA 22209.

*Phi Delta Kappan.* Published monthly by the Phi Delta Kappa Fraternity, Eighth and Union, Bloomington IN 47401.

*Physical Educator, The.* Published quarterly by the Phi Epsilon Kappa Fraternity, School of HPER, Indiana University, Bloomington IN 47401.

*Quest.* Published twice each year as a joint effort by the National Association for Physical Education of College Women (NAPECW) and the National College Physical Education Association for Men (NCPEAM), c/o Dr. Daryl Siedentop, Editor, The Ohio State University, 1760 Neil Avenue, Columbus OH 43210.

*Research Quarterly.* Published four times each year by AAHPER. Can be selected as a periodical by AAHPER members or ordered separately from membership. 1201 16th Street, N.W., Washington DC 20036.

*Today's Education.* Published quarterly by the National Education Association (NEA), 1201 16th Street, N.W., Washington DC 20036.

*Update.* Newspaper printed nine times annually by AAHPER. Can be selected as a periodical by AAHPER members or ordered separately from membership. 1201 16th Street, N.W., Washington DC 20036.

# Index